. . . .

The
Jewish Moral
Virtues

The Jewish Moral Virtues

Eugene B. Borowitz

Frances Weinman Schwartz

The Jewish Publication Society
Philadelphia
1999 / 5759

Manufactured in the United States of America

Library of Congress Cataloging-in-Publication Data

Borowitz, Eugene B.
  The Jewish moral virtues / Eugene B. Borowitz, Frances Weinman Schwartz. — 1st ed.
    p. cm.
  Includes bibliographical references and index.
  ISBN 0-8276-0664-8
  1. Ethics, Jewish. 2. Jewish way of life. 3. Ethics in rabbinical literature.
4. Rabbinical literature—History and criticism. I. Schwartz, Frances Weinman.
II. Title.
BJ1280.B67   1999
296.3'6—dc21

                                                                98–43921

                                                                CIP

     04 03 02 01 00 99   3 4 5 6

Designed by Sasgen Graphic Design

To Joshua Reuben Langowitz

and

Stuart Schwartz

The publication of this book was assisted

by generous grants from

THE KORET FOUNDATION
(San Francisco)

and

ABE ELENOWITZ

in honor of Dr. Eugene Borowitz's

75th birthday

Contents

Acknowledgments

. . . .

*T*his book began as a seminar on the Jewish Moral Virtues that Gene taught at Hebrew Union College–Jewish Institute of Religion (HUC-JIR), based on the untranslated, recent Israeli edition of *Sefer Maalot Hamiddot*. For seven years, students investigated a single virtue from this book, with a particular concern for the talmudic and midrashic texts the author chose not to include in his anthology. The students not only reported on their discoveries, but provided us with research packets of all of their original source material. Because their efforts gave us the first layer of information, we want to share their names. All have since been ordained, so please add the title "rabbi" to each of them: *Ḥokhmah*, Dan Levin and Joel Sisenwine; *emunah*, Susan Friedman and Roz Landis; *derekh eretz*, Leon Morris; *raḥamim*, Jonathan Aaron, Batsheva Gluckman Meiri, and Alan Litwak; *zerizut*, Mary Lande Zamore; *nedivut*, Wendy Drucker Pein; *osher*, Michele Lenke; *tzedakah*, Neal Gold; *anavah*, Eleanor Smith; *tzeniyut*, Camille Angel; *histapkut*, Sharon Foreman; *yetzer ha-tov*, Karen Bender; *boshet*, Ellen Flax and Ariel Friedlander; *ratzon*, Kim Geringer; *temimut*, Janet Offel and Nancy Myers; *shem tov*, Barbara Symons; *shalom*, Lisa Green; *Torah vekiyum mitzvot*, Adam Stock Spilker; *teshuvah*, Rachel Sabath; *tefillah*, Daniel Cohen; *yediat ha-El*, Joshua Davidson and Sarah Reines; *yirat ha-El*, Jennifer Flatte; *ahavat ha-El*, Jennie Castleman Rosenn. Daniel Lehrman ably supplied additional research on many of these topics. We also thank Amy

Schwartzman and Peter Levi, whose rabbinic theses on *gemilut ḥasadim* and *yirat ha-El,* respectively, gave us new insight on these two subjects. We also say thank you to members of the HUC faculty who helped us find certain particularly elusive references: A. Stanley Dreyfus, Norman Cohen, Leonard Kravitz, and Michael Chernick.

Particular thanks are given to Dr. Philip Miller, librarian of the New York School of HUC-JIR, for all of his personal effort on our behalf, as well as for the ready cooperation of his staff. Our special gratitude goes to Amy Helfman, research librarian at the College-Institute, for resolving numerous questions for us. We are grateful to the Ilona Samek Institute at HUC-JIR for making funds available for special student research and other such useful matters. David Franz, reference librarian at the Montvale Public Library in New Jersey, also deserves a thank you.

Our work took on a new dimension after Ellen Frankel, editor-in-chief of the Jewish Publication Society, read our first chapter. Her enthusiastic response encouraged us to keep going; using just the right amounts of praise and persuasion, her intelligent, sensitive editing of early chapters showed us how to proceed. Christine Sweeney, our project editor at JPS, and her able assistant Aideen Quigley, kept us focused and on schedule. Our eagle-eyed copy editor, Debra Corman, directed our attention to a multitude of errors, which somehow crept into the final manuscript. Thank you, thank you!

Without the continued patience, support, and understanding of family and friends, who bore their neglect so lovingly while we attended to our *middot* project, this book would not have come into being. Francie wants to say a special thank you to her father, Frank Weinman, whose lifelong love of Jewish study continues to inspire her; her children Dana, David, and newest family member Jeremy, whose continuous encouragement helped see her through. And most of all, to Stuart, whose expert editing skills, unceasing sense of humor, and all-around wonderfulness always make her smile.

Gene wants to say a special word of thanks to Estelle. For several decades now, she has put up with the heavy burdens inflicted by a husband who wants to write when normal people are relaxing. Having thought that she had mastered that skill, she now has had to endure the special hardships Gene allowed this demanding project to inflict on their lives. Every positive word on love that Gene contributed to this volume was meant as a personal tribute to this incomparable soul.

Sources and Credits

*A*ll possible attempts have been made to contact those holding rights to the material presented in this book and to obtain permission to reprint it. If the appropriate parties have not been contacted, apologies are hereby extended and correct acknowledgments will be made in future editions.

"Each Man Has a Name," by Zelda, from *The Penguin Book of Hebrew Verse,* edited and translated by T. Carmi and published by Viking Press.

From *The Empty Chair: Finding Hope and Joy—Timeless Wisdom from a Hasidic Master, Rebbe Nachman of Breslov.* Copyright © 1994 by The Breslov Research Institute (Woodstock, VT: Jewish Lights Publishing, 1994). $9.95 + $3.50 shipping. Order by mail or call 800-962-4544. Permission granted by Jewish Lights Publishing, P. O. Box 237, Woodstock, VT 05091.

"The Gambler" by Don Schlitz. Copyright © 1977 Sony/ATV Tunes LLC. All rights administered by Sony/ATV Music Publishing, 8 Music Square West, Nashvillle, TN 37203. All rights reserved. Used by permission.

From *The Hasidic Anthology,* translated and edited by Louis I. Newman and published by Schocken Books, Inc.

Abbreviations

*C*itations from the Babylonian Talmud are given with the abbreviated tractate name, folio number, and page side, "a" or "b": Ber. 16a.

Citations from the Jerusalem Talmud are prefaced with "Yer." ("Jerusalem"), followed by the abbreviated tractate name, chapter, and *mishnah:* Yer. Ber. 30.1.

Citations from *Sefer Maalot Hamiddot* come from Yeḥiel b. Yekutiel's chapter devoted to the same topic.

Ar.	Arakhin
A.R.N.	Avot de Rabbi Natan
Avot	Pirke Avot
A.Z.	Avodah Zarah
b.	ben or bar
B.B.	Bava Batra
Ber.	Berakhot
Bez.	Betzah
B.K.	Bava Kama
B.M.	Bava Metzia
Dan.	Daniel
Dem.	Demai
D.E.R.	Derekh Eretz Rabbah
Deut.	Deuteronomy

Deut. R.	Deuteronomy Rabbah
D.E.Z.	Derekh Eretz Zuta
Eccles.	Ecclesiastes
Eccles. R.	Ecclesiastes Rabbah
Ed.	Eduyyot
E.H.	Even ha-Ezer
E.R.	Eliyahu Rabbah
Er.	Eruvin
Est.	Esther
Exod.	Exodus
Exod. R.	Exodus Rabbah
Ezek.	Ezekiel
Gen.	Genesis
Gen. R.	Genesis Rabbah
Git.	Gittin
Hab.	Habakkuk
Ḥag.	Ḥagigah
Ḥal.	Ḥallah
Hil.	Hilkhot
Hil. Tal.	Hilkhot Talmud Torah
Hil. Tesh.	Hilkhot Teshuvah
Hor.	Horayot
Ḥul.	Ḥullin
Isa.	Isaiah
Judg.	Judges
Ked.	Kedoshim
Ket.	Ketuvot
Kid.	Kiddushin
Lam. R.	Lamentations Rabbah
Lev.	Leviticus
Lev. R.	Leviticus Rabbah
Mak.	Makkot
Mal.	Malachi
Matt.	Matthew
Meg.	Megillah
Mekh.	Mekhilta

Men.	Menaḥot
Mic.	Micah
Mid. Prov.	Midrash Proverbs
Mid. Pss.	Midrash Psalms
Mid. Sam.	Midrash Samuel
M.K.	Mo'ed Katan
M.T.	Mishneh Torah
Ned.	Nedarim
Neh.	Nehemiah
Nid.	Niddah
Num.	Numbers
Num. R.	Numbers Rabbah
P. Hashalom	Perek Hashalom
Pes.	Pesaḥim
Pes. R.	Pesikta Rabbati
P.R.E.	Pirke de Rabbi Eliezer
P.R.K.	Pesikta de Rabbi Kahana
Prov.	Proverbs
Ps.	Psalms
R.	Rabbi, Rabban, Rav
R.H.	Rosh Hashanah
S. of S.	Song of Songs
S. of S. R.	Song of Songs Rabbah
S.A.	Shulḥan Arukh
Sam.	Samuel
San.	Sanhedrin
Shab.	Shabbat
Shek.	Shekalim
Sot.	Sotah
Suk.	Sukkot
T.	Tosefta
Taan.	Taanit
Tam.	Tamid
Tan.	Tanḥuma
Tan. B.	Tanḥuma, Buber ed.
T.B.E.	Tanna debe Eliyahu

T.B.K.	Tosefta Bava Kama
T.B.M.	Tosefta Bava Metzia
Tur	Arbaah Turim, and its author, Jacob b. Asher
Yer.	Yerushalmi
Yev.	Yevamot
Zech.	Zechariah
Zeph.	Zephaniah

PART I

The *Musar* Way to "Menschhood"

CHAPTER 1

What Is *Musar?*— An Introduction

*J*udaism, we know, calls for study, prayer, ritual, and good deeds as time-honored practice. Some Jews these days have also made a form of Jewish mysticism their dearest Torah. These actions are sacred, inherited ways to be a good Jew. Yet there is another mode of living the life of Torah that inspires them all and, without drawing much attention to itself, gives Judaism its special charm. It is the way of *musar,* the practical wisdom that has informed Jewish piety through the centuries and does so still today. Insofar as we infuse our everyday affairs with our Jewish values, we add our own style to the unbroken chain of *musar.*

Text and mitzvah are taught through formal study and community practice; mysticism involves a teacher and a discipline. But we learn *musar* quite informally, almost subliminally; perhaps that is why its influence on Jews has been so pervasive. When the Book of Proverbs, that classic of Jewish practical wisdom, admonishes the young: "My child, heed your father's *musar,* and do not forsake your mother's *Torah,*" (Prov. 1:8), it doesn't have home tutoring in mind. Rather, it is reflecting the reality that parents, consciously or not, continually impart wisdom to their children. Their lectures are probably the least effective part of their instruction. It is their example —a good deed done, a promise kept or broken, or even a cutting comment—that reveals their true standards and creates an indelible impression. And all the formal and informal good Jewish sense we take from our parents becomes in a fresh way our own possession, no matter how receptive or rebellious we were regarding religious education or observance.

Our parents and extended family aren't our only sources of *musar*. Our neighbors and teachers in the Jewish community play much the same role. The older we get, the wider our *musar* masters circle becomes, whether as those we seek to emulate or those whose acts we deplore. No wonder, then, that the kind of Jewish community we and our children find has always been a matter of great concern to us as caring Jews.

This love letter extolling Jewish wisdom is not meant to negate other ethnic groups' quite similar efforts. Nor should it convey that *musar* does not often overlap the good sense of others. Thus much of our tradition, like others different from our own, has come down to us in broad, folk form. Some maxims may rhyme—a stitch in time saves nine—or balance neatly—a bird in the hand is worth two in the bush—but these are always concise. Other forms of folk wisdom are expansive, like the cautionary tale—don't talk to wolves in the forest—or praise great exemplars—the young George Washington who cannot lie. Or wisdom can be approached quite thoughtfully, as did the Greek thinkers who called their passion "philosophy," literally, the love of wisdom. All of these examples illustrate a simple truth: the lore of wisdom is universal, part of every culture. As our talmudic sages taught, "If they tell you there is wisdom among 'the nations,' believe them" (Lam. R. 2, 9.13).

So, while we shall be drawing mostly on teachings of Jewish *musar* tradition, we shall also occasionally refer to insights found elsewhere. Yet we believe that we Jews, like other ethnic groups or religions—and we talk about both interchangeably—have given a distinctive shape to our wisdom. Thus the same rabbis who know the commonality of humankind and its wisdom chose to conclude their Lamentations Rabbah dictum in this way: "But if they tell you there is Torah among 'the nations,' don't believe them." And it is, of course, the practical wisdom defined by Torah, refined and amplified by Jewish life over the centuries, that we seek to impart and expand upon here.

Not many collections exist of informal folk wisdom that properly may be called *musar*. We cannot tell whether the aphorisms in the

Book of Proverbs are a collection of folk sayings or the refined formulations of an emerging class of "wisdom specialists"—the book itself claims King Solomon as its author. And not until about a century ago was an effort made to consciously collect epigrams consistently spoken by ordinary people, which makes it possible to cite Yiddish, Ladino, and Iraqi proverbs on a broad range of topics. Unfortunately, we do not have a similar literature from various Sephardic communities but have tried to compensate by drawing on formal works by various Sephardic sages.

If questions still remain about the folk derivation of the Book of Proverbs, most scholars believe that the Book of Ecclesiastes—the second of the three great wisdom books of the Bible—shows the sophistication of an emerging class of teachers who specialized in imparting the various nuances of wisdom. In the Book of Job, the third great wisdom book, any such questions disappear. Job's careful structure and high rhetoric surely must be the work of a single genius or a small group of teachers. Over the centuries, the Jewish people and their gifted teacher-writers reworked and reshaped the tradition of Jewish wisdom to mirror their own thoughts. *Musar,* for all our efforts to capture it in a pithy saying or a complex book, is dynamic, changing, yet somehow the same, like life itself.

You will see that we took most of our citations from the Talmud and the Midrash, the classic sources of Jewish tradition. Scholars compiled the Babylonian Talmud, the Bavli, in the first six centuries of the Common Era; another group previously completed the Talmud of the Land of Israel, the Yerushalmi, more than a century earlier. Both are based on the Mishnah, the code/study book of Jewish law dating from about 200 C.E. The first Midrash books were also composed about this time, and later midrashic material continued to be written well into the medieval period.

Our translations and paraphrases from all the works are quite free, aiming at clear comprehension rather than something approaching literary accuracy. We claim R. Judah b. Ilai as our guide in this matter, for long ago he set out the parameters for properly rendering a text: "If one translates a verse literally, one is a liar, and if one rewrites the verse, one is a blasphemer" (Kid. 49a). The easy flow of our text, however, should not lull you into thinking there are no problems. For example, scholars still energetically argue over how much historical reliability to attach to much of the rabbinic material. When we write that Yoḥanan b. Zakkai or, for that matter, the Baal Shem Tov centuries later "said" this or that, please be aware that we are simply presenting the data as it comes down to us. We aren't claiming that Hillel really tried to teach the would-be convert the whole Torah while he stood on one foot (better, "in one rule") or that the tales from the life of R. Akiba actually occurred. Note the "R." in front of Akiba's name. Because we cannot be certain what titles were used in which periods or circles—e.g., *rabban, rabbi, rav*—the accepted custom is simply to write "R." and say "Rabbi." However, in this book we have gone far beyond "the rabbis," the teachers mentioned in the Talmud and Midrash, to acquaint you with many additional writers of our tradition, down to our own time. So we indicate at their first mention their time and place of origin.

Classic Jewish texts pose a problem that needs to be faced directly. They are male centered and male dominated—in brief, sexist. We may slightly mitigate this damning ethical judgment by reminding ourselves of the time and place in which they were written, or we can praise the writers for those pronouncements that treat women comparatively benignly. Nonetheless, sexist attitudes predominate. And we do not wish to perpetuate the denigration of women while transmitting the greater wisdom of the Jewish sources. So where it seems reasonably clear that our almost universally male teachers meant "people," we render their texts that way, even though they used the masculine terms, which then conventionally included everyone. Alas, often we weren't sure, and we felt we had a certain responsibility to convey our tradition with reasonable accuracy. Then we gave the sexist usage as we found it, so that readers might address the problem shared by so many contemporary Jews, making our teachings and practices reflect our fervent belief in our equality before God.

One author of the many represented in this work merits special mention: Yeḥiel b. Yekutiel b. Binyamin Harofe. We mainly know this late-thirteenth-century Roman Jew as a scribe; Yeḥiel copied our earliest full manuscript of the Yerushalmi. But he interests us here as the author/compiler of a modest-sized anthology, *Sefer Maalot Hamiddot* (The book of the choicest virtues), because with it Yeḥiel created a new genre in Jewish literature. No one before him wrote a comprehensive, analytic treatment about the specific virtues that Judaism esteems. Of course, the Bible and Talmud contain many comments about the traits that should characterize a good Jew, but these are widely scattered rather than thematically arranged. Yeḥiel gathered many of these wisdom passages, plus others from contemporary writers (some we think adopted by the Jewish community but not of Jewish origin), and added his own thoughts to this anthology. *Sefer Maalot Hamiddot* broke new ground and was well accepted by the Jewish community of his time, engendering countless other books about Jewish virtues.

We were particularly attracted to Yeḥiel's work because it helped us overcome the problem of selectivity—why, of all the human traits various biblical and talmudic authors commended, we now chose just these and not those to emphasize. For example, our book has a chapter on "Wealth," but not on "Justice." There is never a fully satisfactory response to that charge, which is one reason people keep turning out new books on this theme, another sign of the dynamic nature of *musar* literature. But if the first author of a well-received book on Jewish virtues selected just these twenty-four virtues rather than others, we felt confident following his lead.

We make no claim that Yeḥiel's list is normative, even though we place a definite article in the title of our book based on his, *"The Jewish Moral Virtues."* Rather we are saying that we find Yeḥiel's selection and treatment marvelously stimulating. One notable feature is Yeḥiel's inclusion in many of his chapters of the vice that is antithetical to the virtue he discusses, helping us to more graphically define it. We follow his lead in this regard as well.

Again and again we realized that some truths about human nature do not change; people today have pretty much the same aspirations and failings as they did seven centuries ago in Yeḥiel's time, or even in the days of the Bible and Talmud. The deep human insight of Jews who lived millennia ago in circumstances so different from our own is often breathtaking.

But we could not simply be satisfied to translate Yeḥiel's work and deem it ripe wisdom for our time. He writes out of the classic medieval mind-set. For Yeḥiel, simply to cite a biblical verse (or pile up a few) is enough to validate the virtue he emphasizes and to motivate his readers to follow it. He is also supremely confident that doing the worthy deed would lead to the tangible as well as the spiritual rewards the Bible says God will give us. And his impregnable faith in all he received and now seeks to transmit—a stance that lends itself to the hyperbole so characteristic of rabbinic writing—often jars the sensibilities of our far more skeptical, self-doubting, uncertain time.

What we have done, then, is to rewrite Yeḥiel's book for Jews setting out on the twenty-first century. To do this we also include many citations by authors from the past seven centuries who wrote their wisdom after Yeḥiel. So while we follow his list of topics to discuss, we arrange them in quite a different order and give them a different exposition and emphasis.*

Still we believe that the *musar* impulse that unites us with Yeḥiel is far more fundamental than what separates us. When Rabbi Noah (1774–1832) succeeded his father Rabbi Mordechai as Rav of Lechovitz, his hasidic followers soon noted that he did many things quite differently. When they asked him about this, he responded: "I do exactly as my father did. He did not imitate and I do not imitate." Yeḥiel was not content merely to teach the Bible and the Talmud, but reshaped the traditional wisdom in new ways. Thus today, in our own style, we too are trying to carry on the timeless *musar* tradition.

In what follows, the reader should not expect to find a clearly rendered portrait of the quintessential good person. This work is no

---

* If you read our book beginning with the first page of the first chapter, you may notice that each virtue follows its predecessor without introductory comment, until Part VII, "Staying Worthy." There is a reason for this. Through chapter 19, we discuss the basics of attaining *musar* competence, ending with Part VI, "Achieving Our *Musar* Goals." We then tackle the difficult process of converting learning to doing—the action phase of *middot* accomplishment. And this, we feel, requires a certain added explanation. The same holds true of our concluding section, Part VIII, "Our Ground, Our Guide, Our Goal," as we honor the Reality that informs all of our learning and doing.

"genome project" mapping fine character. It cannot be, for the boundaries of the virtues we describe are quite fluid. One melds into another, as, for example, do wealth, generosity, and charity or contentedness, lovingkindness, and compassion. And when we do construe some coherence among the virtues, our vision is disrupted by virtues that appear to clash, as do contentment and zeal.

It is best, then, to think of *musar* insights as inevitably partial, consisting of one bit of wisdom after another. Approach this material as you would a huge mosaic (pun intended). Up close, individual stones may or may not be interesting, and their relation to those nearby may seem difficult to describe. But if we are successful, meaning should appear. When Israel, the Rebbe of Rizhyn was asked by his disciples how to serve God, he said, "How should I know?" But he then told this story: Two friends were found guilty of an offense, and the king, who wanted to be merciful, sentenced them to undergo the following ordeal. A rope was strung across a vast cavern; if they could cross on it to the other side they would be free. The first one got safely across, and his terrified colleague yelled across the chasm to find out how he did it. The friend responded, "All I know is that when I felt myself toppling over to one side, I leaned to the other" (Buber, *Tales of the Hasidim*, bk. 2, *The Later Masters*). Putting a life together is a little like that. A certain deed or experience can often supply some immediate insight, but a sense of the whole takes a lot of balance and many years. And the passing of time may yield yet a different perspective, for wisdom is that vigorous.

We hope that our examples encourage you to make *musar* literature a conscious part of your Jewish self, synthesizing it from your own experience and passing it on to others. So let us start our tour of the Jewish moral virtues by exploring the gateway to them all, Wisdom, the value that empowers our actions. We begin this journey by thanking the One who gives us this teaching and enables us to impart it to you:

Barukh atah Adonai, ḥonen ha-da'at. We bless you, Adonai, who graciously gives us wisdom.

CHAPTER 2

Wisdom—*Ḥokhmah*

Wisdom has built her house,
She has hewn her seven pillars.
She has prepared the feast,
Provided the wine,
And also set the table. . . .
"Come, eat my food
and drink the wine I have ready;
Give up simpleness and live,
Walk in the way of understanding."

—Prov. 9:1–2, 5–6

Wisdom and Life—one cannot exist without the other. Even the least complicated organism soon withers and dies if it cannot get the food and shelter it requires. It must have a brain or nervous system that "knows" what to do to survive. Wisdom is fundamental to life, in fact, to all nature. "R. Simeon b. Ḥalafta said: One should ask for wisdom above all other virtues, for it contains everything else" (S. of S. R. 1.1, 9). A popular adage of rabbinic times agrees: "If you lack knowledge, what have you acquired? If you acquire knowledge, what do you lack?" (Num. R. 19.3). Extending his highest praise, Amemar insists that "A wise man is even superior to a prophet" (B.B. 12a).

To be wise about wisdom, we need to distinguish its several "pillars." Wisdom can be as simple as learning how to tie a shoelace (not simple if you're two years old). It can be intensely practical, like knowing how to operate your new VCR or planning how to get along in the business world. As the Yiddish proverb explains: "You don't come into the marketplace with just a little wisdom." It can be technical, like figuring out how to use an unfamiliar ATM, or creative, as the rabbis teach: "If the bread is too high to reach, the sensible person will tie two sticks together and pull it down" (Lev. R. 19.2). It can be as complex as astrophysics or as challenging as playing chess against the IBM computer, Deep Blue.

But the richest, most intricate wisdom of all is knowing how to live properly. The thirteenth-century Spanish sage Jonah Gerondi, echoing the Bible, said the truly wise have the ability "to do good and shun sin" (*Shaarei Teshuvah* [Gates of repentance]). The twelfth-century Spanish ethicist Bahya ibn Pakuda connected wisdom to religious sensibility. He counseled us to seek wisdom by meditating on God and human nature (*Hovot Halevavot* [Duties of the heart]). Yehiel b. Yekutiel, the thirteenth-century Roman sage, characterized practical wisdom as "the great acquisition which does not get lost, the treasure which does not diminish" (*Sefer Maalot Hamiddot* [The book of the choicest virtues]). This *hokhmah,* the medieval Sephardic commentator Judah Bargeloni advised, comes only "after struggle, quest, anguish and effort" (*Perush Sefer Yetzirah* [A commentary to the book of creation]). Acquiring wisdom, and "not too late," as the Yiddish proverb says, should be our lifelong goal. Helping you attain that goal is the aim of this book.

"Hug Wisdom and She Will Exalt You" (Prov. 4:8)

Everyone knows Solomon as the great biblical exemplar of wisdom. Yet all his wisdom could not keep his royal house together, for after his death, the vast kingdom his father David had amassed was divided, a sad legacy indeed. Perhaps wisdom came too easily to Solomon. The Bible tells how, while still a young man, Solomon received *hokhmah* from God. When in a dream God offered to grant his most cherished wish, Solomon responded: "Give me an understanding heart to judge your people, that I may discern between good and bad." God was so pleased with this request that God said: "And I also will give you what you did not ask for—both riches and glory all your life, the likes of which no king has ever had" (1 Kings 3:5, 9–10, 13). Or maybe all those riches and glory clouded his wise heart, so that his wisdom never matured beyond simple book learning, a mere intellectual accomplishment. Our tradition demands that learning be paired with action; without action, our wisdom is neglected and wilts. As the twelfth-century scholar Joseph Kimḥi taught: "Wisdom joined to practice will guide a person until death, but wisdom from which no action flows [dies], leaving nothing" (*Shekel Hakodesh* [The holy shekel]).

The Torah has told us of another uniquely wise person whose legacy still inspires us today: Bezalel, the chief artisan of the wilderness tabernacle. In the Book of Exodus, we learn that God singled him out and "filled him with the spirit of God, in wisdom, in understanding, in knowledge, and in all manner of workmanship . . ." (31:3). Moreover, God put wisdom in the hearts of his helpers. Bezalel must have been quite wise, for he directed the efforts of all these skillful workers in "gold, silver, and brass, and those who could cut precious stones for setting and carve wood in the required ways," (Exod. 35:30–35, 36:1–2). Some rabbis taught that Bezalel fulfilled God's directions so well that God chose him as an ancestor of the Messiah.

"Wisdom Calls, Understanding Raises Her Voice" (Prov. 8:1)

Most of us acquire our wisdom in far more mundane ways. The blessings we say each morning remind us that wisdom grounds our very existence. The rabbis tell us to recite this *berakhah* after going to the bathroom: "Blessed are You, *Adonai,* our God, Ruler of the universe, who formed us in wisdom and created in us an intricate system of ducts and tubes, knowing full well that if one of them should open or close at the wrong time, we could no longer exist before You" (Ber. 11a). Since roosters roused people before the days of digital alarm clocks, the rabbis praised God for creating such discerning creatures: "Blessed are You, *Adonai,* our God, Ruler of the universe, who gave the cock the intelligence to distinguish between day and night" (Ber. 60b). The rabbis did not limit their appreciation of *hokhmah* to mornings or the intimate realm but extended it throughout the day and expanded it to the entire cosmos. In the evening service, the prayer after the *Barekhu* blesses

God, who "by Divine wisdom brings on evening, ordering the planets, the times, and the seasons" (Ber. 11b). In this way we express our sense of wonder at the harmony so evident in the heavens.

But what Judaism identified as spiritual wisdom, science reduces to natural order. Indeed, it's only human for most of us to take the systematic workings of our bodies and our world for granted, as the way things should be, for as a traditional Jewish maxim says: "[Only] fools and the crazy are accustomed to confusion" (Ladino proverb). Yet even those on science's cutting edge seem awed by recent discoveries. Why should DNA, the vital life force that controls primal genetic information, consist overwhelmingly of tightly wrapped "garbage"? And why do we humans have so much of it? Each of us has enough DNA to extend from the earth to the sun and back again! And what kind of human achievement is cloning? If we ever make the leap from cloning sheep to cloning people, will that demonstrate our wisdom—or our folly? Will our wisdom assert itself, teaching us not only how to do something, but also whether it should be done at all?

In our increasingly uncertain world, many scientists admit that their disciplines have limitations, and many theologians are making less extravagant claims for what religion can tell us. Their shared lack of absolute wisdom brings together scientific and religious theorists in a new dialogue, united by their similarities rather than separated by their differences in belief. Chief among these shared ideas is the notion that the universe started with a "big bang." According to Daniel Matt, a contemporary academic scholar of Jewish mysticism, we can find intriguing parallels between cosmogony, the study of the evolution of the universe, and Kabbalah, the Jewish esoteric theology. Scientists agree that all matter started from a single cosmic energy-seed in which conditions were so unique that it is called a "singularity." Our reality begins at the point, scientists say, when the energy-singularity exploded, forming matter and creating our universe. Similarly the kabbalists, following the teaching of the sixteenth-century Safed seer Isaac Luria, trace all beginnings to the Unity we call God. According to the Lurianic myth, the all-pervading power that is God contracted to make room for a physical world, distinct from the Divine. God then put this creative energy into the vacated space. But the condensed force shattered the "vessels" that were meant to contain and thus shape the world. So our imperfect universe was born, ever seeking to return to its ideal, unified state. Our job is to find the divine energy-sparks scattered throughout the material universe and by our actions restore the unity of our cosmos. Matt's imagery defines and thus relates the awe implicit in science and the wisdom religion finds in nature.

Is Silence Always Golden?

So far we have been speaking about wisdom on a grand scale. How does wisdom show itself on a more human scale, in our everyday lives? It is through words that we teach wisdom. Through words we offer comfort to those who have just suffered a loss, or through words we offend mourners if we substitute glib banter for consolation. When Job's friends visit him in one of the first documented *shivah* calls, they so eagerly communicate their "wisdom" that their words plague, rather than comfort him. Finally unable to hear any more, Job cries out in rage and frustration: "Oh that you would just stop talking! And that would be your wisdom" (13:5). Ecclesiastes agrees, pointing to "a time to keep silent and a time to speak" (3:7). The sages of the Talmud, those verbal virtuosos, sensibly connect silence to wisdom. R. Akiba says: "Silence is a fence for wisdom" (Avot 3.17), and R. Hiyya indicates: "It isn't necessary to tell a wise man to hold his tongue" (D.E.Z. 7.4). R. Judah of Kefar Giboraya teaches: "There is no better medicine than a wise silence" (Meg. 18a). And a folk maxim states that even a donkey who keeps silent is considered wise (Ladino proverb). Nonetheless, these sages were not urging us to take vows of total silence, for they knew: "Wise people are recognized by their speech" (D.E.Z. 5.3). "The words of a sage, even when spoken quietly, are better than the shouting of the leader of an ignorant rabble" (Eccles. 9:17). Thus both silence and speech express the many aspects of wisdom.

The Talmud has given us two similarly phrased, but different models of the *hakham*, the wise person. One text reads: "Ben Zoma said: Who is wise? One who learns from everyone" (Avot 4.1).

According to Ben Zoma, we might pick up wisdom anywhere, from the fool as well as from the sage, from the young as well as the old. Ben Zoma's realism teaches how we benefit from teachers we find whenever we seek wisdom. The eleventh-century Spanish poet and philosopher Solomon ibn Gabirol concurs, suggesting that an important part of wisdom is knowing that our search never ends: "If a person imagines he has attained it, he's a fool" (*Mivḥar Hapeninim* [The choicest pearls]). Even contemporary pop culture preaches the same lesson. As the country and western ballad "The Gambler" puts it, we can learn wisdom even from a dying card player: "(You've got to) know when to hold 'em, know when to fold 'em, know when to walk away, know when to run. . . ."

The second talmudic definition of a *ḥakham* expands our understanding. "Who is wise? Someone who can see what's coming" (Tam. 32a). Indeed, we often gain much foresight from experience. How many times have we assured a distressed friend or child that the grim task looming ahead "will all be over by this time tomorrow?" Some people are blessed with that special insight we call "vision," the ability to discern in the welter of the present a clear image of what likely will soon happen. We are indeed fortunate when our leaders are such visionaries.

But we now find ourselves facing a paradox. On the one hand, wisdom is so simple that we learn it everywhere; on the other hand, it is so infinitely complex that, despite strenuous effort, we never really attain it. Will our reach forever exceed our grasp? Is our wisdom then only illusory?

The Wisdom We Are Given, the Wisdom We Acquire

It is fortunate, then, that we do not enter this world as total ciphers. "R. Simlai delivered the following discourse: During the months of our mothers' pregnancy, we are taught the whole Torah from beginning to end. But as soon as we are about to be born, an angel approaches, slaps us on the mouth, and causes us to forget all the Torah completely" (Nid. 30b). The tradition explains that this is why we have an indentation on our upper lip! Tiny and helpless as we are when newly born, we nonetheless emerge with certain instinctive traits to help us survive. When babies need food or the comfort of a fresh diaper, they make that need known exquisitely clear and loud. As children get older, they seem to know intuitively what buttons to push to drive their parents crazy. Yet somehow, they manage to reach adulthood in reasonably sound shape. Perhaps we owe this miracle to the good sense, *hokhmah,* we are born with, as well as that which we acquire through experience.

The authors of the Bible located our understanding within our physical bodies. They associated decision-making with the heart—"Teach us to number our days that we may get us a heart of wisdom" (Ps. 90:12)—or the hand—"If I forget thee, O Jerusalem, let my right hand forget its cunning" (Ps. 137:5)—or the eyes—"A wise person has eyes in his head, whereas a fool walks in darkness" (Eccles. 2:14). Later sages have identified other sites. R. Simeon b. Yohai explained that Abraham came to know the one God despite a father who made idols, because "his two kidneys overflowed with wisdom" (Gen. R. 61.1). When his students left R. Ammi's class they said to him, "May your heart meditate understanding, your mouth speak wisdom, and your tongue induce song" (Ber. 17a). The medieval midrashic anthology *Yalkut Shimoni* claimed: "Wisdom was placed in the heart because all limbs depend on the heart" (*Yalkut Shimoni,* Prov. 929). And the anonymous author of *Orhot Tzaddikim* (The ways of the righteous), writing over 450 years ago, firmly believed that "the soul is wisdom, dwelling in the mind like a king at the head of his troops."

As we continue to acquire wisdom throughout our lives, we discover that it is possible for our critics to become our most important teachers. As we mature, we find that we can come to "love the one who rebukes us so that we may add to our wisdom" (D.E.Z. 9.2). After all, the Yiddish proverb teaches us: "No one is really smart about themselves, but everyone is smart about everyone else." As we keep growing, these encounters broaden our capacity for acquiring wisdom, affirming the biblical adage: "God gives wisdom to the wise, knowledge to them that know" (Dan. 2:21). So Judaism has long honored its elders, recognizing that wisdom ripens over a lifetime. The tart Yiddish mind put it this way: "When beauty's passed, brains last," and "for looking, one wants someone beautiful, but for living, one wants someone wise." "When you need brains, brawn won't do." And finally: "As the Kobriner Rabbi said: Service to the Lord is like wine, best when it is old" (Newman, *The Hasidic Anthology*).

The Wisdom of Women

Because the rabbis usually equated wisdom with knowledge of traditional Jewish law, a field all but closed to women, they tended to overlook the frequent, positive connections between wisdom and women found in the Bible. For there we find vivid portraits of savvy females endowed with both practical street smarts and complex intelligence, able to handle whatever comes their way. Rebecca knows that Jacob, not Esau, deserves Isaac's blessings and masterminds the plot to achieve that result (Gen. 27). Yael entices the Canaanite general Sisera into her tent and kills him (Judg. 4:17–22). Moses' sister Miriam looks after her infant brother as he floats in the Nile River bulrushes and suggests to Pharaoh's daughter that she hire his real mother to nurse him (Exod. 2:4, 7).

But the rabbis were not so sexist that they *never* associated wisdom with women. One midrash tells us that "Miriam took wisdom" as her inheritance and passed it on to her descendant, Bezalel (Exod. R. 48.4). Another relates how Miriam found fresh water to drink after the people crossed the sea to freedom (Taan. 9a). However, the ultimate connection between understanding and femininity is supplied by the Book of Proverbs, which personifies wisdom as a woman: "Wisdom cries aloud in the streets, raises her voice in the squares . . . at the gates she speaks out" (1:20–21). "Say to wisdom 'you are my sister,' and call understanding a kinswoman" (7:4). "She is more precious than rubies, all your goods do not equal her worth. Length of days is in her right hand, riches and honor in her left hand. Her ways are ways of pleasantness and all her paths are peace. She is a tree of life to them that grasp her, and all who hold on to her are happy" (3:15–18).

Proverbs does not only depict woman as an allegorical figure of wisdom; it also praises the living human being in "The Woman of Valor" poem that closes the book. Feminist scholars have faulted some of the poem's verses because they portray the archetypal female as glorying in self-sacrifice: "She rises while it is still night, and supplies provisions for her household. . . . And never eats from the bread of idleness" (31:15, 27). We prefer to see her as an early exemplar of female entrepreneurship, for the text also says: "She sets her mind on an estate and acquires it. . . . She girds herself with strength and performs her tasks with vigor; she sees that her business thrives" (31:16–18).

Some of these early themes have been adapted in more modern times. For example, the eighteenth-century Polish poet Isaac Halevi Satanov writes: "Because God loved wisdom, He adopted her as His daughter and lovingly brought her up. Before God made heaven and earth, she was God's delight" (*Mishle Asaf* [The proverbs of Asaf]). A twentieth-century female incarnation of wisdom may well be the poet and playwright Gertrude Stein, whose wise dying words were, "What is the question?"

Of course, of all women honored by the tradition, we must not fail to mention our first and most influential teacher—our own mother. As our first and most constant connection with life, our mother bequeaths us her insight and her wisdom, which serve as the foundation of our knowledge for all the years to come. Our later teachers are either her surrogates or her colleagues.

The Fool We Hope Never to Be

If our mother ideally knows everything, the fool is someone who knows nothing—or close to it—and doesn't learn much from experience, either. As a Ladino proverb tells us: "A donkey who comes back from Mecca remains a donkey." Or as the Yiddish adage has it: "At a feast and at a funeral one shouldn't allow a fool to make a speech, because he might blurt out the truth!" The Book of Proverbs puts it even more bluntly: "A fool returns to his folly the way a dog returns to his vomit" (26:11). In the Talmud, Rava states: "Be not like the fool who, after sinning, brings an offering but does not repent" (Ber. 23a). An American maxim adds its own bit of wisdom: "Burn me once, shame on you; burn me twice, shame on me." All of us know at least one misguided soul who fits into this category.

When this person heads our way, we wince, for we know there's no way to escape hearing advice we never ask for and could do better without.

Yet even the wisest person among us occasionally acts the fool. For life requires a measure of daring, even foolhardy risk, as the nineteenth-century German poet Heinrich Heine quipped: "Who never acted foolishly also never was wise" ("Lazarus"). Paradoxically, foolishness may sometimes be our best teacher, because learning from it may add to our wisdom. For one who has "wised-up" serves as a more convincing role model than one who has never succumbed to folly's wiles. In our own time, many of us have found that psychotherapy also brings us wisdom, leading us to the kind of self-understanding that can break the habits of foolish living.

Foolish "sages," more naive than wise, populate the literature of every age and society. Our nineteenth-century eastern European ancestors gave us "The Wise Men of Ḥelm," our very own archetypal nincompoops, who brought comic relief to an often harsh and bitter existence. Although an actual town called Ḥelm with a large Jewish population existed in Poland until the beginning of World War II, we unfortunately do not know how its inhabitants became the butt of these funny, silly tales. Here is a sample of their wisdom:

> Why is the sea salty? Because of the herring. The herring is salted and that makes the water salty, too.
>
> Why are summer days long and winter days short? In the summer the days expand because of the heat, and in the winter they contract because of the cold.
>
> Not far from the Ḥelm village square two brightly lit lanterns hung from two high poles. Across the poles was a large sign reading "All Searching Done Here." Before this creation, whenever the Ḥelmites lost something at night, they couldn't find it because the village was so dark. Once the lanterns were hung, anyone who lost something had a lit square in which to look for it. (Simon, *The Wise Men of Ḥelm*)

The Limits of Wisdom

Sometimes we can be too wise for our own good. How often have we told ourselves: "It would have been better had I not known." The Bible expresses this sentiment well: "In much wisdom is much grief. One who increases knowledge, increases sorrow" (Eccles. 1:18). And even though we learn this lesson, we must watch helplessly as our children make the same mistakes we did, just as we repeat our parents' errors, or err on the opposite extreme in trying to avoid them. Perhaps this is one of the special burdens we must bear for being human. "Have you ever seen an ass or a camel convulsed with anguish?" ask the rabbis. "By whom is such pain experienced? By humans. R. Ishmael reminds us: You load the beast with what it can bear" (Eccles. R. 1.18, 1).

Wisdom can also lead us down dark paths. Jeremiah warns us: "Let not the wise man glory in his wisdom . . ." (9:22). More than a millennium later, the late-thirteenth-century commentator Bahya b. Asher teaches that wisdom will not necessarily keep us from error, since it is possible to be both wise and bad (*Kad Hakemah* [A measure of fine flour]). The twentieth-century Polish sage Rabbi Eliyahu Dessler notes: "Uncontrollable knowledge is useless, even dangerous if it brings disaster to its possessors" (*Mikhtav MeEliyahu* [Strive for truth]). In our own time, we have seen wisdom gone awry by computer whizzes who sordidly flood the internet with pornography or maliciously change people's personal data files.

The highest wisdom, then, results from acknowledging limits, knowing what is too much or too little for our minds to manage. Wisdom creates the critical discernment that gives our lives order and balance. Long ago Ecclesiastes admonished: "To every thing there is a season and a time to every purpose under the heaven: / A time to be born and a time to die; / A time to plant and a time to uproot; / A time to kill and a time to heal; / A time to break down and a time to build up; / A time to weep and a time to laugh; / A time to mourn and a time to dance . . ." (3:1–4). How shall we meet each of these times with appropriate wisdom? No single set of rules can fully tell us what we should do in every circumstance or how to navigate our way through new situations. All we can do is to consult that inner good sense we've been cultivating through study and deeds, and hope that it will enable us to balance conflicting claims.

Our Ultimate Wisdom

As we have seen, human wisdom has limits. When we have stretched these limits as far as we can, our tradition teaches us to turn to wisdom's ultimate source—God. We take comfort in knowing that we are not alone when we face life's extraordinary challenges and opportunities. If we can even fleetingly appreciate the One who, as the daily prayer says, "graciously endows humankind with knowledge, and teaches us understanding . . ." we can rely upon a relationship with God that will help us when our own good sense falters. Thus our greatest wisdom is knowing that we can turn to God and, in that intimacy, sense what we should do. "For the Lord gives wisdom, and knowledge and understanding are God's decree" (Prov. 2:6). After Job describes how difficult it is to find wisdom, he finally admits: "God understands the way to it; God understands its source. . . . God says to humanity, 'See! Revering the Lord, that is wisdom, and shunning evil, that is understanding'" (Job 28:23, 28).

From Our Tradition

Teach wisdom to one who knows not, and learn from one who knows. By doing this you will know what you do not know and remember what you indeed know.

—Solomon ibn Gabirol, *Mivḥar Hapeninim*

The Yehudi and Peretz his disciple were crossing a meadow. Cattle put out to pasture mooed and geese cackled. "If only one could understand what all of them are saying!" cried Peretz. "When you get to the point of understanding the very core of what you yourself are saying, you will understand the language of all creatures," said the Yehudi.

—Buber, *Tales of the Hasidim*, bk. 2, *The Later Masters*

Said the Mezritcher: Wisdom is God's garment. Wisdom constantly receives influence from above and gives spirituality below.

—Newman, *The Hasidic Anthology*

I will make the wisdom of the ancients my portion. . . .
When I dive into the sea of their knowledge,
I bring forth pearls to adorn my neck. . . .
They are light to my eyes, music to my ears,
They are honey to my palate, they are a sweet savory scent.

—Moses ibn Ezra, *Selected Poems*

PART II

Living Responsibly

Trustworthiness— *Emunah*

*F*ew modern-day public figures merit our admiration as role-models. Yet when Cardinal Joseph Bernardin of Chicago died of cancer late in 1996, Americans of every faith experienced a profound sense of loss. His willingness to share publicly his most elemental doubts and fears, his warm outreach to so many of different faiths, his simple decency (even when falsely accused of sexual improprieties), convinced people that he was a good man, someone who "kept the faith." Similarly, though Jimmy Carter elicited doubt as well as trust when he was president, his continued idealistic strivings in the years since leaving office transformed him into a figure of great public esteem. His hands-on work building homes for the needy and his willingness to travel almost anywhere to further peace have earned him widespread respect, even from those who don't agree with his politics.

But one need not be prominent to serve as such a role model, to be someone who radiates stability, credibility, and hope. All of us have felt that deep sense of appreciation for those special individuals who we know would never let us down. Over the years we trusted that we could count on them. These rare people exemplify *emunah*, not "faith" as it is commonly understood, but "trustworthiness" as it relates to character.

Building a Sense of Trust

Trustworthiness begins with our learning to trust others. The psychoanalyst Erik Erikson explains that we owe this ability to our earliest relations with our mother. As our first nurturer, she receives our wholehearted trust, fashioning a fundamental relationship that prefigures all others. Luckily for future generations, young women contemplating motherhood are well aware of this responsibility. Even the most ambitious new mother, determined to fulfill herself in the workplace, knows that developing this life-shaping bond is critical to her child's proper development. Therefore she invests herself in this process, staying home with her newborn as long as she can, so that another human being may successfully form the power of trust.

How we fulfill our promises to those we love defines our basic trustworthiness, a reality that hasn't changed much over the centuries. As the talmudic sage R. Zera said, "One should not say to a child, 'I will give you something,' and then not give it to him. He thus teaches the child to lie" (Suk. 46b). It doesn't help to declare, "Do as I say, not as I do." R. Yoḥanan's parable clearly illustrates the problem: "A businessman bought his son a perfume shop on the street of harlots. When the father discovered that his son was frequenting the prostitutes, he began yelling, 'I'll kill you!' Luckily, one of the father's friends witnessed the fracas and spoke up: 'Why are you yelling so? You yourself ruined your son, ignoring all other occupations and teaching him to be a perfumer, and ignoring all other streets, opening a shop for him with harlots as neighbors!'" (Exod. R. 43.7).

Although we learn as we grow up that not everyone merits our trust, it is still heartbreaking to discover that someone we thought we could trust has betrayed us. If such betrayals happen often enough, children grow up hardhearted, unwilling to trust anyone. Bereft of a circle of trusting friends, a person may face a bare and lonely existence. As caring adults, we recoil from such a fate. Thus we need to feel safe enough to shed our emotional armor, confidently allowing lasting relationships to grow.

Learning to Act Responsibly

Growing up, of course, means learning not only how to trust but also how to be trustworthy ourselves. It means accepting increased accountability for our actions. As the third-century sage Resh Lakish taught, "First clean yourself, and then clean others" (B.B. 60b). The Mishnah tractate Demai discusses those persons whose word should be accepted: "If a man is not trustworthy about what he does, how can he be trusted when he attests to what others did?" (2.2). We must guard against unintentional deception. "R. Judah said in the name of Rav, 'You must not keep in your house a measuring vessel smaller or larger than the standard' [Deut. 25:14], even if it is to be used as a chamber pot. Others may use it as a measure by mistake" (B.M. 61b). The author of Psalm 15 demands even more. First raising the question, "*Adonai,* who may sojourn in Your 'tent,' who may dwell on Your holy mountain?" the Psalmist answers: someone "who stands by his oath even to his own loss" (15:1, 4).

The Torah presents two outstanding studies of how trustworthiness evolves, played out in the lives of our patriarchs Jacob and Joseph. When Jacob hears Laban's sons complaining about Jacob's increasing wealth, he hurriedly gathers together his wives and possessions and flees toward Canaan. Laban pursues and finally catches Jacob, first chiding his son-in-law for running away and then accusing him of stealing the household gods. Jacob angrily retorts: ". . . Anything in your herds that beasts ate, I never brought to you; I had to pay for it. You also required me to pay for anything beasts snatched from the flocks during the day or the night. This is how it was: in the day the drought consumed me and at night there was frost so bitter I couldn't sleep. I was in your house for twenty years. I worked fourteen years to marry your two daughters and six more to gain my own flock, and in that time you renegotiated my wages ten times! If God . . . hadn't helped me, you certainly would have sent me away empty-handed" (Gen. 31:39–42).

Jacob's son Joseph embodies a similar ideal of trustworthiness. Trying to rid themselves of this pesky know-it-all, his siblings throw Joseph into a pit. They then sell him to Midianite traders bound for Egypt, where Potiphar, Pharaoh's chief steward, buys the hapless lad. Joseph's new master observes that "*Adonai* made Joseph successful in everything he undertook. Potiphar took a liking to him. He made Joseph his personal attendant and put him in charge of all of his household and all that he owned. . . . He left all that he had in Joseph's hands; with him in charge, Potiphar needed to pay attention only to the food he ate" (Gen. 39:3–6). When Potiphar's wife tries to seduce Joseph, he resists, arguing that Potiphar trusts him too much to betray him this way: "Look, with me here, my master gives no thought to anything in this house, and all that he owns he has placed in my hands. . . . How then could I do this awful thing and sin before God?" (Gen. 39:8–9). Potiphar's wife falsely accuses Joseph, and Potiphar has him thrown in jail, where he again proves so trustworthy that the warden makes Joseph responsible for the whole prison (Gen. 39:22–23). Finally, Pharaoh places the entire nation under Joseph's care, saying: ". . . except by your authority, no one shall lift up hand or foot in all the land of Egypt" (Gen. 41:44).

So we learn that the greater our position of responsibility, the greater must be our trustworthiness. Even Moses, God's "own servant," is not exempt from this rule. A midrash explains that the Torah provides a detailed list of all of the gifts brought by the people to build and decorate the wilderness tabernacle. It goes to such great lengths in order to uphold Moses's reputation for honesty, ensuring that no one charges him with taking anything as a personal payment (*Yalkut Shimoni*, Prov. 28:2).

Trusting Others As We Are Trusted

People appeal to us all the time to trust them, hoping that we won't dig too deeply to discover why we shouldn't. So many scam artists abound in today's world that we are more likely to suspect someone who comes right out and says "trust me," than to grant that person our confidence. In most cases we base our judgment on our estimate of that person's general character. The final arbiter often is no more sound than "gut instinct."

The Bible provides two cases of women whose wise judgment led them to put their lives in another's trust. Abraham's servant Eliezer wants Rebecca to accompany him to Canaan to marry Isaac, a cousin she's never met. Her father Bethuel and her brother Laban want Rebecca to stay with them a while longer, so they "call the maiden and ask her to speak for herself." In response to their question, "Will you go with this man?" Rebecca replies, "I will go" (Gen. 24:57–58). Rebecca thus relies on an indefinable intuition and judges Eliezer so trustworthy that she leaves her family to go with him, traveling for several hundred miles to begin a new life in an unknown land.

After Naomi's husband and two sons die in Moab, she decides to return to her people in Israel. Naomi urges her Moabite daughters-in-law to return to their father's homes. Orpah obeys, but Ruth will not abandon her mother-in-law: "Entreat me not to leave you or turn back from following you. For where you go, I will go; and where you lodge, I will lodge. Your people will be my people, and your God, my God. Where you die, there will I die, and there will I be buried. Let *Adonai* do what He wants with me if anything but death parts me from you" (Ruth 1:16–17).

Trusting Naomi, Ruth offers to her this classic gift of self. We can't explain why; the biblical authors provide these stories to show us that sometimes we must give ourselves to that component of *emunah* we call faith, as Rebecca and Ruth did. And we hope to become the kind of person who deserves such trust. We can't program ourselves with a specific set of behaviors to elicit such feelings, yet we sense that, if our basic characters are worthy enough, they will shine through and speak for themselves, as Eliezer's and Naomi's did.

Trusting Enough to Accept Criticism

All of us occasionally need to listen to some harsh truths about ourselves. The Book of Proverbs says, "Reprove a wise man and he will love you for it" (9:8), to which R. Yose b. Ḥanina adds, "A love without reproof is no love" (Gen. R. 54.3). But few of us are mature enough to rise to this level. Because we are so eager to deflect the wounds that criticism inflicts on our pride, we quickly turn from defense to offense, impugning our critic's motives.

Our *musar* teachers have long argued that to have and be a faithful friend merits a trust that won't easily dismiss unwelcome comments. The hasidic rabbi Yeraḥmiel Yisrael Yitzḥak Danziger counseled: "To be worthy of offering advice to another, one need not be an expert. It is sufficient to be a trusted friend" (Elkins, *Melodies from My Father's House*). And the anonymous author of *Orḥot Tzaddikim* wrote more than 450 years ago: "Don't be ashamed to receive the truth from anyone, even from the smallest of the small," a point Hans Christian Andersen made unforgettably in his story, "The Emperor's New Clothes." For who would have thought that a mighty king would only hear the truth from a little boy, who blurted out before any adult could stop him that he was parading down the main avenue in the royal buff!

Coping with the Treacherous

The world is full of people we can't trust; that is why we learn street smarts early as critical survival tools. For some time after Francie's wallet was stolen in the New York City subway she remained apprehensive, afraid that anyone who pushed against her or even avoided her glance intended to do her harm. How many of us leave our cars unlocked, even in our suburban driveway? And most of us wouldn't dare leave a key under the doormat or in the mailbox, "just in case. . . ." We have become prisoners in a culture of fear.

Musarists distinguish three levels of untrustworthiness: deceit, hypocrisy, and the most villainous, betrayal. Though the least harmful, deceit still causes damage, for we say or do something while purposely hiding our real motive. In hypocrisy we dissemble even further, pretending to be virtuous while hiding our true, evil intention. Betrayal is most harmful because it is most hurtful. It relies on the trust of the blameless other, only to demolish it by duplicitous acts. While we rail against such moral dishonesty in all its forms, we define this descending pattern to put everyone who is still unsuspecting on notice—remain gullible at your own peril.

How Shall We Deal with Deceitful Behavior?

Biblical authors excoriate the deceiver: "Anyone who lives by crooked speech is a scoundrel and an evil person" (Prov. 6:12). "Like a madman scattering deadly firebrands as arrows is one who deceives his fellow and says, 'I was only joking'" (Prov. 26:18–19). "An enemy dissembles with his speech but inwardly he harbors deceit" (Prov. 26:24). Lying seems so much a part of human behavior that a person who tries to be sincere prays wholeheartedly: "*Adonai,* deliver my soul from lying lips, from a deceitful tongue" (Ps. 120:2).

The field of commerce seems almost to encourage experts of deceit, giving them a ready-made forum to practice their trickery. Acknowledging this reality, the rabbis long ago developed a substantial body of law to shield unsuspecting souls from the sinful manipulations of these ancient "used-car salesmen." Our sages regarded deceit in the marketplace as *genevat da'at,* "stealing" someone's mind, and *ona'at devarim,* fraudulent representation: "There is a teaching, 'A man must not plow with his ox at night, and hire it out by day, nor may he himself work at his own affairs at night and also hire himself out by day. And he must not undertake a fast, or self-imposed privation, for he thereby diminishes the amount of his work for his master'" (Yer. Dem. 8.4). R. Simeon b. Gamaliel ruled: "A shopkeeper must clean his measures twice a week, and wipe his weights once a week, and cleanse his scales after every weighing of liquids" (B.B. 88b). In general, "a merchant may not tell a customer that his product has some intangible advantage it does not have" (B.M. 59b). So in their idealized story of R. Simeon b. Shetaḥ's purchase of a donkey, the rabbis admonish us to go to the opposite extreme. When R. Simeon examines the animal he has bought, he discovers a precious stone tied to its neck. Though his disciples try to dissuade him, he returns the stone to its original owner, insisting that he purchased a donkey, not a jewel (Deut. R. 3.3).

Hypocrisy: "Lord, Lord, How This World Is Given to Lying" (I Henry IV)

Hypocrisy intensifies deceit, for the hypocrite pretends to believe one thing while intending to act quite differently. Thus the rabbis warn: "The Holy One, blessed be He, hates a person who says one thing with his mouth and another in his heart" (Pes. 113b). "Hypocrites are one of the four kinds of deceivers who may not come into God's presence" (Mid. Pss. 101.7). "There are seven sorts of thieves. The first comprises people who deceive their neighbors by urging them to be their guests when they don't really want them, or those who push a gift when they know the neighbor won't accept it" (T.B.K. 7.8). "The law, 'You must not set a stumbling block before the blind,' [Lev. 19:14], includes the sanction, 'You must not hide part of your intention in giving someone advice.' You must not say 'Sell your field and buy a donkey,' when you are really manipulating things so you can buy his field" (Sifra Ked. 88).

These days it is difficult to name public officials who aren't masters of hypocrisy. Fifty plus years after the Holocaust, some Swiss bankers may actually return a fraction of the funds they've long said they never had. In addition, the Swiss government, which claimed neutrality during World War II, might finally assume fiscal responsibility for doing profitable business with the Nazis. Or shall we speak of the American government's hypocrisy: its decades-long treatment of poor, black men in the Tuskegee medical experiments with syphilis; its refusal to acknowledge the harm caused to troops exposed to nerve and other toxic gases during the Gulf War?

People lie for various reasons. Some convince themselves that they should tell us only what they think we need to know. Others believe that a sin of omission—giving an incomplete version of the truth—is a lesser vice than a sin of commission—saying and doing whatever they think they can get away with. No wonder the infamous "credibility gap," a phrase made popular during the Vietnam War and Watergate, continues to widen. Our sages reject such convenient rationalizations. They have always demanded scrupulously high standards, especially of our leaders.

Scam artists who prey on the poor, the lonely, and the elderly are particularly reprehensible. Gene's candidate for arch-hypocrite is a once-highly regarded accountant. While president of a traditional New York congregation, he invested the funds of individual members, initially providing a high return. Lured by his guarantees of continued high dividends, many widows also entrusted their money to him. Sometime later he acknowledged that there was nothing left in their accounts. He couldn't be prosecuted because his victims had trusted him enough to give him total discretion over their investments. His community didn't need to formally excommunicate the man—since almost no one in the congregation would wish him so much as "Shabbat Shalom," he soon left the area.

Betrayal: The Deepest Trust May Beget the Most Painful Deceit

We despise governmental dissembling; hypocrisy fills us with revulsion. But even more vile is being betrayed by one we love. For love, the ultimate trust, arises only when we feel secure enough to drop our innermost defenses, exposing everything we are to pledge lifelong faithfulness to another. We pray that this unique communion will help us to forgive, if the person we trust hurts us badly. But sometimes that person knows us so intimately that he or she wounds us too deeply for our love to survive. Jewish tradition has long taught that adultery constitutes such a treachery. Despite our culture's recent fling with permissive sexual activity, we still cry "How could you?"—a cry of the soul's pain when cut to its primal core. "R. Simeon b. Menasyah says: What qualifies as 'That which is crooked cannot be made straight' [Eccles. 1:15]? If a man steals, he can restore the theft and make amends. . . . If a man expropriates something deposited with him or withholds the payment due a laborer, he can similarly make restitution. But one who cohabits with a married woman . . . is driven from the world . . . for he cannot restore the old marriage" (Num. R. 9.6). Today, not many would accept this rabbinic ruling against taking back a wife who strays. Still, few marriages remain the same after one of the partners commits adultery.

Spousal or child abuse is another ultimate betrayal. When the person we trust most destroys that relationship by inflicting physical pain, by sexual violation, or by abandonment, the soul is as outraged as the body. This abuse of power may be our generation's most heinous sin. Its viciousness reaches new depths if betrayal is the response to our love.

Rabbinic Realism: When It's All Right to Lie

But none of us is an angel or a saint. Total honesty and total trust clash even, perhaps especially, in our most important relationships. While the rabbis sought scrupulously to follow the guidance of Proverbs 13:5, "The righteous man hates lies," they were realistic enough to rule that one may sometimes lie in order to make peace (Yev. 65b) or preserve human dignity: "Our sages taught: What does one chant before the bride? Shammai's disciples say: Sing something about her as she really is. Hillel's disciples say: O beautiful and graceful bride. Said the school of Shammai to the school of Hillel: And does one say this of her if she is lame or blind? Didn't the Torah say, 'Keep far from a lie' [Exod. 23:7]? Said the school of Hillel to the school of Shammai: If someone makes a peculiar acquisition in the market, should one praise or deprecate it? Surely one should praise it. Based on this the sages taught: One should always try to be pleasant with people" (Ket. 17a). So too, "If sexual relations with your wife make you late to the synagogue and people ask why you were delayed, ascribe it to something else" (B.B. 23b).

The twentieth-century *rav*, Eliyahu Dessler, concurs: "Sometimes it may be wrong to 'tell the truth' about our neighbor . . . and sometimes it may be necessary to change details, when the plain truth would injure" *(Mikhtav MeEliyahu)*. When Francie's late mother-in-law suspected that she had a life-threatening illness, she trusted her family to lie to her rather than scare her with the doctor's grim prognosis. Not telling her the medical "truth" about her condition was not totally honest, yet it supported a worry-free atmosphere that assuredly extended her life.

There are other times when you must respect a loved one's final wishes and not betray a trust, though every fiber of your being wants you to do so. Francie's mother, the only person in her immediate family to survive the Holocaust, wanted to be cremated as they had been. She also asked that her ashes be scattered, so that no cemetery headstone would mark her earthly remains. She trusted her husband and daughters to carry out these difficult tasks, even though this would hurt them and was contrary to traditional Jewish law. Fulfilling that trust more than twenty years ago was perhaps the hardest task Francie ever faced.

Trusting God As the Foundation for Trusting People

At the most elemental level, Judaism teaches that trustworthiness is essential to our character, because God, in whose image we are created, is worthy of our trust. If nature, God's creation, was not basically orderly, we could not learn to predict its changes or accommodate ourselves to it. We express wonder at the orderliness of things as simple as the sequences of days and seasons. Such wonder translates into praise of the One who gave nature its unity. And as Mordecai Kaplan emphasized, we base our lives on that unity and the orderliness that critically supports human development. Abraham Heschel pointed out that in living our lives, our wonder becomes joined by our gratitude for all that we're given. We trust that our Giver will never tire of bestowing beneficence upon us or become irritated when we take these benefits for granted. We trust that each day our bodies will work, our minds will reason, and our hearts will feel this simple trust in God that forms the bedrock of Jewish piety.

Yet there are moments when we wonder whether we are too trusting. When those who inhabit God's world hurt each other unbearably, we question whether the one our tradition calls *El Emunah*, the Faithful God, is deserving of that name. Why aren't we able to give a rational explanation of everything that God does or allows? Why does God seem so aloof? Like Job, some directly confront God with their anger and their hurt, demanding God's attention. These responses are time-honored Jewish ways of showing our trust in God, for trust does not always imply passivity. We shall say more about this topic in our chapters on knowing, revering, and loving God.

Here we wish only to call attention to another feature of our primal trust: the way that trusting God exemplifies our own potential for goodness. A world bereft of this trust, with life utterly indifferent to righteousness, would reduce trustworthiness to random, ad hoc occurrences. Cynics, in fact, live as though this were true—or say they do. Most Jews, most people, may not think of themselves as great believers. Still, without a fundamental attitude of trust toward the predictable workings of the universe, we cannot hope to create a unified humanity. Simply put, "In God We Trust," the motto on United States currency, forms the universal basis of our trusting ourselves and others.

It is this faith in God that may help us survive, long after our faith in humanity ceases. Our friend Helga Newmark was a young child when she was liberated from the Bergen-Belsen concentration camp in April 1945. Fifty years later as a rabbinic student, she revisited the camp for the first time as part of an American-German Interfaith seminarian exchange. There she composed a prayer that she read at a memorial service dedicated to all Jews who died in the Holocaust: "Blessed are you, our Eternal, Who enables our eyes to see a new day, . . .Who enables us to reach out to others in pain, to trust again, and to heal the wounds of the past."

From Our Tradition

The letters that form the word *emet* in Hebrew are spaced far apart in the Hebrew alphabet, while the letters that form *sheker* (deceit) in Hebrew closely follow each other. This suggests that it is difficult to act in truth and in trust, while deception is as close as one's ear.

—*Yalkut Bereshit,* on Shab. 104a

Rabbi Simḥa Bunim of Przysucha was asked: "What is the law?" He replied, "It is forbidden to deceive your neighbor." "And what is going above the letter of the law?" "Not deceiving yourself."

—Sherwin and Cohen, *How to Be a Jew*

The essence of trust is a tranquillity of soul enjoyed by the truster.

—Baḥya b. Joseph ibn Pakuda, *Ḥovot Halevavot*

The Sadigurer Rebbe said: In the time of the Baal Shem Tov, robbers lived in the forests, and therefore he lived there in order to protect those who passed through. Today, however, the robbers live in the city, and the Tzaddik is compelled to live there as well in order to protect the weak, if he can.

—Newman, *The Hasidic Anthology*

R. Giddel said in the name of Rav: If a man of Naresh kisses you, count your teeth; if a Pumbeditan escorts you, change your lodgings.

—Ḥul. 127a

The truth is known only to God, and to me, a little.

—Yiddish proverb

Lovingkindness—
Gemilut Ḥasadim

he Oral Law is quite explicit: there are some commandments that we must do. And the Oral Law is also quite unequivocal: it refuses to set limits that restrict their doing. So the Mishnah tractate Pe'ah [The Corner], tells us: These are the things about which the Law prescribes no acceptable amount—how large a corner we must leave in our fields for the gleaners to reap, the number of first fruits we need to bring to the Temple, how great an offering we must bring when we come to the Temple on the three pilgrimage festivals, acts of *gemilut ḥasadim,* and how much we must study Torah (1.1). Moreover, the Talmud names specific acts whose merit provides "income" we will enjoy in this world, while their "capital" awaits us in the world to come: honoring one's father and mother, acts of *gemilut ḥasadim,* early attendance at the house of study morning and evening, hospitality to guests, visiting the sick, providing a bride's dowry, escorting the dead, praying at the appointed times, making peace between people—but the study of Torah is equal to them all (Shab. 127a). The mitzvot in both these lists are quite specific and thus understandable, and everyone knows what Torah study is—but what *gemilut ḥasadim* involves is the subject of intense, yet instructive rabbinic argument.

The Beginnings of the Enigma

Why didn't our teachers simply translate the well-known Hebrew terms *gemilut* and *ḥasadim* and thus resolve their difficulties? For

41

starters, the word *ḥesed* (the singular of *ḥasadim*), though frequently used in the Bible, has a rather imprecise meaning. Scholars say it can mean goodness, kindness, mercy, affection, piety, loveliness, charity, loyalty, or covenant faithfulness. It obviously refers to a deed stemming more from a feeling than from a rule. And this emotion moves us to do good, like helping someone struggling in the supermarket with an unwieldy load of groceries and wheeling it to the parking lot, even loading up the car. So *ḥesed* is a most attractive human quality. While we can't define it, we know it when we see it.

The root *g-m-l,* from which *gemilut* comes, also has many meanings: deal out, do good/evil to, reward, repay, ripen, wean. Put *g-m-l* into Hebrew to form an abstraction and link it with acts of *ḥesed,* and the resulting phrase connotes a positive, benevolent act attached to a strong sense of obligation. But just how the term *gemilut* became connected with *ḥasadim* in the first place—it doesn't occur in the Bible, though it seems well established in early rabbinic literature—is a mystery we must leave to scholars to decipher. Fortunately, as with much else in Judaism, we are commanded to live it, not define it. The author of the eighth-century Jewish mystical work *Otiot R. Akiva* instructs us: "The world couldn't exist for even one hour without acts of kindness."

The Two Paths of *Gemilut Ḥasadim*

When our sages debated *gemilut ḥasadim,* they argued over the subtle but critical distinction between commending a general behavioral trait and commanding a specific list of things we must do. Should Judaism emphasize it as a comprehensive, overarching super-virtue, motivating us to perform innumerable benevolent deeds? Or should it mandate certain exemplary acts, whose performance fills people with its essence?

One: The Generalists Want Ḥesed to Infuse Our Lives

Rabbinic generalists on this issue object to a finite list of deeds that fulfill the commandment of *gemilut ḥasadim.* Human nature being what it is, our evil urge would quickly skim it and then refuse to do anything more. And that is no way to relate to a duty that

Simon the Righteous describes as one of the "three pillars that uphold the world: Torah, worship, and *gemilut ḥasadim*" (Avot 1.2). Specifying certain acts in the name of lovingkindness would restrict its effective scope. We should, rather, follow the guidance of R. Yoḥanan: "Be always like a helmsman, on the lookout for good deeds" (Lev. R. 21.5).

This position gets considerable support from biblical examples of the individual Hebrew words that make up the phrase. Thus in the Book of Proverbs, the root *g-m-l* describes the capable woman's relation to her husband in general terms: "She does him good, not evil, all the days of her life" (31:12). So, too, the root *ḥ-s-d* is used when David, fearing for his life, begs Jonathan to act "kindly/graciously/lovingly" by telling him whether his father Saul intends to kill him (1 Sam. 20:8). Whatever we think of the characters involved or the contemplated act, we have to agree that the favor David is asking of Jonathan goes far beyond one friend's ethical duty toward another.

When these two open terms combine, they create a value with an even broader reach than they have separately. This lies behind the special English term created to relate what neither "loving" nor "kindness" does by itself: lovingkindness. Our sense of what we are stretching for is so great that we do not use a hyphen—loving-kindness—but link the two words in synergistic intimacy. Surely, say the generalists, attaching a particular inventory only diminishes this soaring responsibility.

Two: The Particularists Want Concrete Jewish Objectives

A bumper sticker Gene once saw goes to the heart of the problem. It said: "Do random acts of kindness"—a striking way to remind us that acts of *ḥesed* shouldn't wait for special moments but ought to be a regular part of our lives. Yet without specific actions, our dedication loses its urgency and becomes random. If we don't provide detailed ways to do *gemilut ḥasadim*, we leave people up in the air about precisely how to perform this critical mitzvah. The rabbis try to straighten out the confusion: "R. Judah b. Shila said in R. Assi's name in R. Yoḥanan's name: There are six things whose fruit we enjoy in this world: hospitality to wayfarers, visiting the sick, meditation in prayer, early attendance at the Study House, rearing one's sons to study Torah, and judging one's neighbor in the scale of merit. But didn't we have a tradition that said that only four things have that effect: honoring parents, *gemilut ḥasadim,* peace-making, with Torah study equal to them all? Does this latter statement mean that only these four merit special reward? Of course not, for all the extra matters are included under *gemilut ḥasadim*" (Shab. 127a–127b). "R. Ḥama b. R. Ḥanina taught: What does the text mean, 'Walk after God's ways' [Deut. 13:5]? As God clothed the naked, visited the sick, comforted mourners, and buried the dead, so should you" (Sot. 14a). To these talmudic injunctions, the great twelfth-century Spanish philosopher Maimonides adds dowering the bride and rejoicing with the bride and groom (M.T., Hil. Evel, 14), and the thirteenth-century Spanish moralist Jonah Gerondi charges us to give counsel and advice to the poor as well as aiding them (*Iggeret Teshuvah* [A letter about repentance]).

Allowing for different emphases, we follow those teachers who list eight acts that merit the quite special attainment of *gemilut ḥasadim.* But before turning to them, let us anticipate a question. Since almost all these acts are mitzvot in their own right and we are already commanded to do them, why are they particularly mentioned with regard to the duty of *gemilut ḥasadim?* Our answer: These eight deeds singled out here are doubly meritorious. They not only create the goodness that every mitzvah does, but also share that extra holiness of *gemilut ḥasadim.*

Rejoicing with the Bride and Groom

We begin our discussion of the eight exemplary acts of lovingkindness on an utterly joyous note. Judaism grants special merit for raising others' already happy moods. There is something beautifully odd about this; joy increases, the more others enjoy our delight. We recognize that sometimes we just aren't in the mood to celebrate other people's triumphs, or we still resent the way they treated us three years ago at the family picnic. And some people are so emotionally stingy they just can't loosen up and get happy because others are happy. Our sages want us to dispel glumness by becoming the kind of people who amplify other people's glee. In this case, always acting formally polite is not the preferred mode of behavior.

"R. Samuel b. R. Isaac danced with a stick before the bride and groom to amuse them. When R. Zera saw this, he left the room, saying, 'Look how this old man is embarrassing us.' When R. Samuel died, thunder and lightning boomed for three hours. A heavenly voice then proclaimed, 'R. Samuel b. R. Isaac, who always performed acts of *gemilut ḥasadim,* has died.' When it was time to perform the *ḥesed*-act of burying him, a fire in the form of a stick came from Heaven and placed itself between his bier and the people. The rabbis then said, 'Come see this old man—how his stick now vindicates him!'" (Yer. Pe'ah 1.1).

In these instances, Judaism counsels us to live a bit vicariously, genuinely appreciating the good fortune of others. We should allow ourselves some unrestrained happiness; of the eight double mitzvot included in *gemilut ḥasadim,* this is the only celebrative one. Yet the same good will that animates joy-giving manifests itself in the seven sobering, even somber activities to which we now turn.

Visiting the Sick, *Bikkur Ḥolim*

"A master said that the Torah's phrase about a man injured in a fight, 'He must walk' [Exod. 21:19] is, by implication, the source of the commandment that we must visit him until he is up and about. As that master also taught, the *bikkur ḥolim* of a person the same age as the sick one takes one-sixtieth of the stricken one's illness away with him when he leaves. Although even that slight exposure to illness might deter people from visiting the sick, we have a text indicating that he still must visit him" (B.M. 30b). According to the Ḥafetz Ḥayyim, the late-nineteenth-century Polish sage, visiting the sick has no fixed measure of stature or time. "Someone who is quite distinguished is required to visit a person of more ordinary accomplishment. Should it be desirable, this mitzvah is to be performed even several times a day" (*Ahavat Ḥesed* [Love of kindness]).

A non-rabbinic *kal ve-ḥomer* argument (reasoning that proves from the trivial what is true in a weightier matter): Forward-looking physicians, experimenting with ways to help the elderly keep their dignity as they get frail, have discovered that occasional but regular visits by very young children revitalizes nursing home residents, despite significantly raising noise and activity levels. Their research has also found that cuddling dogs and cats and responsibly caring for plants positively affect the quality and length of life of the aged. If even superficial contact with plants, animals, and kids is beneficial to the elderly *(kal),* how much the more so would be visits by adults of their acquaintance *(ḥomer)?*

Giving Comfort and Advice

People with serious problems feel isolated. When such persons listen as we speak to them and show our concern, we discover that they appreciate our reaching out as much as the words we use. Judah the Pious of Regansburg, the thirteenth-century Franco-German musarist, explains this Jewish duty: "All Jews are like mothers and fathers to each other, so they should look after and care for each other as if other Jews were their children" (Judah Heḥasid, *Sefer Ḥasidim* [The book of the pious], 589).

Discovering that someone cares can mean a lot. "Everyone enjoys a ready response, and a word rightly timed is especially good" (Prov. 15:23). Perhaps that is why many of us remember our earliest mental picture of God as a kindly, bearded, grandfather type, seated somewhere in heaven, beckoning us to share our problems. (Of course, now that we have become sophisticated adults, we never imagine the Deity this way!) In our mobile age, few of us are physically close enough to always give the hug that matters. So just hearing a sympathetic voice on the other end of a telephone may be a great help. As computer know-how becomes common, most of us are only an e-mail's click away. Somehow our rabbis knew the magic of communication on any level, for they wrote: "If you have nothing to give him, console him with words" (Lev. R. 34.15).

Lending to the Needy

Has there ever been a time when some good people weren't in serious need of money? Ashkenazic and Sephardic folklore are ripe with astute wisdom on *gemilut ḥasadim*. How sensible is the Yiddish maxim: "Everyone is quite capable of falling by himself. But to get up again needs the hand of a good soul." This Ladino proverb provides a tone of elegant sacredness: "Lending to the poor is like offering a sacrifice to God." Charity is, we hope, second nature to Jews; it should be a matter of simple duty to help when we hear of great need. But to do so out of an intuitive feel for others that goes far beyond simple duty earns the special commendation of *gemilut ḥasadim*. It is a tired cliché to disparage those for whom writing a check is about as religious an act as they ever do. Do you know any truly worthy cause that could not use a few more checks to do God's work?

Of course, our age of comparative affluence has made plain that one can be "needy" in other than financial ways; today, "lending" often involves giving of oneself. Are you that rare person who does not have a list of people with whom you really should have kept in touch? Sitting and chatting about nothing momentous heals both the souls involved. The sixteenth-century Polish ethicist Isaiah Horowitz understood how needy we all are when he commented: "No one should let a day pass without doing a specific act of lovingkindness, whether by giving money or by personal endeavor" (*Shenei Luḥot Habrit* [The two tablets of the covenant], pt. 2, 27).

Clothing the Naked

We usually think of "clothing the naked" as mere metaphor. But for much of Jewish history this phrase had a far more literal meaning. Jews lived on poverty's fringes; subject to rulers' whims or mob violence, they easily found themselves stripped of their goods. The rabbis had no difficulty associating the duty to "clothe the naked" with God's exemplary act in Eden. For when Adam and Eve ate from the Tree of Knowledge, they knew that they were naked and needed makeshift clothes to cover themselves: "*Adonai Elohim* made tunics of skins for Adam and his wife, with which God then clothed them" (Gen. 3:21). Rabbinic preaching asks us to imitate God and care for the unfortunates among us.

When disaster strikes, we take the duty to clothe the naked quite literally. Whether monsoons or earthquakes devastate communities thousands of miles away, or floods or hurricanes ravish areas closer to home, the losses are immense. For all that governments and private agencies do to help, they can't completely carry the burden when many people lose just about everything. Then we also feel the imperative not to let those people go naked, but provide as best we can the basic necessities of food, shelter, and clothing. And even when nature is relatively benign, there are always those who, for whatever reason, can use what no longer suits us.

But we cannot neglect saying a word about a far more pervasive problem: people who, one way or another, are stripped of their dignity. "Outsiders" of every variety are regularly degraded. And even those who seem integrated into the mainstream of their communities suffer at the hands of the many who debase others. Creating humane working conditions, respectful teacher-student relationships, sensitively egalitarian marriages, a politics of merit—these are the great challenges for *gemilut ḥasadim* today.

Accompanying the Stranger

"Three young disciples of R. Elazar were late for their study with the master. He said, 'Where were you?' They said, 'We were occupied in performing a mitzvah.' He replied, 'As worthy as that is, were there no others to do it so that you could attend to the mitzvah of Torah study?' They said, 'No, for the man was a stranger.' With that, R. Elazar knew he had taught them well" (Yer. Pes. 3.7).

Francie vividly remembers trying to find her way in unfamiliar surroundings and becoming increasingly lost and frustrated. She stopped and asked directions from two people on the street. The first person called over to say that he was too busy to stop jogging long enough to point her in the right direction. The second person not only gave her great verbal directions but went with her to her destination, which took him several blocks out of his way. One does not have to literally accompany a stranger nowadays to fulfill this aspect of *gemilut ḥasadim*. But graciously taking the time to help out, even if it means temporarily veering off our schedules, seems doable even living our hectic lives.

So, too, removing obstacles from the way of stranger also becomes exemplary. The Bible tells us not to place a stumbling block before the blind (Lev. 19:14). Today this surely includes land mines. On a simpler level, today's strangers are often those who have just moved into a new neighborhood or are making their first visits to our synagogue. And, since we speak so much these days about "corporate culture"—a phrase describing almost any institution—mentoring those who do not "know the ropes" (as if we still had great sailing ships) is a small but significant part of our practice of lovingkindness.

Burying the Dead—*Levayyat ha-Met*

Long before "embodiment" became a buzzword, Jewish teachers spoke of the importance of respect for the corpse, *kibud ha-met.* Every Jewish community in the Middle Ages had a volunteer organization to administer the final Jewish "needs" of our loved ones; membership in this *ḥevrah kadishah,* the holy society, indicated belonging to the community elite. Even in our time of professional Jewish funeral directors, such organizations bring loving hands and dedicated hearts to this humble, touching duty. In many cities, organizations like the New York Hebrew Free Burial Society make sure that Jews so indigent they must be buried in our equivalent of a "potter's field" have fitting Jewish care and funerals. "The highest form of benevolent action is that undertaken toward the dead, since there is no thought of reward. . . . A poor person may someday be able to repay one who gives him a loan or aid, but the dead can never repay us" (Tan. B. Vayeḥi 107). Yeḥiel b. Yekutiel, the medieval Italian sage, said: "If one eulogizes a dead person and bears him to burial and occupies himself with his burial, this is absolute *gemilut ḥasadim" (Sefer Maalot Hamiddot).*

Our Yiddish ancestors phrased it with their usual matter-of-fact directness: "Even to die one needs help; no corpse ever buried himself" (Yiddish proverb). And that means help from the entire community; going to a funeral of someone you don't know is as true a mitzvah as burying a family member. When few attend a funeral, we feel bad; when many come, it assuages our sense of loss and our intimations of our own mortality. And that attitude has created our new interest in hospice care. Respectful, loving attention in the face of the ultimate void that is death shows that *gemilut ḥasadim* is more than duty, but an extended, felt kindness in which, once again, we emulate our Creator: "And God buried Moses in the valley" (Deut. 34:6).

Comforting the Mourner

"When anyone entered the Temple by way of the Mourners' Gate and his lip was covered, [a custom unknown to us], they knew he was a mourner and they said: 'May He who dwells in this house comfort you.' If he entered by way of the Mourners' Gate and his upper lip was not covered, they knew he had been excommunicated. To him they said: 'May He who dwells in this house allow you to hear the words of your friends and relatives, that you repent and again are accepted in the community, so that all Israel can fulfill their obligation of *gemilut ḥasadim*'" (*Torat Haadam* [The law of humanity]).

Naḥmanides, the medieval commentator, legal authority, and mystic, gives his version of this often-quoted counsel a different spin. By insisting that the Jewish community acknowledges the pain of even someone who forfeited the right to community membership, Naḥmanides points out just how important it is to treat everyone with lovingkindness. So today we pay a *shivah* call to those in our community whom we may not know well, to let the presence of a few more persons help heal their grief. The greater virtue is attached to those later "how-are-you-doing" phone calls, not forgetting that the pain of loss lingers after the official period of mourning ends. Following classic Jewish instruction, we try to sense when to remain silent and when to speak, when to just listen and when more extended aid would comfort. In these acts of goodness, the feeling heart must be our guide.

Are There Really Two Ways of Doing *Gemilut Ḥasadim?*

Our tradition solves the problem of the general and specific approaches to lovingkindness in typically Jewish fashion. Preferring the realities of life to logic, it reports both points of view, implicitly asking us to work out what suits us best at any given moment. "R.

Elisha b. Abuyah said that a man who has learned much Torah and has good deeds is like a horse with reins. But someone who knows what needs to be done and doesn't do it is like a horse without reins, soon throwing the rider over his head" (A.R.N. 24.4). Without far-ranging ideals, the soul shrivels; without deeds, our interactions with others are empty. For *gemilut ḥasadim* is about relationships and about the give and take that defines and nurtures them.

We know that we must reach beyond our face-to-face acquaintances to a much wider community. As the medieval Spanish philosopher Solomon ibn Gabirol challenges us: "Act with kindness both with him who deserves it and with him who deserves it not. For if he is deserving, you bestow it in its proper place; and if he is not deserving, you will deserve it, for God commanded humanity to do good and practice kindness" *(Mivḥar Hapeninim)*. Thus whether we don't know much about someone or know the person well, we still need to give of ourselves, perhaps from a sense of social responsibility or, more deeply, from a sense of our people's covenant with God. This basic other-directedness, so critical to our understanding of Judaism, is our response to Isaiah's prophetic revelation: "For the mountains may move and the hills shake, but My lovingkindness shall never depart from you" (Isa. 54:10).

It is *gemilut ḥasadim* as the giving of our very essence that our sages say we must do without measure. As the father of modern Orthodoxy, the nineteenth-century German rabbi Samson Raphael Hirsch, put it, "It is a self-involvement which goes far" *(Commentary to the Torah)*. It is doing the laundry even if that chore belongs to your roommate; it is car-pooling even when it is not your turn—unforced gifts of self, joining others as helpfully as we can, performing acts of loving deeds. Yeḥiel b. Yekutiel explains: "What is lovingkindness—that one be friendly and benevolent to everybody, rich and poor, living and dead. . . . If you include in this drawing close to those who are distant; how much the more so should you do it to your close ones?" *(Sefer Maalot Hamiddot)*.

From Our Tradition

Our rabbis taught: In three respects is *gemilut ḥasadim* superior to charity. Charity can be done only with one's money; *gemilut ḥasadim* can be done with one's person and one's money. Charity can be given only to the poor; *gemilut ḥasadim* can be given to both the rich and the poor. Charity can be given to the living only; *gemilut ḥasadim* can be done for both the living and the dead.

—Suk. 49b

For the merit of three things rain comes down: the earth, *gemilut ḥasadim,* and suffering.

—Yer. Taan. 3.3

Faithfulness will spring up from the ground below, and righteousness will look down from the sky.

—Ps. 85:12

For the Lord said: "The world will be built with lovingkindness" [Ps. 89:3]. Building on this quote from the Book of Psalms, Yeḥiel b. Yekutiel says: If one does lovingkindness with a friend, it is accounted to him as if he built the world.

—*Sefer Maalot Hamiddot*

Common Decency—
Derekh Eretz

*R. Akiba once followed his teacher, R. Joshua, into the
outhouse, and there learned three things: when relieving
oneself, one may not turn to the east or the west; one must
undress sitting down; one never wipes oneself with the right
hand, only the left. R. Ben Azzai heard about this and said
to Akiba: "How did you dare take such liberties with your
master?" Akiba replied: "This, too, is Torah, and I need to
learn it."*

*R. Kahana entered his master's bedroom to hide under his
bed. He heard his teacher laughing with his wife as they
made love. Suddenly his teacher realized that someone else
was in the room and said: "Kahana, is that you? Leave—
you are rude—have you no sense of decency?" Kahana
replied, "This, too, is Torah, and I need to learn it."*

—Ber. 62b

What's going on here—what are these stories
doing in a book on Jewish virtues, especially a
chapter commending manners, courtesy, and etiquette? Surely the scholarly Akiba and Kahana were outrageously
disrespectful when they spied on their teachers engaging in very
private activities! Two other vignettes from the Jewish tradition may
help explain. The first is attributed to Rabbi Leib, son of Sarah, who
said: "I didn't travel to my master, the Maggid of Mezritch, in order
to hear Torah from him, but to see how he laces his shoes" (Buber,
Tales of the Hasidim, bk. 1, *The Early Masters*). And the second invites

the reader to eavesdrop on a typical conversation between parent and child. "R. Huna asked his son why he did not attend the lectures of R. Ḥisda, whose teaching reputedly was quite ingenious. The son said that Ḥisda spoke of mundane matters, functions of the digestive organs, and how one should behave in regard to them. Said his father, 'Ḥisda occupies himself with the life of God's creatures, and you call that mundane!'" (Shab. 82a).

Most people acquire some social graces, since even the blackest scoundrel occasionally needs to display acceptable behavior. We shake our heads in bewilderment over the antics of R. Akiba and R. Kahana, as they insist that learning how to act when moving one's bowels or engaging in sex takes precedence over common decency. Obviously the rabbis introduced these exaggerated scenarios to underscore the limitless breadth of Torah; by doing so, they also emphasize the importance of *derekh eretz* in our social encounters. And while both messages are indeed timeless, they demand updating for our modern societies, where people use indoor bathrooms, not outhouses, and attend school, rather than apprenticing themselves to a teacher. Besides, we have come to see privacy as a critical element in human dignity. So our sense of when it might be right to violate it, as did the two "peeping Tom" rabbis—even for Torah—requires radical rethinking.

Gene suggested that he and Francie jot down modern versions of *derekh eretz* while culling the classical Jewish sources. It was so valuable (and a lot of fun) that we suggest you continue reading with pen and paper close by, to update the traditional examples with those from your own experience. For instance, Francie agrees with the statement in Derekh Eretz Zuta that one should use the toilet in a timely fashion, so as not to keep the next person waiting (8.12). Her present-day gloss on bathroom manners would include supplying enough toilets for women to get rid of those interminable lines at public functions. And, gentlemen, how about putting down the seat after each use, in consideration of the ladies who must use the same facilities?

Many of our citations in this chapter come from the two "minor tractates" of the Talmud devoted to our theme, Derekh Eretz

Rabbah (D.E.R.) and Derekh Eretz Zuta (D.E.Z.). A brief explanation about them is in order. They are two of fourteen such works that in modern times have been included in editions of the Babylonian Talmud. These tractates are considered "minor" because most were written later and do not share the legal authority of the "major" talmudic books, which directly comment on the Mishnah. Scholars have suggested that the Rabbah, which gives a general orientation to the theme, was written first, while the Zuta, which discusses proper etiquette befitting scholars, was written somewhat later.

Encouraging Agreeable Communal Life

Derekh eretz means respecting the social conventions of the community. As R. Meir taught: "When you enter a town, follow its customs" (Gen. R. 48.14). Thus, the sage Samuel counseled Jews some fifteen hundred years ago to refrain from spitting in another's presence (Hag. 5a). That's still proper etiquette today, and we extend it by showering regularly and using deodorant as part of our hygiene regimen. Our desire not to offend those with whom we come in contact in the community continues to rule our bathroom behavior, establishing standards of simple decency that our ancestors would find quite foreign.

Let's face it. With the exception of those few who seek solace in a solitary existence, all of us echo the teaching of Genesis: "It is not good for people to live alone" (2:18). Judaism has long taught that humans were created as social beings. Hillel's statement that we should not separate ourselves from the community (Avot 2.4) still rings true. Our generation, for all its privatism, knows well that it is psychologically unsound to spend too much time isolated from others. So the current rage to commune profoundly with our computers, substituting a screen for the bodily presence of a co-worker or friend, is troubling. The virtual reality of e-mail and chat-room conversations cannot match meeting people face to face, when body language, gestures, and silences are often more significant than the words we swap.

"With Good Manners You Can Open Any Door" (Yiddish Proverb)

When we were still small we learned that a wide gulf separated what we might get away with at home and how we were expected to behave in public. As we grew older, most of us became disciplined enough to show respect for our friends' parents and their property, even if we occasionally "mouthed off" to our own family and inadvertently demolished their stuff. We made arrangements to play at friends' houses; often our mothers placed the first phone call to make sure that "it wouldn't be any trouble." That's a contemporary version of Derekh Eretz Rabbah's advice: "One should never enter a friend's house suddenly" (5.2). It says further: "If one enters a house by invitation, whatever the host tells you, you must do" (6.1).

Growing up, we soon learned the importance of flexibility, even if we are never specifically taught that we need to accommodate others to keep our friends (and get invited back). So as adults, we watch people's interminable travel slides and videos or hear about the endless "adorable" antics of our friends' children or grandchildren. Two hundred years ago the Vilna Gaon reworked a linguistically cryptic text to say: "Be not like a doorpost which can injure the face by crashing into it, or like the doorjamb which can hurt the legs and ultimately falls, but be like a doorstep that everyone treads on, but remains in place even if the whole building collapses" (D.E.Z. 3.11). If we have *derekh eretz*, we're polite and affable and don't go around bumping into others, either physically or emotionally.

But that's not so easy. We regularly concede the truth in the Yiddish maxim: "It's harder to stay on good terms with people than with God." Too often we witness the hurtful behavior Rabbi Barukh of Medzibezh has in mind when he says that people are very careful not to swallow an insect, but not at all careful about devouring a person (Elkins, *Melodies from My Father's House*). Common courtesy, the everyday concern that flows from "Love your neighbor as yourself" (Lev. 19:18), too often gets lost as we engage in the conduct that Gluckel of Hameln describes in her memoirs in 1690: "Nothing pleases a person more than ruining his neighbor" *(The Memoirs of Gluckel of Hameln)*. Hillel counsels a tamer but more ethical realism, recommending: "Anything you hate having done to you, don't do to your neighbor" (Shab. 31a). Few things are more commonly irksome today than trying to negotiate city streets when people double- or triple-park, so we try not to be guilty of it ourselves. And walking from a distant parking place, we can't stand those who are clearly physically fit yet insist on zooming into a parking place plainly reserved for the handicapped.

Clothes Make the (Hu)man

Our almost slavish zeal to make the correct social statement often focuses on the clothes we choose. The rabbis, more interested in character than fashion, nonetheless demanded that our clothes not detract from what we ourselves represent. Scholars were expected to avoid shabby attire and to maintain a high level of cleanliness (D.E.Z. 5.3). With typical rabbinic hyperbole, R. Yoḥanan admonishes his disciples: "A Torah scholar who leaves grease on his clothes deserves death" (Shab. 114a). He adds that it is disgraceful to come into the marketplace with heavily patched sandals. Such disregard of self is in fact a denigration of the Torah. An aggadic narrative from the Jerusalem Talmud applies the same logic to the following interchange between two senior scholars: "Once when R. Ḥanina visited R. Judah the Patriarch, he came out to greet Ḥanina in his linen undershirt. R. Ḥanina said, 'Go back and put on your woolen over-cloak'" (Yer. San. 2.6). A passage in Derekh Eretz Rabbah says: "Be presentable in entering and leaving" (4.1).

Gene has never forgotten two lessons in *derekh eretz* Abraham Heschel taught him. In his bachelor, Cincinnati days, Dr. Heschel lectured at Hebrew Union College and lived in its dormitory. One day he saw Gene about to enter the bathroom carrying a Hebrew book. "Gene," he said, "one doesn't take a *sefer* into a bathroom." On another occasion Gene was acting on a "rabbis-need-not-be-bourgeois" attitude by wearing a shirt with a quite frayed collar. Dr. Heschel took note of this and said, "Gene, a scholar shouldn't appear in public with torn clothing." Of course he was right; people in positions of authority, even rabbinic students, mustn't go around inappropriately attired. And, since we are all created in God's image, we need to exercise a certain care in how we present ourselves. We come back to the theme of our chapter—"This too is Torah, and we need to learn (and do) it."

While today we are more relaxed about what we wear and when we wear it, Francie and her friends, like so many others, still call before big social events to make sure they know what manner of dress will most complement their host's mood. It is quite a sickening feeling to enter a social gathering and discover that your unsuitable clothing may even momentarily offend those who invited you. These days our kids often seem to care more about what they wear to school than about what they study once they get there. But the rigorous rule of Francie's youth—no white clothing or black patent leather shoes worn before Memorial Day or after Labor Day—has disappeared with hula hoops. Of course, clothing styles change more frequently than other social conventions, and many of us still eagerly thumb through fashion magazines at the beginning of each season. Fortunately an inflexible rule of etiquette no longer requires us to change from day to dinner to evening dress, as dictated by a self-indulgent designer drumming up business for the conglomerate that bears his or her name.

Nor do we give as much social credence to the old, formal rules once attached to proper visiting. Time was when it was *de rigueur* for women to be "at home" at certain hours to "receive" guests, who were expected to present printed name cards that announced their arrival. Today, when we agree with our rabbis that we should not go out alone (Tan. Emor 2), it is for personal safety rather than social reasons. Abaye's rule that one shouldn't unduly raise one's voice in normal conversations still holds (Yoma 86a); now we also apply it to proper computer etiquette and are careful NOT TO TYPE USING ALL CAPITAL LETTERS, BECAUSE IT APPEARS THAT WE ARE RUDELY SHOUTING.

"Thou Shalt Not Be a Boor When Eating or Conversing"

Animals gorge themselves regularly; human beings should eat with more care and decorum, associating dining with human dignity. The Bratzlaver Rabbi said that even when eating alone, a person should eat slowly and with proper etiquette (Newman, *The Hasidic*

Anthology). Our Pesaḥ seder, an idealized banquet, took its present form during Roman times and therefore emulates an aristocratic meal of that era, with attendees languorously propped up by pillows. More than a thousand years later, the twelfth-century German sage Eliezer b. Isaac of Worms passed on the following advice to his children: "Snatch not at flesh while the steam is rising from it, whether the meat is roasted or boiled. Eat no food prepared in a pan in which no cooking had been done for 30 days" *(Hebrew Ethical Wills)*. We snicker when we see the British monarch Henry VIII depicted as slobberingly stuffing food into his mouth, forgetting that silverware is a rather recent invention.

A vulgarian not only eats like a pig but converses like "those who moon like doves and roar like bears and wave their hands and stamp their feet" (Yeḥiel b. Yekutiel, *Sefer Maalot Hamiddot*). That's just not *derekh eretz*. Loutish speech is characterized by interrupting or answering others hastily or by speaking on a subject other than the one being discussed (Avot 5.7). Our medieval musarists put it positively. R. Asher b. Yeḥiel admonishes us to "weigh our words by the scale of our intelligence before we speak" (*A Treasury of Judaism*). The thirteenth-century scribe Yeḥiel b. Yekutiel advises: "Think of what you are going to say before you say it. Once the words leave your mouth, you will not be able to retrieve them, just as the archer cannot call back the arrow once it leaves the bow" (*Sefer Maalot Hamiddot*). R. Ḥidka offers a pithy rule of thumb for chatting with others: "Love the term 'perhaps,' and hate the expression 'So what?'" (D.E.Z. 1:11).

A Sense of Dignity, a Sense of Style

Derekh eretz is particularly important for those in a relatively high socioeconomic category, as important for someone who employs an occasional household helper as for an executive with dozens of underlings. R. Jeremiah b. Elazar said that if God could oversee Adam's wedding arrangements, even people of great eminence should not consider it beneath them to deal with lesser folk with respect (Ber. 61a). While a certain elitism led the rabbis to say, "Love each according to his station" *(Sefer Maalot Hamiddot)*, they tempered their somewhat snobbish mind-set by also suggesting, "Let your tongue be soft." A scholar, and therefore a paragon of Jewish behavior, should be "meek, humble, alert, modest, and filled with the desire to learn" (D.E.Z. 1.1). While scholars spent most of their time studying and teaching Torah, they still had to know how to act in the general community. And since the literal translation of *derekh eretz* is "the way of the world," we are not surprised at R. Gamaliel's strong phrasing to his colleagues: "When the study of Torah is not combined with ordinary work, the learning becomes neglected and even causes sin" (Avot 2.2).

True, the rabbis did not advocate a society without hierarchies; they were too realistic for that. So they set limits regarding what people of some eminence ought to do. "R. Huna said in the name of Samuel: To maintain the dignity of his position, a man appointed to high office may not do manual work in the presence of three or more persons" (Kid. 70a). "R. Yoḥanan saw R. Ḥanina b. Sisi splitting wood. He said, 'This does not befit your dignity.' R. Ḥanina said, 'But I have no disciple to do this for me.' R. Yoḥanan replied, 'If you did not have the means, you should not have accepted high office [in the Patriarch's court]'" (Yer. San. 2.6). While R. Yoḥanan was concerned with economic means, today an increasingly important issue is whether senior officials handle human relations as successfully as they juggle numbers on a balance sheet. Recently we read that the chairman of a multi-billion-dollar company was asked to leave because his way of doing business was no longer acceptable; even his friends admitted that he was controlling and arrogant, the antithesis of a team leader. His conduct sharply contrasted with the more conciliatory tone of his peers, which inhibited his subordinates rather than bringing out the best in them.

Refining Social Convention

We have two versions of the sages' sense of "the way of the world." "This is the general rule: a man should not act differently from the practice of his fellow" (D.E.Z. 5.5). "This is the general rule: a man should not deviate from the custom of his companions or from society" (D.E.R. 7.7). Both affirm that, by and large, our social conventions make sense. But the rabbis' basic conservatism conflicts with the ethical ideals of many modern, middle-class Jews, since it suggests a more passive, status quo attitude than our current moral sense demands. We do not counsel tacitly accepting social customs that perpetuate injustice, as any feminist or African-American will remind us. So once again, the issue of balance comes to the fore; after all, zeal is also a commended virtue. The rabbis sought to refine the etiquette of their time, raising people's conduct above the commonplace, seeking the sacred. Let us trace this theme through several levels, ranging from simple, public behaviors to our most complex, private, spiritual concerns.

Rabbi Simḥa Bunim said, "Even as we should eat slowly, so too we should not gulp down a glass of water, but should drink it slowly" (Newman, *The Hasidic Anthology*). The rabbis said that drinking a whole goblet of wine in one gulp brands us as drunkards (D.E.R. 6.5). They admonished us not to bite from a loaf of bread and then return it to the serving tray or give the piece to another diner (D.E.R. 9.1). We should not eat while standing, or lick our fingers at the table, or belch in the presence of others (D.E.Z. 5.1). Obviously, the spectacle of a "food fight" would have been as unacceptable two thousand years ago as it is to us today. The rabbis took exception to other publicly accepted vulgarities. R. Aḥa b. Ika taught: "Proper people do not go around scratching their backs against a public wall" (B.K. 30a). To which we add: nor do they publicly scratch other, more private parts of their anatomy.

We also seek to refine coarse mannerisms. The most common example is crude speech: "R. Eleazar b. Jacob said: A person who uses rough language is like a pipe spewing foul odors in a beautiful room" (D.E.R. 3.3). Contemporary equivalents such as "gangsta rap" and the undeleted expletives that increasingly punctuate "normal" street usage quickly come to mind. We also include the sleaze that fills radio talk shows and the public confession format on much of daytime television. A Jew should strive to be known for *nikayon peh*, literally, "a pure mouth," what we more figuratively call "clean speech."

Once again, the realism of the rabbis grounded their efforts to elevate our words above our naturally earthy thoughts. "R. Ḥanan b. Raba said: Everyone knows why a bride enters the bridal chamber. But if a man sullies his lips by speaking of it, then, even if 70 years' prosperity have been decreed for him, it is reversed. Rabbah b. Shela said, in the name of R. Ḥisda, For him who uses obscene language, hell is deepened. And this applies even to one who listens to such talk without protesting" (Shab. 33a). "Why are the fingers tapered like pegs? So that if one hears anything improper, we can insert them in our ears" (Ket. 5b). "R. Joshua b. Levi said: We should never let an unseemly expression fall from our mouths" (Pes. 3a). Knowing the damage the tongue can do, R. Joseph b. Zimra said that God tried to restrain it: "All the limbs of the human body are vertical, but I made you horizontal; all of them I put outside the body, but you I put inside; and I have even surrounded you with two walls, one of bone and one of flesh" (Ar. 15b).

The sensibility Judaism seeks to create is not easily described these days, since American culture is so intermingled and dynamic. Some types of behavior that were once acceptable we now consider crude, just as things that we find innocent may offend those from other cultures. We hug and kiss each other with a charming liberality that certain religious fundamentalists or Asian societies deplore. Yet we no longer inhale snuff, and most of us think it intolerably unrefined to chew tobacco or spit tobacco juice. We are not quite that socially prohibitive with cigarette smoking, though most public establishments these days do control it. Many of us ask our potential cigarette- or cigar-smoking guests not to do so inside our homes. However, Francie remembers that the very first thing she learned after pledging her college sorority was the "proper" way to light a cigarette, so that it wouldn't dangle out of her mouth, unlit.

Sexual temptations activate a good deal of reactive *derekh eretz*. While our chapters on "Modesty" and "Inclining toward the Good" give considerable attention to this topic, we want to point out that social convention tries to limit sexual excesses. Men, traditionally considered more sexually proactive than women, were strongly admonished to avoid behaviors that might lead to sin. Thus, a man shouldn't carry on casual conversations with women (Avot 1.5), shouldn't listen to them sing (Ber. 24a), shouldn't touch a woman—not even to shake hands in greeting, and should never walk behind a woman, forcing him to see her swaying hips (Ber. 61a). Some even say a man should avoid gazing directly at a woman not his wife: "One should not look intently at a beautiful woman, even if she is unmarried, or at a married woman even if she is ugly" (A.Z. 20a). And women were counseled not only to stay indoors but never to let their hair be seen in public (Ket. 72a). Yeḥiel b. Yekutiel cautions from his medieval vantage point: "Anyone who stands naked by the light of a candle or the moon is issuing an invitation to commit a major sin" *(Sefer Maalot Hamiddot)*.

Toward Reaching Our Spiritual Potential

At its best, *derekh eretz* serves as an inner disposition that infuses every ordinary human activity with a touch of transcendence. Again, Yeḥiel puts it nicely: "Without *derekh eretz*, we are nothing but a beast of the wilderness" *(Sefer Maalot Hamiddot)*. Centuries later, Rabbi Bunim makes the same point: "We are not mere animals. Though we must feed our bodies, we must do so in a mannered way, to display our superiority over the animals" (Newman, *The Hasidic Anthology*).

This is not to deny that people often behave bestially. We are all painfully aware of humanity's genius for evil. In fact, some ethicists accuse their fellow humans of speciesism, finding little reason to elevate ourselves so highly above other creatures. Insofar as they suggest we humans become more humble, a Jewish virtue we discuss in this book, and draw our attention to our minuscule part in an encompassing natural order, we welcome their message. But not to conquer dreaded diseases like polio or cholera so people may live, perversely denies the sacredness of all life. And to suggest that our ethical obligations toward our own children are not utterly distinct from those we owe even adorable dolphins or poodles seems counter-intuitive. Judaism knows that animals are included in the sacred realm, and we must live with them in Jewish piety. But people are different.

People are different because we are the only animals who know we are animals and still have the power to rise above our animality. That is what makes human bestiality so different from that of a marauding tiger. We don't have to act that way. We could do the good. The rabbis even encourage us to help those who wished to do us harm: "After disarming your enemy, and he comes hungry and thirsty to your house, give him food and drink" (Mid. Prov. 25:21). Think how we rescued Germany and Japan economically after defeating them militarily in 1945.

Derekh eretz is the virtue of letting that understanding of our specialness refine our routine interactions. It is the quiet accompaniment to the respectful way we conduct ourselves with family and strangers alike. It is the hint of God's image in us that makes us, creatures of dust and ashes, a little lower than the angels.

From Our Tradition

R. Joshua took some disciples with him when he went to transact some business with a lady with whom the great ones in the city consorted. When they got near her house he took off his tefillin, went in, and shut the door. When he came out he bathed and then taught his disciples, saying to them: "When I took off my tefillin, what did you suspect?" "That you believed that holy objects should not be brought into an unclean place." "And when I shut the door?" "Perhaps you had state business to transact." "And when I bathed?" "Perhaps spittle from her mouth may have fallen on your clothes." He replied, "Thus it was, and as you judged me favorably, so may God judge you."

—Shab. 127b

R. Eleazar b. R. Simeon was coming home from his teacher's house, self-satisfied for having mastered much Torah. On the road a particularly ugly man greeted him respectfully, but R. Eleazar did not respond pleasantly. Instead he vented, "You boor, are all the fellows in your city as ugly as you?" The man answered, "I don't know, but go to the Craftsman who made me and tell Him what ugly work

He produced." The man refused to accept the rabbi's profuse apologies, and when they got to town, he wouldn't listen to the people who paid the rabbi homage. Even after hearing how R. Eleazar had insulted the man, the citizens still asked him to forgive because of Eleazar's reputation as a great Torah scholar. Finally the wronged man said, "I shall forgive him for your sake, but only if he stops behaving like that."

—Taan. 20a

This story is told of R. Simeon b. Antipatros, with whom many used to come and stay. When he pressed them to eat and drink, they vowed by the Torah that they would neither eat nor drink, but later they did. When they left, R. Simeon had them flogged. R. Joshua was sent to investigate, but though he stayed for a while he was not whipped. He asked R. Simeon why he had flogged other guests, but not him. R. Simeon said, "You are a great sage and you have good manners. You do not vow by the Torah not to eat and then break that vow by eating." Said R. Joshua: "May heaven bless you! Whoever behaves so badly, give him forty lashes on your account and another forty on account of the sages who sent me."

—D.E.R. 6.1

CHAPTER 6

. . . .

Compassion—
Raḥamim

*I*f you, dear reader, will be compassionate, we propose to solve two mysteries by the end of this chapter: (1) who really wrote Shakespeare's plays and (2) how the most famous English poem extolling mercy, from *Merchant of Venice*, could be directed against a Jew, the moneylender Shylock. As the Talmud often says (e.g., Bez. 32b, Yev. 79a), the children of Abraham are congenitally compassionate, making it impossible for one of them to ever suggest that a pound of human flesh is an appropriate fine for being a bit tardy in repaying a loan!

We invite you to enter our world of fantasy to learn how we solve these two conundrums. Shakespeare's character Portia has a sensitivity to mercy which obviously echoes classic Jewish teaching. Thus her speech, and the whole play, clearly show the mind-set of an early Jewish feminist. And since Jews were expelled from England almost three hundred years before Shakespeare wrote, Portia obviously comes from one of the thousands of Jewish families forced to flee the Spanish Inquisition. Her great-grandparents settled in England and pretended to live as Christians, all the while secretly observing Jewish ritual. Shakespeare found this gifted ghostwriter (never mind how) and blackmailed her (don't ask why) into publishing her work under his name, introducing various revisions that conceal her real identity. As our culminating proof, we present her original draft, with our commentary.

The quality of raḥamim *[mercy] is not strain'd,*
It droppeth as the gentle rain from heaven
Upon the place beneath; It is twice blest;
It blesseth him that gives and him that takes:
'Tis mightiest in the mightiest: It becomes
The throned monarch better than his crown;
His sceptre shows the force of temporal power,
The attribute to awe and majesty,
Wherein doth sit the dread and fear of kings;
But raḥamim *is above this sceptred sway,*
It is enthroned in the hearts of kings,
It is an attribute to God himself;
And earthly power doth then show likest God's
When raḥamim *seasons* din *[justice].*
Therefore [Shylock], thou savage unbeliever,
Though din *be thy plea, consider this,*
That in the course of din *none of us*
Should see salvation: We do pray for raḥamim;
And that same prayer doth teach us all to render
The deeds of raḥamim.

(Merchant of Venice, *act 4, sc. 1*)

"The quality of *raḥamim* [mercy] is not strain'd,
It droppeth as the gentle rain from heaven
Upon the place beneath"

One need not know much Hebrew to realize that the words translated as mercy, *raḥamim*, and womb, *reḥem*, come from the same root, *r-ḥ-m*. Critical nurturing takes place during pregnancy, allowing these women to experience an intimacy that the rest of the population can only imagine. It transfers to the general art of forming successful relationships, based as they are on mutual, compassionate understanding. Over the millennia, females seemingly developed an extra "*raḥamim* gene," making them more prone to compassion's mastery than males. So Portia's success at winning Shylock's sympathies was predetermined, as was this example from biblical tradition: "Why did King Josiah in his time of peril send a delegation to Hulda the prophetess and not to [the prophet] Jeremiah? The members of the school of R. Shila replied, 'Because he knew that women are merciful'" (Meg. 14b). Or, as our folklore put it: "You did not suckle at my breasts, you never felt my mercy, so why do you now call me 'Mother'?" (Iraqi Jewish proverb).

Once out of the womb, all of us quickly are taken up by life's incessant demands, as relationships evolve into complicated mixes of emotional power as well as purely positive feelings. Our first bonding experience usually takes place with those in charge of parenting us. But at times their expectations exceed our limits, causing us to disappoint or wrong them. As we get older, we find ourselves in similarly unhappy situations with others we deeply care for. To get back on good terms, the one who errs must express sorrow for what happened, and the other must find enough compassion to accept this apology. Then mercy takes over, for without it, no relationship long endures.

Yet its giving cannot be forced. Asking someone to overlook a wrong is like seeking the soothing embrace of a guileless understanding, a freely given gift, an unexpected hug. Compassion for another stems from such a gentle stirring of the soul. As Rabbi Nahman of Bratzlav taught: "Many merciful deeds themselves require mercy. They lie in a cramped corner of our lives and no one takes pity on them" (*Otzar Harayonot Vehapitgamim* [Treasury of concepts and proverbs]). Only when we find the inner power to lovingly take back the one who hurt us can we overcome estrangement. There is an ancient Jewish model for this: "When Moses asked to see God's face [Exod. 33:18], Moses was really asking, 'Show me the attribute You use that helps You rule the world.' God said, 'I will cause all my goodness to pass before you.' When God passed before Moses, He said of Himself, '*Adonai, Adonai, El rahum ve-hanun . . . ,* *Adonai, Adonai* is a God of mercy and graciousness'—I do not owe any creature anything, but I give to them gratuitously" (Tan. B. Vaet'hanan). The thirteenth-century Roman sage Yehiel b. Yekutiel said: "God loved Israel, so God gave the people mercy as a gift" (*Sefer Maalot Hamiddot*)—just as God sends rain to Venice.

**"It is twice blest;
It blesseth him that gives and him that takes"**

More of us are now finding that our duties to care for others extend far longer than we might have thought. For though children may still need us, our parents do as well, giving the term "sandwich generation" true poignancy. Roles suddenly reverse, and we assume parental responsibilities for those who raised us. Painfully, we may have to come to terms with difficulties in our relationship that have lain dormant for decades. Perhaps we're able to find help from the experts we consult, the books we read, and the advice of friends in similar situations. More likely we will reach a point when only our compassion can sufficiently ease our pain, allowing us to accept and fulfill our responsibilities. And if our loved ones have any insight into what we freely give them, this most primal of all relationships can find new richness and strength.

All of us want to take part in life's relationships just as long as we are able; yet in the end, we know that we must let go. Even death is less painful when mercy has flowed freely. Francie lost a friend who knew that death was near. But as he grew weaker he could not let go of his work; his love and concern for the well-being of his wife and three teenaged children drove him to provide for them. His anguish palpably increased as his body shut down, until he finally realized he was unable to go on. Then, one Friday evening, at home with family and dear friends surrounding him, he managed to ask his wife if she would be able to continue without him, raising the children to become the adults he would never see. Was he not really asking her to forgive him for dying so young and leaving her alone? And being the loving soul she is, she unhesitatingly promised, compassionately telling him at the same time that no forgiveness was required, since no offense had been committed. Several hours later he died peacefully in her arms, one week short of his fiftieth birthday. The early-modern Italian sage Samuel David Luzzatto wrote: "The quality of mercy is its own reward, for the person who feels it aches with his neighbor's pain and cannot rest until he has bound up his wound and healed his blow" (Rosenbloom, *Luzzatto's Ethico-Psychological Interpretation of Judaism*).

**"'Tis mightiest in the mightiest: It becomes
The throned monarch better than his crown;
His sceptre shows the force of temporal power,
The attribute to awe and majesty.
Wherein doth sit the dread and fear of kings;
But *rahamim* is above this sceptred sway,
It is enthroned in the hearts of kings"**

In the Elizabethan England of Shakespeare's day, queens and kings ruled by divine right, assuming almost unlimited power. Believing that they ruled by God's fiat, sovereigns felt empowered to be completely ruthless. The rabbis describe similar political realities of their own times: "It is universally believed, that a king of flesh and blood against whom his subjects unsuccessfully rebel, who then kills all the surviving rebels, is considered cruel. If he slays only half of them, he is merciful. An exceptionally merciful king merely chastises the rebels' leaders" (San. 39a).

Recognizing the arbitrariness and vindictiveness of most monarchs, Portia nonetheless daringly identifies *rahamim* as a ruler's most significant virtue. Even though we live in more merciful times, we have seen corporate CEOs frequently replacing royalty as the controllers of our destinies. Ours is a time of corporate downsizing, when employees with years of dedicated service are dismissed with little more than a notice. And if this sad event happens just before the end of the year, with its holidays, or just before we are due to receive pensions or other financial benefits, the cries for compassion will be as loud as they will probably be futile. The "bottom line" can be that cruel. Our Yiddish-speaking ancestors indicated the simple compassion required: "A stick won't help as much as good words" (Yiddish proverb).

"It is an attribute to God himself"

Contemporary corporate muckety mucks beware—all your earthly influences are mere shadows of the One who created us all, teaching and inspiring us: "Abba Saul said that the verse, 'This is my God and *anvehu,* I will glorify Him' [Exod. 15:2] should read, 'This is my God and *ani ve-hu,* I and He,' teaching that 'I am to be like God.' As

God is gracious and compassionate, so I should be gracious and compassionate" (Shab. 133b). "The prophets regularly remind God: 'Just as a father has mercy on his children . . . so must You have mercy on the sinners of Your people Israel'" (Exod. R. 46.4). "Consider how plentiful are the mercies of the Holy One for the people of Israel . . . for when God sees the sufferings that the wicked wreak on the righteous, He weeps into His folded arms" (T.B.E., E.R., chap. 17, p. 87).

Portia, our "secret" converso Jewess and alleged authoress of this play, quite likely knew some of the more familiar pieces of the Jewish liturgy. She might well have known God's self-description by heart: "*Adonai, Adonai* is a God compassionate and gracious, slow to anger, abounding in kindness and faithfulness, extending kindness to the thousandth generation, forgiving iniquity, transgression, and sin" (Exod. 34:6–7). As we see, mercy, *rahamim,* is not just another attribute of God, but the very first mentioned. *Adonai*'s compassion reaches out to all of us, regardless of our gender or age: "When the daughters of Zelophehad [Num. 27] heard that their late father's land was to be divided only among the male descendants of the various tribes, excluding the females as was customary, they gathered together to take counsel. They said: God's compassion is quite different from the compassion of mortal kings. Human kings have more compassion for males than for females. However, the One who spoke and the world was, is not that way. Rather, God's mercy extends to the women and to the men, indeed, to everything, as it is written: 'God gives bread to all flesh' [Ps. 136:25] and 'God gives food to the animals' [Ps. 147:9], and 'God is good to all, and God's mercies are over all' [Ps. 145:9]" (Sifre Num. 133).

The authors of the Bible and their devoted successors, the rabbis, do not hesitate to describe God's *rahamim* in quite human terms. They often find it in parents who seem to have endless resources of love, able to cope when their children misbehave. "Said R. Samuel: It is the way of the father to have compassion, 'as a father has compassion on children' [Ps. 103:13]. It is the way of the mother to comfort, 'as one whom his mother comforts' [Isa. 66:13]. And because God meant to be both mother and father to Israel, the Holy One used 'I' twice in the verse, 'I, even I, am the One that comforts you' [Isa. 51:12]" (P.R.K. 19.3).

"And earthly power doth then show likest God's When *rahamim* seasons *din* [justice]"

Anyone who has stood before a judge, even if only to plead "not guilty" to a parking ticket, wants the judge to rule compassionately and waive all penalties. The writer-philosopher Francis Bacon, Shakespeare's contemporary, echoes this universal hope when he writes: "Judges ought in justice to remember mercy, [casting] a severe eye upon the example, but a merciful eye upon the person." Projecting their own problems in being merciful to those who wronged them, the rabbis often depict God as needing to make this same effort: "R. Yohanan says in the name of R. Yose: The Holy One says prayers. What does God pray? R. Zutra b. Tobi said in the name of Rav: May it be My will that My mercy may suppress My anger, and that My mercy may prevail over My attributes of justice and of recompense, that I may deal with My children in the attribute of mercy and, stopping well short of the line of strict justice, acting for their well-being" (Ber. 7a). Particularly when reciting their High Holy Day petitions, the rabbis beseeched God to "get up from the throne of judgment and move to the throne of mercy, using Your attribute of mercy toward Israel rather than that of judgment" (Lev. R. 29.6).

Of course, we cannot live without a considerable measure of justice in our lives—but how much better it is when we can season it with a considerable measure of compassion! Think of the anguished physician who must choose when to implant a life-saving organ in one critically ill person and thus deny it and perhaps life itself to an equally desperate sufferer. Everyone concerned can better accept the awesome decision if they know that it was made not only after exercising careful judgment, but with warm compassion as well. And we marvel at people who have just lost a loved one, yet are able to muster heart-laden compassion to donate a still-healthy organ of their dead to one who may be granted a new life due to their *rahamim*. Yehiel b. Yekutiel, who lived centuries before such operations were possible, anticipates such saintly individuals in his words:

"Happy are the righteous, for they transform their inclination to strictly follow the law to an inclination to reach out to others in compassion" *(Sefer Maalot Hamiddot)*. As the rabbis never tire of telling us, we shall find "the gates of mercy are open all the time, and anyone who wishes to enter through them may do so" (B.K. 38a).

> **"Therefore [Shylock], Thou savage unbeliever,**
> **Though *din* be thy plea, consider this,**
> **That in the course of *din* none of us**
> **Should see salvation"**

Sternly dispensed justice, lacking *rahamim's* softening touch, would make the biblical "eye for an eye" punishment literal, denying one of our most compassionate legal defenses, "extenuating circumstances." Following the letter rather than the spirit of the law does not allow for excuses or explanations. "*Adonai,* if you would keep an account of our sin, O *Adonai,* who would survive? But You also have the power to forgive us and that is why we hold You in awe" (Ps. 130:3–4). The rabbis staunchly reaffirm the Psalmist's theme: "A king possessed some delicate glass vessels. He said: 'If I pour hot water into them they will break. If I put cold water into them they will crack.' What did the king do? He mixed hot and cold water, poured it into them, and they held. So, too, God said: 'If I create the world on the basis of mercy alone, people will be great sinners. If I create it on the basis of justice alone, it will not endure. I will create it with both justice and mercy and would that it then endure'" (Gen. R. 12.15). "Said R. Levi: If justice is what you want, God, there can be no world, and if you want to have a world, You cannot have strict justice" (P.R.K. 19.3).

This is not a plea to live entirely out of mercy. The rabbis, those "realistic" idealists, knew that just as too compulsive an application of justice denies us our humanity, too much *rahamim* denies us our very breath. "Our masters taught: There are three kinds of men whose life is no life: those who are overly compassionate, those who are prone to instant anger, and those who are relentlessly fastidious" (Pes. 113b). Yet our folk wisdom insists, since much of it was born in a far less compassionate world than ours: "Sometimes you have to make your heart into a stone" (Yiddish proverb) and "If you unsparingly go about helping others, you will end up with nothing yourself" (Ladino proverb).

Judaism unequivocally commends the pursuit of justice through institutions of the law; without them, God's will cannot be satisfied. It is easy to forget that the civil rights of Jews became national commitments relatively recently and that the civil rights of still others have come about only by even more recent legislation. One glance at the morning newspapers reminds us that horrendous acts happen all the time; only a fairly functioning legal system can bring those who commit them to justice. But just about every legal system allows some leeway, and this is what our tradition calls compassion. Can we call it justice when some jurisdictions are too freehanded with capital punishment, demanding the death penalty with an almost automatic regularity? And when we exercise our individual powers to tyrannize subordinates or dependents, don't we negate the very impulse that we find so compelling when we are on the receiving end of such treatment?

> **"We do pray for *rahamim;*
> And that same prayer doth teach us all to render
> The deeds of *rahamim*."**

Mercy is so strong a part of our tradition that a substantial body of Jewish law and practice prohibits any kind of cruelty to animals, a duty that the rabbis said was commanded by the Torah (Shab. 128b). The acts forbidden because they generate *tzar ba'alei hayyim,* the pain of living things, have their source in the narratives as well as the legislation of the Bible. Rebecca tended to Eliezer's camels as soon as she saw that he had slaked his thirst. This so impressed Abraham's servant that he knew she was the right woman to be Isaac's wife (Gen. 24). "R. Judah said in the name of Rav: A man may eat nothing until he has fed his animals. For the Torah first indicates, 'I will give grass in your fields for your cattle,' and only later says, 'You shall eat and be satisfied' [Deut. 11:15]" (Ber. 10b). A related law prohibits a person from buying an animal unless he first has enough food to feed it adequately (Yer. Yev. 15.3). "It says something about a person's goodness when his animals are well fed and satisfied" (Sifre Deut. 43).

A talmudic tale about Judah ha-Nasi, the Patriarch of the Palestinian Jewish community in the late second century C.E. and the chief compiler of the Mishnah law code, stresses the importance of these laws. "The sufferings of Rabbi came because of an act he did that lacked compassion, and left because of an act that he did that was full of compassion. One day a calf was being taken to the slaughterhouse. It broke away and hid under Rabbi's robe. 'Go,' said Rabbi, 'for this you were created.' Because of this hardheartedness, sickness came upon him. Some time later, Rabbi's maidservant was sweeping his house when he saw that she was about to sweep away a nest full of weasel pups. 'Let them be,' he said to her, for it is written, 'And God's compassion is over all God's works' [Ps. 145:9]" (B.M. 85a).

The detailed laws of the kosher slaughtering of animals, *shehitah,* rest upon this compassion for animals, requiring that when we kill them for food, we make sure that they die instantly and painlessly. Thus we must use a perfectly sharpened knife, one free of any nicks or rough edges (Aaron, *Sefer Hahinukh* [The book of instruction], 451). To this day the *shohet* must test his knife before using it. Should he find an imperfection, he must immediately sharpen it away or set it aside and use another knife. In the same spirit, citing the negative example of the biblical hunter Esau, the rabbis prohibit killing merely for sport (A.Z. 18b).

Rahamim Combines *Musar* with Law, for Humanity and for God

If Jewish teaching demands such compassion on animals, how much the more so does it require showing it toward human beings, enveloping our legal activities in our highest ethical goals? The Talmud contains the following edict: "A judge can rule only in accordance with what his eyes see" (San. 6b). The eleventh-century French commentator Rashi interprets this to mean that a judge must strive to apply the law both "justly" and "truly" (Rashi, on San. 6b). So we strive to listen to and act according to our tradition, emulating Portia as we monitor our deeds and behavior with the virtuous eyes of compassion. And we hope that God will do the same. "In the days of R. Tanḥuma there was a terrible drought. . . . While they were distributing funds to the poor they saw a man give money to his divorced wife, and they complained to R. Tanḥuma about this apparent breach of decency. When R. Tanḥuma questioned the man about this he responded, 'I saw she was in great distress, and so I became filled with compassion for her. I assure you, I had no ulterior motive.' Whereupon R. Tanḥuma turned his face to heaven and exclaimed, 'Sovereign of the universe. This man, upon whom this woman has no claim for sustenance, nonetheless saw her in distress and was filled with pity for her. O You who are full of compassion and graciousness, we who are Your children and the children of Your beloved Patriarchs, should You not now be filled with compassion for us?' Immediately the rains came and the world enjoyed relief" (Gen. R. 33.3).

From Our Tradition

Biblical law provides for sparing the feelings of animals: No animal may be slaughtered on the same day as its young (Lev. 22:28); do not take away a young bird from its nest until you first shoo the mother away (Deut. 22:7). This is traced to God in the story we read each Yom Kippur. When God does not destroy the city of Nineveh because the people repented for their evil, Jonah is angry at the compassion God shows. God retorts: "Should I not care about that great city with its many people, and its many beasts as well?" (Jonah 4:11).

R. Yehudah said in the name of Rav: If an animal falls into a stream on Shabbat and is unable to pick herself up, one may bring pillows and cushions and place them beneath her so she can step up on them and climb out.

Shab. 128b

*T*wo donkey drivers who hated each other were going down a road when the donkey belonging to one could no longer bear its load. The other driver saw this and at first walked by. But then he remembered: "If you see the donkey of one who hates you lying under its burden, release it with him" [Exod. 23:5]. So he returned and helped his enemy in loading and unloading. Then peace came between them. The two entered an inn, ate and drank together, and became fast friends.

—Tan. B. Mishpatim 1

R. Berekhiah said: When the Holy One was about to create Adam, God saw both the righteous and the wicked who were to issue from him. God said: If I create [humans] the wicked will issue from him; if I do not create him, how are the righteous to be born? So God shielded the way of the wicked from His eyes, embraced His quality of mercy, and then created Adam.

—Gen. R. 8.3–4

*O*nce when Abba Taḥnah the Pious was entering his city on Sabbath eve at dusk, a bundle slung over his shoulder, he came upon a man afflicted with boils lying [helplessly] at a crossroads. The man said to him, "Master, do an act of compassion—carry me into the city." Abba Taḥnah replied, "If I abandon what I have in my bundle, how shall I and my household support ourselves? But if I abandon this man afflicted with boils and leave him outside the city, I will forfeit my life!" Abba Taḥnah set his bundle on the road and carried the man into the city. Then he returned for his bundle and reentered the city with the last rays of the sun. Everyone was astonished to see someone so pious carrying a bundle, with Shabbat about to begin. He too felt uneasy; was it possible that he had desecrated the Sabbath? The Holy One, feeling his suffering, caused the sun to continue to shine a while longer, delaying the onset of Shabbat until Abba Taḥnah arrived home with his bundle.

—Eccles. R. 9.7, 1

PART III

Making a Contribution

CHAPTER 7

Zeal—*Zerizut*

*S*ome people know how to get things done. The rest of us count on them to keep the local soup kitchen going, to give us a lift when our car won't turn over, or to coordinate the temple bazaar. And then there are those who mean well but have an internal jump-start mechanism regularly stuck in the "off" mode. The Bible makes it clear: Diligence is a cherished virtue and sloth a derided vice. The classic statement is surely Proverbs 6:6–11:

> *"Look to the ant, you sluggard,*
> *Study its ways and learn.*
> *Without leaders, police, or rulers*
> *It lays up its stores during the summer*
> *And gathers in its food at the harvest.*
> *How long will you lie there, lazybones?*
> *When will you wake from your sleep?*
> *A bit more sleep, a few extra winks,*
> *A bit more hugging yourself in bed,*
> *And poverty will come calling on you,*
> *And want, like an officer with a shield."*

The rabbis embellish that image as they seek the balance that defines a *zeriz*, an industrious soul, but not too much so: "The ant's house has three levels. She doesn't store grain in the upper one because rain may enter through the roof, nor in the lower one because dampness may seep through the floor, but in the middle" (Deut. R. 5.2).

Useful Business

A Jew is supposed to stay usefully busy. Our legendary first ancestors weren't plopped down in paradise to develop the perfect suntan or watch the fruit ripen: "*Adonai Elohim* took Adam and placed him in the Garden of Eden to work it and tend it" (Gen. 2:15). He and Eve were expected to plant and to reap, to sow and to harvest—how else could they feed themselves? And then their apple-eating caused God to make the ground difficult to till, prone to thorns and thistles, so that "the sweat of your brow" became the only way to get bread from the earth (Gen. 3:17–19). As the Yiddish proverb puts it: "Roasted chicken doesn't simply fly into your mouth." Our sages, who deemed very little to be more valuable than study, knew that only a concentrated amount of labor makes learning possible. "Rava said to the rabbis: Don't come to me to study during the month of Nisan [harvest time] or the month of Tishrei [when grapes and olives are ready for pressing]. Do your work then so you won't be threatened by poverty" (Ber. 35b).

The rabbis believe diligence arises not simply from nature or from our personal needs, but from God's very purpose in creating the world. Isaiah 45:18 provides the critical phrase: "*Adonai,* the Creator of heaven, the only real God, the one who formed the earth, said this, *Adonai* set up the land and made it as it is. But *Adonai* did not create it to be a waste, but *lashevet,* for habitation." When the rabbis want to say that we have a religious obligation to be constructively busy, they simply say, *lashevet.* We are God's partners by working on concrete projects that create decent places to live and raise families. This carries through from an individual to a communal activity. Midrash describes this spirited model for Jewish zeal: "Israel entered into the work of building the tabernacle with zest, doing it joyfully and enthusiastically" (Exod. R. 48.16).

True, life doesn't often find us enjoying our work so heartily. Still, in the days before two-career families—as if tending to one's family isn't itself a "career"—many of us had mothers or grandmothers who lived their own versions of "women of valor": "[She] rose while it was still night and got food ready for everyone in the house. . . . [She] girded herself with strength and set about her chores, checking that her projects were going well, even if that meant working by a lamp at night" (Prov. 31:15–18). Their floors shone, their laundry was bright—and starched stiff—and exhaustion wouldn't delay a feast. All that our fathers and grandfathers had to do was to earn enough to move us from immigrant poverty to middle-class ease and beyond! Gene still remembers his mother gently chiding his father for coming home with torn shirt shoulders, even though, as the one in charge of a large factory, he needed only to tell others to move heavy bundles and it would have happened.

Our children grow up in another world. Much of the physical labor we once routinely did has been radically transformed by automatic or automated equipment, "fast food," and generally, more laid-back standards to rate our worth. Nonetheless, we still want the next generation to know the importance of staying useful, and so we demand that our children take care of certain household chores. They often grouse about them—as we do about various adult responsibilities—but this is how they learn, by actively doing. We may then hope with the Bible: "Initiate young people in the way to live, and even when they grow old they will not depart from it" (Prov. 22:6).

Diligence is not just a value for young, vigorous adults but stays with us as we mature. So becoming elderly merely downshifts our efforts to a less frenetic pace. There is still much to do: baby-sitting the grandkids, volunteering at the hospital, or occasionally delivering meals to a homebound friend. At the very least we try to live by the Hippocratic oath, "First, do no harm," or take Nancy Reagan's lead and "just say no" to the things that diminish us and those around us. There is great virtue in living by negative commandments, as our rabbis taught us by claiming that their famous 613 mitzvot had far more negative (365) than positive (248) precepts.

In any case, one needs to do what one can. "R. Judah b. Batira stated: What should one do if there is nothing that must be done?

If he has a waste plot or a desolate field, let him go and make something of it. R. Yose said: A person only dies from sheer idleness" (A.R.N. 11). But the rabbis did not suggest activity as a sure road to success and power. With their customary realism they cautioned: "Some are diligent yet lose, and some indolent ones win" (Pes. 50b). "There are those who are lazy and profit, and those who are industrious and suffer loss" (Ned. 36a). They knew *zerizut* was important, but energy alone could not vanquish all obstacles. As the eighteenth-century Italian mystic Moses Ḥayyim Luzzatto put it: "For people of true understanding, the incentive to zeal comes from a sense of duty and the realization of the worth of the good deed itself" (*Mesillat Yesharim* [The path of the upright]). Luzzatto thought *zerizut* important enough to devote four chapters of his *musar* work to this virtue; we therefore quote him liberally in this chapter.

The Vice of Laziness

Once it is clear that we are not talking about the amount one does or the speed with which one acts, but a basic attitude toward life, a fundamental disposition of the self, it is safe to face the withering satire and biting contempt much of our tradition aims at the slothful. Here is a rabbinic interpretation of Ecclesiastes 10:18: "By slothfulness—by being too lazy to wear a hat—the ceiling falls down—one gets rheumatism—And because of idle hands—by being too lazy to dry properly after washing—the house caves in—one's body breaks out in sores" (Lev. R. 19.4). The Book of Proverbs says: "The lazy rationalize, 'There are bears on the road, lions in the city squares! They turn on their beds like a door on its hinge,'" which drew this late-medieval gloss: "If you tell the lazybones that his teacher has come to a nearby town and he should attend lectures, he will answer you, 'I am afraid of the bear on the way.' If you tell him his teacher has come to his town and he should attend his lecture, he will say, 'There is a lion in the streets.' If you say he is at home, he will say the door is locked. If you tell him it is open and he has no further excuse, he will admit: 'Whether the door is open or locked, I just want to snatch a little more sleep'" (*Yalkut Shimoni*, Prov. 26:13–14). The authors of Proverbs hyperbolically suggest that one who totally lacks *zerizut* is in danger of starvation while staring at a bowl of food: "The sluggards may get their hands into the food bowl but [due to their laziness] they can't manage to get them back to their mouths" (Prov. 26:15).

Our teachers don't think that anyone is born indolent, but believe that laziness and its consequences increase with inaction. The thirteenth-century sage Yeḥiel b. Yekutiel used two telling similes for the insidiousness of sloth: "It is like a small tear in a garment which will destroy the whole thing if not attended to, or like a slight leak in a water pipe which may ultimately cause the whole house to flood" *(Sefer Maalot Hamiddot)*. Luzzatto suggests that the vice begins when one does not exert oneself sufficiently, so one who doesn't put enough effort into the study of the Torah may misconstrue and misunderstand what the Torah teaches us *(Mesillat Yesharim)*. Another path to loss of character comes from being too lazy to acquire wise friends or, having once enjoyed the company of such companions, finding it too hard to stay in touch with them (*Orḥot Tzaddikim* [The ways of the righteous]). The condemnation of indolence is universal, as witness the fable of "The Little Red Hen," left alone to plant, reap, and bake her bread, but flooded with volunteers to help her eat it, or that of "The Three Little Pigs," or the grasshopper who played away the summer, only to find himself with just a thin shirt to ward off winter's wind and snow.

Need we point out the predicament all of us experience at one time or another, when we're left to scramble because someone who said they would do, didn't. "One who is slack in his work is like a brother to a vandal" (Prov. 18:9). "If you send someone lazy on a mission, you might just as well put vinegar on your teeth and smoke in your eyes" (Prov. 10:26). We all can swap exasperating stories of someone who just couldn't manage to get around to doing something they promised to take care of.

"If You've Got It, Hold It; If You're Capable, Do" (Yiddish Proverb)

Much of the classic disgust with laziness stems from the punishing economic conditions in which most people lived until quite recently. Want or the threat of want severely limited our choices, making our communal leaders, seeing the general neediness, add their own controls. But deprivation no longer informs our zeal as it once did. With our means expanded, with society itself more open, our limitless number of choices now intrudes on our ability to choose to do just this or that. And our tolerance of diversity has ballooned so greatly that we no longer summarily dismiss what once seemed indecent. In short, the temptation of inaction has now found a powerful ally in indecision.

Martin Buber described our situation well when he said that as we evolve, we can be bowled over by infinite possibilities: "The plenitude of possibility floods over [one's] small reality and overwhelms it . . . the chaos of possibilities of being . . . becomes a chaos of possibilities of action" *(Images of Good and Evil)*. The resulting inability to choose just one course of action brings all doing to a screeching halt. We can remember dismaying childhood experiences that probably distressed us to tears: with our limited money, we could buy just one of the many different kinds of candy or toys displayed before us. The super-rich have the obverse form of our indecision. Having "been there, done that," they easily fall into ennui, the boredom that also brings inaction. Yet everyone knows affluence shouldn't keep us from doing, even though rabbis told us that wealthy married women could "lounge in easy chairs" (Ket. 59b).

Another source of temptation diminishes our zeal: our sense that there must be some good in everything. Why should we take sides on issues when both sides make a certain amount of sense? It becomes increasingly difficult to identify with absolute conviction who is fully right and who fully wrong. If someone tries, we are suspicious of them and their certainties. That, we say, is merely their opinion, something we're all entitled to, a liberality of appreciation that questions our momentary commitment to a given cause and saps our devotion to it. Is it any wonder, then, that recent years have seen a decrease in ethical activism? If we tolerate everything, what will happen to even our most strongly held beliefs? Or will indecision dominate and induce the inevitable spiritual flab?

"Don't Pull the String Too Taut" (Yiddish Proverb)

Yet, giving diligence full rein can be as destructive as inaction. Instead of affluence making us less tense about work and leisure activities, it encourages a more fevered intensity. We now identify participants in a new class of addiction that many of us proudly affirm, smugly labeling ourselves "workaholics." We are not content to give 100 percent of our energy to our work, but regularly speak of investing 110 percent of ourselves, as if that were even possible. Luzzatto knew the consequences of this folly: "He who has become a slave to work is no longer his own master and cannot act differently, even should he want to do so" *(Mesillat Yesharim)*. Those of us who would not consider ourselves compulsive willingly accept the need for long hours and high dedication to succeed at our jobs, or to even hold on to them and their perks. Families search for ingenious ways to create quality time simply because there is so little opportunity to hang out together. Volunteer agencies bemoan the lack of those helpers who once gave so agreeably and gained so much in the process.

Nonetheless, the result of exceptional diligence can be admirable. Several years ago, much of America thrilled to Cal Ripken, Jr.'s feat, as he broke Lou Gherig's record for the number of consecutive baseball games played. One might say that the response was utterly disproportionate, since all he did was show up for work every day, prepared to do the job he earns megabucks to do. Yet that does not appreciate the special problems even a superbly conditioned athlete faces, taking the field day after day. Gherig's record stood for decades because the inevitable muscle pulls, virus attacks, and general indisposition—or lessening of performance—that sidelined every other ball player were somehow overcome by Ripken's zeal and dedication.

Tragically, it becomes easy to cross the thin line separating good, hard work from absurd overextension. John Edward Curtis was known in his community as a thoroughly admirable human being. He had just been appointed the CEO of Luby's Cafeterias, a publicly held company. The night before he was to preside over his first board meeting, after saying his usual evening prayers with his wife of almost thirty years, he drove to a motel, where he committed suicide. Apparently Curtis was overwrought by the need to report a quarterly profit margin of 6 percent, rather than the 9 percent increase his predecessor achieved. To us, this points to zeal gone mad. Yet sociologists assure us that Curtis's action, though extreme, is symptomatic of "executive suicide" syndrome, in this case literally so. Misapplied zeal distorts our humanity and renders it misshapen. It appears that too many of us take this Ladino proverb too literally, too often: "The successful can put their hands in a sack and pull out a tower." To descend further to the level of mere cynical realism, here is some of the tart wisdom that eastern European Jews applied to such warped priorities: "Even God didn't make the world in one day"; "With one pair of feet you can't dance at two weddings"; "No matter how long you live, you won't have time for everything"; "Don't run too fast, and you won't tear up your shoes."

In allocating our energy, we continually make judgments as we decide the relative importance of each given area or project. Of course, making money is a highly regarded Jewish goal, as we hope to point out in our chapter on "Wealth." But surely it isn't the most important one. That ought to be our sense of Ultimate Reality, what constitutes the underlying foundation of everything we care about and everyone we love: in brief, God. Being diligent about the life of Torah helps us understand how God wants us to reach these most worthy goals.

Our *Zerizut* Models

Women, by their industrious accomplishments over the past quarter-century, are our finest contemporary examples of *zerizut*. Reserve and reticence once characterized the "good girl," implicitly training women to play down their talents and put aside their aspirations. Francie remembers a grade school teacher admonishing her overzealous efforts by reciting this awful platitude to her: "Just be good, and let those who can't, be clever." But the zeal of certain particularly focused females helped to halt this passivity. The writing and speeches of Betty Friedan, the late Bella Abzug, and Letty Cottin Pogrebin (a few of many), galvanized women of all ages, injecting massive doses of confidence into the American female psyche. Now females fill at least half of law, medical, and liberal rabbinical school classes. That women should be as ambitious as men in pursuing career paths seems natural and accepted by all but the most traditional. Women's continued *zerizut* on their own behalf will keep society from slipping back into its old sexist ways, perpetuating a fundamentally unethical pattern out of sheer inertia.

In the Bible's quite patriarchal tradition, Abraham is *zerizut's* great exemplar. We note how his zeal emphasizes velocity as he provides hospitality for God's messengers: "Abraham went quickly into Sarah's tent and said, 'Hurry, make cakes.' Then Abraham ran to the herd to select a tender and choice calf, and gave it to a servant, who hastened to prepare it" (Gen. 18:6–7). Some sages find zeal in Abraham's response to God's awesome command to sacrifice Isaac: "Abraham rose early the next morning, saddled his ass, took two lads and his son Isaac, split the wood for the offering and set out for the place . . ." (Gen. 22:3). No wonder the classic description of proper religious vigor is *zerizim makdimim le-mitzvot,* the diligent rush to do a mitzvah (Pes. 4a). Judah b. Tema states this dramatically: "Be as strong as the leopard, soaring as the eagle, fleet as the hart, and mighty as the lion to do the will of our Father in Heaven" (Avot 5.23). And of course we must mention those five diligent B'nei Brak rabbis who got so engrossed in performing the *maggid* (storytelling) step of their seder that they continued their discussion until dawn. As we read each Pesaḥ, "everyone who extends the telling is praiseworthy."

But the rabbis did not promote religious *zerizut* unconditionally. Consider the enigma of the highly esteemed second-century teacher Ben Azzai, who said: "Run to fulfill even a slight precept as you would to perform a great one" (Avot 4.2), a clear invitation to scrupulosity. When Ben Azzai died, the religious leaders of the day called him "the last of the industrious scholars" (Sot. 9.15). But for some reason, he was never ordained. Did they sense that his devotion had subtly evolved into a compulsion to feed his pride?

Whatever the case, in eight separate talmudic citations the rabbis debate whether taking on special stringencies of observance, *ḥumrot,* leads to pridefulness, a grievous vice that should be shunned. It is possible to become so meticulous about observing a law that one loses all sense of its never-changing purpose: building a Jewish relationship with God. One famous late-medieval

Lithuanian halakhist, Solomon Luria, recorded the opinions of those who believed that it made no difference whether such practices were done publicly or privately—the person who did them should be put under a ban (*Yam Shel Shelomo* [The sea of Solomon], B.K. chap. 7, par. 41). Luzzatto summed it up well: "No one should carry zeal or confidence to excess" (*Mesillat Yesharim*).

Reason-Defying Zealotry

Religious zeal can go one terrifying step further and become zealotry, such a certainty in one's own faith that one compels others to accept it—or else. Most American Jews embrace religious diversity; they cannot fathom that "their" Judaism, like all religions, can be read to coerce the unbelievers and the unobservant. But the occasional outbreak of intra-religious intolerance by the ultra-Orthodox Israeli rabbinate makes this strand of our faith frighteningly real. As some interpret it, loving one's "neighbor" like oneself applies only to fellow Jews, and only those who are "like you" in proper observance.

That permits hating not only some co-religionists but, in quite exceptional cases, actually condones striking out against other Jews. To contemporary zealots, the honor of the Torah demands such *zerizut;* the rest of us assert vehemently that such religious zealotry blasphemes God and violates the Torah's goal of creating peace. The overwhelming majority of Diaspora Jews are long experienced in living peacefully with others whose views and practices differ from our own. Living in democracies has taught us the spiritual value of pluralism, helping us to incorporate this as a significant principle of our faith.

Because of these aberrations of religious zeal, some cynics argue that religion creates more trouble than good. They want it stripped of all urgency to act, and reduced to the privacy of contemplative belief. Others negate *zerizut* by insisting that only universal precepts rightly command us. We have all heard some well-intentioned person say this, or something similar: "As long as we all get along and work together, why take particular practices so seriously?"

As Always, Striving for Zealful Balance

But though religious zealotry in any form is deplorable, a slothful approach to virtue is even more dangerous, as one glance at our society indicates. While doing "the good" may be difficult to discern and specify, its visibility and genuine power still rouse us to action. And acts aren't worth much if they are done in a vague, general manner; they must be done quite particularly. Thus we make room at our seder table for the person who wouldn't have anywhere else to go and try to make Shabbat dinner a family night. We promise ourselves that this year we really will build a *sukkah* in the back yard, read a Jewish book, and attend an adult education class at temple.

Without zeal's demanding, energizing spark, everything we care about, like decency, compassion, and trustworthiness, become mere daydreams, damning indictments of secular aspirations. Judaism is a religion of distinctive deed. No wonder, then, *Orḥot Tzaddikim* teaches: "The quality of zeal is an ornament to other virtues; it corrects them and makes them real."

From Our Tradition

R. Josiah said: Just as you must not allow matzah to rise, ferment, or sour by lack of promptness in its baking, so you must not let a *mitzvah* sour by delaying its performance, by letting it wait.

—Mekhilta de R. Ishmael, Bo 9

Admire the man who is diligent in his work, for he shall stand before kings.

—Prov. 22:29

Said the Kotzker Rebbe: The lazy and the deliberate are both unhurried in their action. The deliberate one keeps thinking over the merits of the required action. The indolent one delays action until it becomes imperative, and then doesn't have the time to give the matter due thought.

—Newman, *The Hasidic Anthology*

You can talk all you want, but it gets nothing done.
A meowing cat catches no mice.
Laughing is easy, doing is tough.
Nobody is born a virtuoso.
Nothing comes easily.
Hit a cold stone, and you'll get a hot spark.

—Yiddish proverbs

The tailor and the idler are always losing either the thimble or
    the needle.
An idler is always busy hunting flies.
The unsuccessful are always busy running—in place.
Cooking is hard; eating is easy.
If you want to eat an almond you first have to crack open the
    shell.
Early risers are blessed with luck.

—Ladino proverbs

On the eve of the New Year Rabbi Menaḥem Mendel of Rymanov
entered the synagogue. He surveyed the many people who had
come to pray. "You are a fine crowd!" he called out to them. "But I
want you to know that I cannot carry you all on my shoulders. Every
one of you must work for yourself!"

—Buber, *Tales of the Hasidim*, bk. 2, *The Later Masters*

Generosity—*Nedivut*

*Someone can feed his father capons and for it be destined to
go to Gehenna, while another person can tie his father to the
millstones to pull them, yet be destined to go to the Garden of
Eden.*

*How does one feed his father capons and be destined for
Gehenna? A man once gave his father delicious fat chickens
to eat. When his father asked him how he got them, the son
replied, "Old man, eat and shut up, just like dogs that eat
and shut up."*

*How does one tie his father to the millstones, yet be destined
for the Garden of Eden? A man once worked as a miller,
pulling the mill wheel himself to make grain for bread.
Someone from his family had to serve in the army. So he said
to his father, "You pull the wheel instead of me—I will go
into the army. Then, if the officers order a disgraceful act, I
will do it, not you, and if someone has to get a beating, let it
be me, not you."*

—Yer. Kid. 1.7

*I*n Judaism, generosity, *nedivut,* is as much concerned
with "how" as "how much." Thus, "R. Yohanan b.
Zakkai told his five disciples to find the chief charac-
teristic a person should cultivate. R. Eliezer said, 'A friendly eye.' R.
Joshua said, 'A good friend.' R. Yose said, 'A good neighbor.' R.
Simon said, 'Seeing the consequences of one's acts.' R. Elazar b.
Arakh said, 'A good heart.' R. Yohanan responded, 'I prefer Elazar's
answer because it will lead to all the rest'" (Avot 2.9). R. Yohanan

understood that, with the proper intention, the correct "how," other positive behavior follows almost automatically. So too, the hasidic master Rabbi Menaḥem Mendel of Kotzk taught: "The Torah, speaking of God's commands, says, '. . . which you shall do, and live thereby' [Lev. 18:5]. That means, perform them with liveliness and enthusiasm'" (Elkins, *Melodies from My Father's House*).

From Yoḥanan b. Zakkai to the Kotzker Rebbe, our sages stressed the value of *nedivut* as referring to quality, not quantity, because rich Jews were such a tiny minority (though an important one) among us. Much of what they said also applies to us, a generation blessed with sufficient means to elevate shopping to a seriously pursued avocation. Our tradition instructs us to guard against such selfishness and greed, teaching us that sharing ourselves is every bit as important as sharing our funds. So Francie remembers how "Jewish" a song from her NFTY camping days seemed: "Love is nothing till you give it away. . . ." Indeed, most of us have found ourselves fervently agreeing with the prayer of our Yiddish ancestors: "May God save me from the stingy of heart!"

"Don't Keep Your Goodness in Your Pockets" (Yiddish Proverb)

Our teachers have long pointed to hospitality as a favorite example of the open, generous heart. It is easy to understand why. Not so long ago, the world was not equipped to welcome outsiders. There were few road maps or atlases, no hotel or restaurant chains, and certainly no plastic to substitute for currency. Although inns existed, they were poor alternatives for genuinely offered hospitality after a long day. Travelers welcomed the sight of an open door and a friendly face. Strangers became friends when invited to "break bread" together. Even those with little to spare stretched their meager provisions for the sake of hospitality. Gene fondly remembers how newcomers were soon seated around the kitchen tables in his grandmothers' tenement apartments. As the sage R. Dimi taught: "Hospitality is greater than going to the Study House," or, in the words of Rav: "Hospitality to wayfarers is greater than welcoming the Shekhinah" (Shab. 127a). Yeḥiel b. Yekutiel, the thirteenth-century Roman ethicist, suggests that this is so natural, we might

even learn *nedivut* from the rooster: "When he chances on something to eat, he calls his fellows to eat with him. Sometimes he even
chooses food and places it before them" *(Sefer Maalot Hamiddot)*.

Because our patriarch Abraham showed legendary hospitality to
the three men/angels who came to his tent, the rabbis name
Abraham as the classic exemplar of *nedivut:* "Let me fetch a morsel
of bread that you may refresh yourselves . . . and Abraham ran to his
herd and selected a tender and choice calf . . ." (Gen. 18:5, 7). The
rabbis note that Abraham did not send a servant, but he himself
"ran" to provide his guests with food. Our teachers cannot praise
Abraham's *nedivut* enough: "All who possess these three attributes
are disciples of our father Abraham: a good eye, a humble spirit,
and a modest soul" (Avot 5.22). The medieval ethical work *Orḥot
Tzaddikim* says: "There are three kinds of generosity: generosity with
money, generosity with one's body, and generosity with one's wisdom—and all three are found in Abraham." The hasidic rebbe
known as the Yehudi, Yaakov Yitzḥak of Przysucha, goes even further, attributing to our first patriarch almost divine capabilities:
"Why does the Torah say incongruously: 'Abraham stood over the
angels and they did eat' [Gen. 18:8]? Angels have virtues and flaws,
and men have virtues and flaws. The virtue of angels is that they cannot deteriorate, but their flaw is that they cannot improve. Man's
flaw is that he can deteriorate, but his virtue is that he can improve.
However, someone who practices *nedivut* acquires the virtues of his
guests. Thus Abraham acquired the virtue of angels, that of not
being able to deteriorate. And so he stood over and above them"
(Buber, *Tales of the Hasidim*, bk. 2, *The Later Masters*).

A Good Eye, a Narrow Eye

The rabbis of the Talmud use "code words" to describe those who
display the virtue of *nedivut* or its opposing vice. People who have a
"good eye" are called *tov ayin;* those with a "narrow eye" are known
as *tzar ayin.* Looking closely at these figures of speech, we can learn
much about the understanding behind the rabbinic metaphors.

When we feel a certain solidarity with others, we want to share
our possessions and, more importantly, ourselves with them. We call

on the universal human capacity for empathy, what the German Jewish philosopher Hermann Cohen calls our ability to transform another person into a "fellow-being." Then we identify with the other's situation so closely that we give whatever and whenever we can. Such generosity takes place even in the most horrific circumstances. Consider the testimony of the late Viktor Frankl, a Viennese psychiatrist who based his new form of psychotherapy, called logotherapy, on his experiences in Nazi concentration camps. He came to realize that his strength to survive stemmed from his need and willingness to help his fellow victims. While many others simply gave up, unable to find a reason to continue, Frankl's empathy helped him to keep going *(Man's Search for Meaning)*.

The rabbis observe that our empathy can become stunted in our far more ordinary, day-to-day lives, stopping us from doing the right thing even though we know we should. So, for example, when someone who has wronged us unexpectedly wants to apologize, do we "narrow" our eyes so that we cannot relate to that person's sincere regret? Or, seeing the other in full humanity, do we earnestly try to be generous and accept the apology with an open spirit? Can we conquer our reluctance, as the medieval Spanish philosopher and poet Solomon ibn Gabirol advises: "When you see that someone is about to offer you an apology, let go of what separates the two of you. Pardon your friend, whether you believe his request for forgiveness is genuine or false" *(Miṿḥar Hapeninim)*.

According to rabbinic tradition, Moses exemplifies the *tov ayin,* the person whose acts are prompted by a "good eye." A story from the midrashic collection, Numbers Rabbah, points out that Moses generously accepts Joshua as his successor in leadership, never an easy task: "*Adonai* said to Moses, 'Single out Joshua, the son of Nun, a man who has spirit in him, and place your hand [*sic*] on him' [Num. 27:18]. But Moses responds with such *nedivut* that 'he placed both his hands on Joshua' [Num. 27:23] (Num. R. 21.15). So too, R. Yose b. R. Ḥanina teaches: "The Torah was originally given only to Moses and his descendants. But Moses generously shared it with all Israel. Thus the Bible refers to Moses when it says: 'He that has a generous eye shall be blessed' [Prov. 22:9]" (Ned. 38a). Few of us will have the chance to emulate such extraordinary *nedivut;* however, Yeḥiel b. Yekutiel provides us with an example of a *tov ayin* acting in more routine circumstances: "If a mitzvah presents itself, [such a person] summons his resources so that he may do it with a good eye, specifically including the humility not to do it for the sake of receiving a reward (and therefore being proud in his heart), or making a show of his merit before others" *(Sefer Maalot Hamiddot).* In other words, a person with a "good eye" recognizes the opportunity to do a good deed as soon as it appears, and then matter-of-factly acts on it.

Not so for the *tzar ayin,* the one of "narrow eye." Here our English idiom aptly characterizes those who avoid seeing others who ask for help: "What's wrong with them? Are they blind?" For if they really saw what was going on, how could they not lend a hand? Social scientists call this critical boundary between "us" and "them" the "ethical horizon," the point where solidarity changes to distance and suspicion, if not enmity. People who have a "narrow eye" don't want to see too much; they shrink their ethical horizons and contract their humanity. Such actions remind us a little of how "gangsters" behave, quite loving with their families and intensely loyal to their peers, but capable of showing quite another standard in their relations with their adversaries and victims. Many of us live similarly—though our distinctions between "us" and "them" have much less violent consequences.

The rabbinic midrash to the Book of Ruth presents a surprising portrait of a *tzar ayin* in Elimelech, Ruth's father-in-law. Almost immediately after telling us that a famine in Israel forced the whole family to flee to Moab, the biblical story recounts that Elimelech died, without offering an explanation. The rabbis see this as a sign of God's justice: "Why was Elimelech punished? He was like a certain prominent man who was so rich that people figured he could sustain them, even if there were ten years of famine. But when a famine actually came, he cannily sent his maidservant to the marketplace with an empty basket in her hands. So, too, Elimelech was one of the notables of his era and a leader of his generation. But when famine came, he said to himself: 'Now all of Israel will come knocking at my door, each one with a basket, begging for food.' So he ran away from them to Moab" (Ruth R. 1.4). The rabbis' critical quid pro quo, while not really acceptable to most of us today, underscores their rage against those who might help others less fortunate than they are but consciously choose not to.

Proverbs teaches that, even if your enemy is hungry, you must feed him, giving him bread to eat (25:21)—one with a "good eye" acts that generously. In a remark as insightful as it is judgmental, R. Joshua b. Korḥa declares: "One who shuts his eyes to those created in God's image, so as not to see an occasion for giving charity, is not much better than an idolater" (Ket. 68a). R. Joshua b. Levi expands R. Joshua b. Korḥa's single sin into two: "If you accept anything from the narrow-eyed, you transgress two negative commandments: 'Do not eat' and 'Do not desire.' So even if you are sure that the *tzar ayin* will set many delicacies before you, don't enter his home. . . . He will inwardly make a note of every morsel that you eat and drink" (Sot. 38b, Prov. 23:6–7).

Our ethicists would not tolerate such selfishness. The thirteenth-century sage Judah the Pious says of the tightfisted: "If someone is niggardly with the poor, and not only doesn't share his bread or money, but as good as steals from people, then 'may none pity his orphans' [Ps. 109:12]. And how much the more should we not pity him" (Judah Heḥasid, *Sefer Ḥasidim,* 1,027). The medieval ethical work *Orḥot Tzaddikim* bluntly describes a *tzar ayin* as "stingy with money and altogether a worthless human being." Stinginess of self is similarly scorned: "If a man gives to his fellow all the good gifts of the world but does so with a grumpy demeanor, the Bible regards it as if he had given nothing. But if he receives his fellow cheerfully and kindly, the Bible regards it as if he had given him all the good gifts of the world" (A.R.N. 13).

"If God Has Given You a Living, Let Others Live a Little" (Yiddish Proverb)

Thus far we have intentionally practiced a little *tzar ayin* of our own by remaining silent about an inevitable reality: most often, *nedivut* requires giving generously of our money. For even the most "narrow-eyed" among us understands that contributing to worthy people or causes, and getting others to do so, is a central Jewish obligation. To paraphrase Hillel: "All the rest is commentary. Go and be generous."

Here we offer a little "commentary" of our own, borrowing counsel from our teachers, who explain why we should be generous with our funds: "His disciples asked R. Neḥunya b. Hakanah the cause of his long life. He said, . . . 'I was generous with my money.' Another rabbi said: 'I never took presents, I never stood upon my legal rights, and I was generous with my money.' It is said that Job was also generous. When he bought only half a *perutah*'s worth of merchandise, he would still leave a whole *perutah* with the storekeeper" (Meg. 28a). Eliezer Papo, a nineteenth-century Sephardic sage, wants even our business dealings to reflect *nedivut,* a virtue not ordinarily associated with the canny wiles of commerce: "When you can, lower your prices so that your customers will also profit. Sell at cost to the poor or to Torah scholars, and if you hire them, pay them generously" *(Pele Yoetz).*

Nedivut in Our Community and in Its Leadership

But we must not think of *nedivut* as limited to something that only one person can do for another, that is, only one-on-one generosity. That would be a "narrow eye" indeed! Nor should we limit our vision only to our own often-suffering people. Rather, our hand should extend to humanity as a whole, giving *nedivut* a widespread, social dimension. The organization known as Mazon, which calls itself "The Jewish response to hunger," gives open-handedly to both Jewish and non-Jewish groups, enabling communities to assist their own needy. The founders of Mazon may have been inspired by the following biblical story. In its account of how the former Hebrew slaves built and decorated the *mishkan,* the wilderness sanctuary, the Torah gives us a striking example of communal generosity: "Moses spoke to the entire community of the children of Israel, saying: "Let us all give gifts to *Adonai;* that is, let everyone whose heart moves *(nediv)* him to do so, bring them. Furthermore, let all among you who are skilled, come and make all the special things that *Adonai* has commanded we have. . . . And everyone who excelled in ability and everyone whose spirit moved him came, bringing *Adonai's* offering for the work of the Tent of Meeting. . . . Thus the Israelites, all the men and women whose heart moved them, brought freewill offerings to the Lord" (Exod. 35:4–29).

In his recent translation of the Torah, the biblical scholar Everett Fox notes that synonyms for the Hebrew word "all" are used fourteen times in the above verses—the people's participation was that inclusive *(The Schocken Bible: Vol. I)*. No less impressive is that in five places, some form of the Hebrew root *n-d-v* is used to describe the openhearted spirit of the contributors. And there is yet another truly astonishing aspect to this story. As the narrative continues, we learn that the people gave so much, so quickly, that the artisans came to Moses and said: "'The people are bringing more than is needed!' . . . Moses had proclaimed throughout the camp, 'Stop giving. . . .'" (Exod. 36:3–7). Anyone who has ever been involved in a fund-raising campaign will appreciate how rare such behavior is. When people are generous, miracles happen.

Nedivut also involves giving in a timely fashion. The rabbis note that, although the Torah describes the lavish sacrifices that the tribal princes brought to the dedication of the *mishkan,* it says nothing about their earlier contributions to its construction. So the rabbis conclude that the offerings of the tribal princes were rejected because they were given only after the magnanimous donations of the general population. They were no longer needed because the common folk had already brought more than enough. Consequently, the princes were embarrassed that they had not given to help build the *mishkan* earlier (Num. R. 12.16).

We expect our leaders to set an example and give their means as well as their time and expertise. The author of *Orḥot Tzaddikim* sets those standards quite high: "A person cannot be called generous unless he is willing to give, regardless of the season of the year or the time of the day." And it is more important to cultivate a habit of giving than making a one-time great show of philanthropy: "If on one occasion you give a thousand gold pieces to a worthy person, you are simply not as generous as someone who also gives a thousand gold pieces, but does so on a thousand different occasions."

"The Longest Distance Is to One's Pocket" (Yiddish Proverb)

And then there are those who seem almost congenitally unable to let go of any of their money at all: "These are the traits of the miser: He does not give charity, he does not have mercy on the poor, and in business, he does not yield at all. He does not feed or clothe or give pleasure to anyone but himself. And he doesn't trust God, who gave him his money" *(Orḥot Tzaddikim)*. Having an atrophied sense of solidarity with the rest of humanity, the miser sneers at those who must receive as well as those who willingly give. "R. Judah said: The miser responds to the poor man with an evil disposition: 'Look at those thighs—Look at those legs! See how fat you are! Why don't you go out and work for your food?'" (Lev. R. 34.7). Since the miser thinks only of himself, he says: "I will cut down this fruit tree for its lumber" (Pes. 50b). He is not only indifferent, but downright disdainful of such a tree's promise to produce an edible yield over and over again. By worshipping money, the miser violates the commandment: "You must not make gods of silver or gods of gold for yourselves" (Exod. 20:20). By rejecting the divine spark within everyone, misers commit blasphemy, reducing God to a being as little and mean-spirited as they are.

No culture has ever had anything good to say about misers, certainly not the wisdom that springs from the Jewish folk. Here are some Ladino maxims: "A miser lights a candle for no one," "A miser is like a tree with no shade," and "If you shake a stingy miller's beard, a cake will fall out." An Iraqi proverb says: "A miser has a withered hand." And our Yiddish-speaking forebears heartily concur: "Better to kill your wife than be miserly with her," and "A miser protects his money like a dog a bone." To which we add this medieval Italian observation: "A miser is like a dog. When a dog stands over a carcass that might feed many dogs and then another dog comes to eat, the first barks and drives him away, insisting there is not enough to satisfy him" (Yeḥiel b. Yekutiel, *Sefer Maalot Hamiddot*).

"If You Rush to Give on the First Day, You May Rue It on the Second" (Ladino Proverb)

Our sages were too practical to suggest that *nedivut* should be our chief virtue. They did not expect us to give away all of our funds. Yeḥiel b. Yekutiel makes that point through this poignant story: "A certain worker was so magnanimous that he did all of his work without pay. People soon took it for granted that they did not need to pay him, so they no longer asked him what they owed, but thanked him and walked away. He became so poor that he had no money even to feed his dog, who starved and died. The man then understood what he had done, and told his customers, 'Just as my dog died from your gratitude to me, I cannot be sustained by it either. A person cannot feed himself with the gratitude of others, without also receiving another good—money'" *(Sefer Maalot Hamiddot)*. Thus the Talmud imposes specific minimum and maximum limits on our monetary giving: "Donate 10 percent of your net income to charity. Should you want to be generous, do not give more than 20 percent of your income, lest you come to need charity yourself" (Ket. 50a).

And give only to those people and causes that truly deserve our generosity. As the Yiddish proverb says, "Don't be too sweet, or the world will eat you up." A heart-rending story does not guarantee a righteous cause, just as an impressive letterhead may conceal more than it reveals. Not so long ago, we learned that only about 20 percent of the monies collected by the long-respected Jewish National Fund ever got to the State of Israel. Happily, that situation has been remedied. Our naturally generous inclination should not blind us to possible abuses by groups that do not practice full disclosure, just as our suspiciousness should not excuse miserliness.

The Spirit of *Nedivut*

But money must not be our last word concerning *nedivut*. In truth it takes quite little, monetarily speaking, to be "good-eyed" and openhanded. A stranger in an unfamiliar city welcomes a home-cooked meal; a lift home from a co-worker beats waiting for an overcrowded bus on a stormy night. Generosity does not begin with a lot of cash, but with that wealth of spirit that shows others we care. We esteem those who give with *nedivut,* as did the biblical poet who said: "He who gives freely to the poor, his beneficence lasts and lasts, and his strength is exalted in honor" (Ps. 112:9).

From Our Tradition

Rabbi Israel Salanter saw a servant maid carrying two pails of water on her shoulders. When dinner was ready he performed the ritual hand washing before eating sparingly. When asked why he did not use more water, he replied, "One must not be generous with a mitzvah on another person's shoulders."

—Newman, *The Hasidic Anthology*

Rabbi Mordecai of Neskhizh saved all year to afford the perfect *etrog* during Sukkot. On his way to the market, he saw a water vendor standing in the middle of the road, lamenting that his horse just collapsed. He gave the man all his money to buy another horse. "What does it matter?" he said to himself as he turned to go back home. "Everyone will say the blessing over an *etrog;* I will say mine over this horse!" But when he reached his house, he found a beautiful *etrog* that friends had bought him as a gift.

—Buber, *Tales of the Hasidim,* bk. 1, *The Early Masters*

Abba the Cupper [Healer] used to receive greetings daily from the Academy on High. Why? Outside his office, he had a discreet place where small coins were to be deposited as his fee. Whoever had money put it there; whoever had none could come to him without feeling embarrassed. When he treated someone who he felt sure had no means, Abba would hand him some coins as he was leaving, and say: "Go and use the money to regain your strength."

—Taan. 21b

When a man is gentle, his family is gentle. If a poor person stands at the door and says, "Is your father in?" they reply, "Yes, enter." Then hardly has he entered before the table is prepared.

—A.R.N. I, 7

Wealth—*Osher*

An elderly Jewish man was hit by a bus. In the hospital, a kind nurse put a pillow under his head and asked, "Are you comfortable, Mr. Cohen?" "Thank God," he whispered, "I make a nice living."

—Blue and Magonet,
The Jewish Guide to the Here and Hereafter

*F*ew of us consider ourselves wealthy. The average Nicaraguan or Bangladeshi might envy what we see as our average lifestyles, and consider the way that we live luxurious. But compared to billionaires like Bill Gates or Warren Buffet, our assets seem meager to us. What seems like wealth to one person may be barely acceptable to another—riches are relative to their beholder. Not so long ago, our families struggled to survive in eastern Europe. They would joke about a more prosperous neighbor: "He's rich—he owns a whole head of cabbage" (Yiddish proverb). Two thousand years ago, R. Tarfon knowingly exaggerated when he claimed that you weren't really wealthy unless you owned 100 vineyards, 100 fields, and 100 slaves to work your vast holdings. In contrast, Tarfon's colleague, R. Akiba, said that a man was rich if his wife was "comely in deeds." And R. Yose, speaking practically, said that anyone was wealthy if his outhouse wasn't far from his table (Shab. 25b).

How Can Having Money Be a Religious Virtue?

Money so easily spoils us that many people believe we can only be pious if we are poor. They tacitly agree with Jesus's advice to the rich man who wanted to learn how to fulfill the law. Jesus told the man that, by giving all of his money to the poor in this world, he would guarantee that he'd be eternally rich in the world to come. Jesus taught his disciples: "It is easier for a camel to get through a needle's eye than for a rich man to get into the Kingdom of Heaven" (Matt. 19:24). Some Christians, like the saintly Mother Theresa, took vows of poverty, devoting their lives to the holy tasks of helping the poor and the sick. Buddhist monks and Hindu ascetics own little more than their begging bowls and prayer mats and consider themselves the more holy for it. So it shouldn't surprise us if we occasionally look at self-denial as a path leading us to true piety. Karl Marx, however, pointed out how nice it was for the rich when the clergy preached that poverty was a great virtue. This stopped the poor from protesting their condition or trying to change it, and maintained the gross economic inequalities that served as the status quo in most societies.

Many Jewish teachers agree that hungering after money makes us less sensitive to the needs of others. "When the rich man counts his money, the poor man's candle goes out" (Ladino proverb). Medieval *musar* writer Baḥya ibn Pakuda asks God to protect him from "the disorders of the soul that would occur if money were found in every riverbed and village" *(Ḥovot Halevavot)*. In the nineteenth century another Sephardic sage, Eliezer Papo, said in apparent agreement: "Wealth is a greater test of character than poverty" *(Pele Yoetz)*. We've seen countless examples of marriages collapsing or lives seriously gone awry once people become financially successful. And while these problems surely aren't funny, they've occurred with such frequency that droll Sephardic pundits couldn't restrain themselves: "When a Jew becomes wealthy, he suddenly considers his wife ugly and his house too small" (Ladino proverb). The rabbis occasionally said something positive about being poor, since so many Jews were without means. Thus R. Akiba commented, "Poverty is as becoming to the Jews as a red ribbon on the neck of a white horse" (Lev. R. 35.5).

But mainstream Judaism did not consider poverty a virtue to be sought. Early in our tradition, we see hints that God does not look kindly on us if we impose radical self-denial on ourselves. In biblical times, Jewish practice allowed men to take vows abstaining from wine or cutting their hair, like the legendary Samson. For a specific length of time, such individuals took on the special status of a Nazirite. Yet when the term of their vows ended, they were required to bring an offering to the Temple. The rabbis said that this sacrifice atoned for their sin—not enjoying the full pleasures of the world, which God had created. When the Italian ethicist Yeḥiel b. Yekutiel praised wealth as one of the virtues that was so vital to Judaism, he reflected the dominant, though usually unspoken position of our tradition.

The Lesson of Jewish Realism—It's Hard to Be Poor and Devout

The reason for Judaism's relatively positive view toward wealth seems plain enough. Throughout our history, most Jews lived in grinding poverty and learned firsthand that neediness does not encourage holiness. An Iraqi proverb is quite blunt: "A *mi shebeirakh* prayer will not feed our children." Poverty easily overwhelms us, forcing us to focus all of our energies on our physical survival. No wonder Sholom Aleichem's fictional character Tevye became so beloved! When he gladly gave up being a dairyman in the shtetl of Anatevka to immigrate to the unknown of America, he exemplified the dreams of several million poor Jews who fled eastern Europe. Tevye was the prototype of all those hoping to escape unrelenting hunger and fear to seek their fortune elsewhere.

One needn't be Jewish to share this realism. George Bernard Shaw's play *Pygmalion* cynically denies the link between penury and spirituality. When Eliza Doolittle's father demands a payoff from Professor Higgins and Colonel Pickering because his daughter is living in their flat, Pickering is outraged. He self-righteously demands, "Have you no morals, sir?" Doolittle unabashedly responds, "Can't afford 'em, Governor. Neither could you if you was as poor as me."

Any notion of a positive connection between religiosity and deprivation was shattered by the events of the Holocaust. By forbidding everything, the Nazis sought to destroy the Jewish soul before murdering what remained of the Jewish body. In his autobiographical novel *Night,* Elie Wiesel indicates how this often led to a total moral breakdown, with sons abandoning or physically attacking their own fathers just to snatch another crust of bread. In *Night,* when the boy's father finally dies of protracted starvation, the teenager, half-dead from hunger himself, cannot pray. Instead, he can only think of how the death of his father frees him from any obligation to another, perhaps thereby extending his own life.

The Talmud is full of maxims decrying the negative effects of poverty. The rabbis said, "Poverty is one of three things that drive a person out of his mind" (Er. 41b). R. Pinḥas b. Ḥama considered poverty in one's house harder to bear than fifty plagues (B.B. 116a). Resh Lakish equated "the poor with the dead" (Ned. 64b). Acknowledging the loss of human dignity that comes with impoverishment, most of the rabbis of the Talmud worked at a trade, often a quite humble one. They considered labor, no matter how unglamorous, vastly preferable to poverty. As Rav said to R. Kahana: "Take a job skinning carcasses in the public street and don't say, 'I am a great man, this work does not befit me'" (B.B. 110a). R. Akiba said: "Make your Sabbath like a weekday, with no special meals, rather than need the help of others" (Pes. 112a). Nearer to our time, Eliezer Papo explains many of the migration patterns of the Jews when he writes: "If you can't make a living in one town, move to another. . . . But do not leave your family behind" *(Pele Yoetz).*

In short, making money—to provide for oneself and one's family— is a critically important mitzvah. This must be one reason why our people have long been considered good at it. There was no other way for them to survive. But Judaism, being a religion of partnership, also teaches that we owe much of our success to God. Thus we unhesitatingly pray in *birkat hamazon,* the prayer said after meals: "Please, Lord our God, let us not need other people's gifts or loans, but only the help of Your full, yet open hand. . . ." And our tradition teaches that, after the talmudic master Rav completed saying the required petitions of the *Amidah* prayer, he added a personal request for "a life of riches and honor . . . a life of blessing and a life of sustenance" (Ber. 16b).

Wealth, the Grand Seductress

Though poverty is bad, riches are not wholly good. Wealth's incredible power can be perilous; it was no accident that the calf Aaron fashioned for the Israelites to worship in the wilderness was made of gold. And having riches seems to suddenly make us wise. We say with good reason, "money talks." Baḥya b. Asher, the thirteenth-century commentator, frankly describes personal riches as "lending weight to one's words, so that the opinion of the wealthy individual will be heard" *(Kad Hakemah)*. As the author of Ecclesiastes notes: "People despise the wisdom of the poor and don't listen to what they say" (Eccles. 9:16). A Ladino proverb proudly asserts, "My father's assets cover my hunchback." Trust our poor eastern European ancestors to pay homage to the virtues of wealth in their proverbs: "Gold glitters, even in the mud." "A rich man's daughter is always beautiful." "If you have money, you are wise, handsome, and you sing well, too." "All locks open with a golden key." "Money is the best soap—it removes the greatest stain." "It's good to be rich—the rabbi himself delivers your eulogy." And the classic maxim: "The world stands on three things: money, money, money." To deny these observable aphorisms condemns Jewish piety to a fantasy world.

Wealth indeed confers power and influence. In so doing, it can encourage the rich to try to get away with bending the very rules that they staunchly enforce on poorer people. It's easy to agree with F. Scott Fitzgerald—"the rich are different"—because they expect different treatment and are treated differently from the rest of us. This Ladino proverb knowingly describes the frustrations of the poor: "Even a rooster lays eggs for a rich man, but even a poor man's hen won't." It seems that the Internal Revenue Service often settles with the very wealthy at terms they never offer to those with more modest means. When the rich appear in court, their public relations people and expensive legal talent can perform miracles of exoneration. And, we wonder, what have they done that they have successfully hidden, that never makes the supermarket tabloids? Worst of all, the wealthy may begin believing they are above the law and assume they are exceptions to the ethics the rest of us live by.

"Moral" Rich

What a joy, then, to hear about extremely wealthy people who use their riches to further the common good. Financier John Loeb, Sr.'s charitable gifts totaled more than 200 million dollars; publisher Walter Annenberg spends much of his time choosing the institutions that will benefit from his extraordinary financial successes. And we can't even guess what they and other equally generous souls have donated privately. Yet these people stand out because they are so charitable. Alas, studies have confirmed that the truly affluent usually give relatively modestly. They realize that their high social status depends more on maintaining their net worth than on the good they might do by giving much of it away.

Wealth is most destructive when the love of money encourages a desire that feeds on itself, or provokes a dread that at any moment we may lose it. "As hard as it is to climb, coming down is harder" (Ladino proverb). Thus Ecclesiastes can write: "The rich person's affluence doesn't let him sleep" (Eccles. 5:11). More than one thousand years later, the philosopher Saadiah Gaon laments: ". . . Once one passionately seeks wealth, one discovers that it entails immense efforts of thought and exertion, keeping one awake at night and plagued by responsibilities by day, so that even when one has acquired what one desires, one can't sleep properly" *(Book of Beliefs and Opinions)*. What once seemed extraordinary is now never quite enough. R. Akiba observes: "No one leaves this world with half his desires gratified. If he has 100 he wants 200, and if he has 200 he wants to turn them into 400" (Eccles. R. 1.13). Bahya ibn Pakuda compares this compulsion for riches to a "fire, which blows more fiercely the more wood is added to it" *(Hovot Halevavot)*. And while we Jews may be proud of our talent for making money, we must also face the ugly truth that Jews have been convicted of monetary crimes in numbers disproportionate to our percentage of the total society. A passion for riches becomes our most common kind of idolatry.

"Abundance Doesn't Cause Headaches" (Ladino Proverb)

Yet despite all of the pitfalls, our sages teach that the risks of wealth are likely to be less destructive to caring Jews than the risks of poverty. What distinguishes humanity is our desire to live decently. We count on having acceptable clothes to wear, food to eat, a place to live, and some hope that these will continue. As important, if we have money, we have the means to do much good. That is why Jewish communities consider it their duty to provide for the indigent. We also believe that governments must provide safety nets without gaping holes in them. Simply said, this extends our public humanity.

The sixteenth-century Polish sage Samuel Edels, known by the acronym Maharsha, suggests three motives for seeking wealth (*commentary* to Shab. 125b). The first is to gain the honors that wealth brings. Although such a goal may seem selfish and deceptive, we can see its virtue if those who do the honoring have admirable Jewish standards. The second reason, to provide for our family, conveys no ambivalent messages. Think how much better we'd feel if we knew our children's educational needs were provided for and that we and our parents would not outlive our funds. The Maharsha's third reason for seeking wealth is the independence it brings. Most children eagerly anticipate the day when they no longer need to rely on their parents for financial support. Aging parents dread having to come to their children for help. Being able to provide for others as well as ourselves gives us a precious dignity.

The Maharsha may have taken yet another goal for granted: we Jews need money to carry out the commandments and customs of our faith. We don't need much to purchase a prayer book, rather ordinary candlesticks, and candles, wine, and a simple *mezuzzah*. We may probably have a few cents left over to give to charity. But it certainly would be nice to buy beautiful ritual objects and to make donations generously. No law says we must eat both fish and chicken at a Sabbath eve dinner, but for centuries we have enhanced our Jewish celebrations with our feasting. The commandment of *hiddur mitzvah* states that beautifying the objects we use to perform Jewish duties adds a spiritual richness to our observance. The rabbis derived this from the poem "The Song of the Sea," which Moses sang immediately after the people fled Egypt: "This is my God, and I will glorify Him!" (Exod. 15:2). R. Simeon b. Gamaliel, who spent 1,000 dinars for the most gorgeous, lemony *etrog* he could find to use in his observance of Sukkot, may have been the chief exemplar of *hiddur mitzvah* (Suk. 41b). When a beautifully adorned Torah is paraded through the synagogue or we light our Hanukkah candles in a stylishly appointed menorah, our thrill is almost palpable. Throughout our history, prosperous individuals fulfilled this commandment by commissioning artful *kiddush* cups and beautifully designed seder plates. As the hasidic rebbe, Naḥman of Bratzlav taught: "We demonstrate the depth of our faith by our willingness to spend money to perform a good deed" (Newman, *The Hasidic Anthology*).

Money Empowers Us to Do Deeds of Lovingkindness

The Torah relates that our patriarch Abraham "was blessed by God with everything" (Gen. 24:1). His great wealth thus allowed him to perform, without financial worry, what later became a time-honored Jewish act. He bought his first parcel of land in Canaan, not as a legal ploy or as a long-term investment, but to bury his wife Sarah. Bargaining with the landowner Ephron to purchase the cave of Machpelah, Abraham accepted the very first, very high price Ephron quoted. Because he had the money, Abraham knowingly overpaid and secured not only a burial ground but good relations with his new neighbors (Gen. 23:3–20).

Abraham was the first to perform a classic Jewish mitzvah. A long line of wealthy Jewish donors connects Abraham to the contemporary industrialist, Aaron Feuerstein. Fire nearly destroyed Malden Mills, his complex of textile manufacturing plants located not far from Boston. Rather than retiring on the insurance money, he immediately began to rebuild his factories. He also paid the salaries and health care premiums of his 3,000-person work force for three months, until most of his employees were once again working full-time. Feuerstein saved their families from great hardship; he also saved and actually strengthened the economies of the cities of Lawrence and Methuen, Massachusetts. Only a mean-spirited individual would argue that Feuerstein, an Orthodox Jew in his seventies, did these acts to benefit his corporate balance sheet. Having been raised in the tradition of *gemilut ḥasadim,* the duty of acting with lovingkindness, he could fulfill that mitzvah because he had the means.

"If I Were a Rich Man . . ."

What if we had enough money to realize our most cherished ambition, the sort of dream that makes us run to buy lottery tickets? A Ladino maxim puts it so well: "The poor have big eyes!" In *Fiddler on the Roof*, Tevye fantasizes that he would sit with the learned men of his village and study sacred texts for hours each day. (Though unschooled in all but the basics, he takes comfort in knowing that his riches would make up for his ignorance.) He'd also fulfill his wife's ultimate desires, even building a great house with a grand staircase going nowhere, but looking utterly elegant.

We chuckle at Tevye's antics, as Sholom Aleichem meant us to— but what would several suitcases full of one-hundred-dollar bills enable each of us to do? Pursue another career? Develop the artistic side of us that we always had to suppress, because we were too busy earning a living? Perform a good deed on a major scale, like building a memorial to our parents, a shelter for the homeless or battered, or a community garden? Whatever the good we manage to do now, wealth could empower us with the ability to do so much more.

And What of Our Social Responsibilities?

How poor a world it would be, Judaism teaches, if each of us were only interested in self-fulfillment. We are social creatures, and thus society's needs must make their demands on us. In some Jewish communities, even those who benefit from communal funds must make token contributions to help others. A prayer from late talmudic times that some still recite after the Shabbat Torah reading sums up our concerns for the whole community:

> May He who blessed our forefathers, Abraham, Isaac, and Jacob, bless this entire holy congregation along with all other holy congregations; them, their wives, sons and daughters, and all that is theirs; and those who dedicate synagogues for prayer and those who enter them to pray, and those who give lamps for illumination and wine for

kiddush and *havdalah,* bread for guests and charity for the poor, and all who are dedicated to meeting the needs of the community. May the Holy One, blessed be He, reward them and remove their every illness, heal their entire body, forgive them their sins, and cause their every endeavor to be blessed and successful, they and all their fellow Jews. And let us say Amen.

Contemporary Jewish prayer books may modify the language, but we still find it important to pray for the wise use of wealth for our community.

There is another reason for our Jewish respect for money. Well into modern times, large bribes, given to the appropriate government official, saved many Jewish communities from persecution. Local rulers used the threat of expulsion or pogrom to extort money from "their" Jews. Naturally, modern political leaders claim to be well beyond all that. Still, the value of Jewish wealth and clout is not lost on them. In 1996, five hundred years after expelling its Jews, Portugal finally rescinded its edict of expulsion and apologized, acknowledging how this loss inflicted great economic and cultural harm on the country. Today, Jews often have a disproportionately large political voice because of the substantial financial support we give to candidates and causes.

Some Traditional Jewish Safeguards Diminish Wealth's Dangers

The rabbis believed that if we took our Judaism more seriously, we could resist the evils of wealth more readily. Thus not only this chapter but our entire book provides the setting for a discussion of the Jewish view of riches. Here we've chosen four aspects of Jewish piety that most logically connect to wealth: realism, self-denial, a proper sense of value, and closeness to God.

Realism

If the promise of money is security, the reality of money teaches that, for all the comfort it may bring us, it may also easily slip away. How else can we explain that, while many Americans are more well-to-do than they ever dreamed, they still worry far more than they used to about their possessions? They may swear they don't believe in superstition or the Evil Eye, but they fear the very real condition of "Here today, gone tomorrow." As shtetl dwellers might have said: "Money is round; it rolls away from you." This is such an old obsession that we find similar sentiments in the Bible: "Don't exhaust yourself trying to make money. You see it and then it's gone. It grows wings and flies away" (Prov. 23:4–5).

Self-Denial

Judaism helps us impose ethical limits on ourselves through the religious rituals we practice. Chief among them is a commitment to Shabbat. No matter how much *oneg*, joy, we bring to this celebration, its fundamental meaning remains, quite literally, "Cease." Two thousand years ago, the Roman conquerors of ancient Israel called Jews lazy for taking one day off in every seven. Yet we learn through that very interruption that we need not play by the rules of the dominant culture. The more we do *not* work on Shabbat, or shop, or take care of undone errands, or continue the bustle of our workday week, the more distance we get from the prevailing culture's compulsions, and the better we understand how some denial actually liberates. Similarly, our Yom Kippur fast, our Pesaḥ rejection of bread, our daily insistence that holiness governs what we do and don't eat, all contribute to the pattern. And while such observances don't automatically guarantee that people of means will restrain themselves from excess, they encourage them to make self-control for worthy ends a habit. Such habits ultimately bring all of us closer to holiness.

Perspective

A Jewish mind-set will also help us keep our priorities straight. How often have we heard wrenching stories of Holocaust era European Jews who refused to emigrate because they couldn't leave behind material "treasures," and so sealed their fate. But we don't need the threat of a Hitler to give our possessions their proper value. Death's certainty should do that for all of us. A Yiddish proverb applies this to money when it says: "Shrouds are made without pockets." Jewish practices, without being morbid, seek to overcome our natural desire to deny death's finality. We remember our dead at every worship service and are commanded to attend funerals. We know that personal pangs of emotion must not prevent us from making a *shivah* call. These and other observances remind us what is real and lasting and what is fleeting and insubstantial.

A Sense of God

No matter what our view of God, all Jews agree with the ancient Hebrew lyricist: "The earth is *Adonai*'s and everything in it, the world and its inhabitants. For God founded it upon the waters and established it upon the floods" (Ps. 24:1–2). The metaphor is telling: everything belongs to God, and we humans are only God's tenants. Or, if you prefer financial language, we are God's fiduciaries, entrusted with God's assets only if we also accept special mandates and accountabilities. Fiduciaries are expected to manage prudently and to exercise good judgment, not for their own best interests, but for those of the owner. Good Jews will manage their wealth, in whatever amount, as God's agents. That is how riches become a component of positive Jewish piety. Thus we may follow our patriarch Jacob's lead and say: "God has shown me favor, and I have everything" (Gen. 33:11).

From Our Tradition

Said the Gerer Rabbi: We read [Ps. 105:37], 'And God brought them out [of Egypt] with silver and gold; no one among God's tribes stumbled.' The Psalmist wishes to tell us that money did not spoil them.

—Newman, *The Hasidic Anthology*

Wealth which comes to us with justice, trust, and uprightness is one of the desirable eminences. . . . For when we have wealth we can sustain ourselves without suffering, without great effort, and without great deliberation in the areas of livelihood, economy, and welfare.

—Yeḥiel b. Yekutiel, *Sefer Maalot Hamiddot*

Rabbi Moshe Leib of Sasov said: How easy it is for a poor person to depend on God! What else has he to depend on? And how hard it is for a rich person to depend on God! All his possessions call out to him: 'Depend on us!'

—Buber, *Tales of the Hasidim,* bk. 2, *The Later Masters*

Alexander the Great was given an eyeball. He weighed all his silver and gold against it, but found they were not equal to it. He said to the rabbis, "How is this possible?" They replied, "It is the eyeball of a human being and this is why they are never satisfied."

—Tam. 32b

Ben Zoma said: Who is rich? One who is happy with what one has.

—Avot 4.1

Charity—*Tzedakah*

$\mathcal{A}$s we have seen in these pages, we acquire general wisdom from folklore, street smarts, or from the actions and words of our great teachers. *Tzedakah*, however, is such a well-established Jewish obligation that it needs little reinforcing from these usual sources. We turn instead to another character shaper, halakhah, Jewish law. By guiding you through some passages on *tzedakah* in the three great Jewish legal codes, we will show you how these particular laws inform the Jewish soul.

Maimonides, a Sephardic Jew and our most subtle philosopher, was also a supreme legal genius. His *Mishneh Torah* virtually invented the idea of a full-scale, logically ordered, easy-to-understand code book of Jewish law. To write it, Maimonides studied and then abridged centuries of talmudic reasoning, gaonic considerations, and subsequent local rabbinic interpretations for his late twelfth-century contemporaries. Jacob b. Asher's *Arbaah Turim* (the "Tur"), composed in the fourteenth century, took Maimonides's work a step further. Omitting all the laws that were no longer followed, like those pertaining to Temple sacrifices, it provided a digest of Ashkenazic rabbinic rulings. Finally, in the sixteenth century, the social and spiritual ferment that followed the expulsion of the Jews from Spain and Portugal persuaded Joseph Karo, another Sephardi, to write a synthesis of previous codes, the *Shulḥan Arukh*, which fostered Jewish unity. It was so masterful a summary of functioning Jewish law that it has never been superseded, though it is still commented upon and supplemented.

As you read their texts in the following pages, remember that these codifiers did not create the basic laws and practices they discuss. To the extent that they "made law," they did so through their methods of transmitting and interpreting prior legal rulings. Since the mandated practices of *tzedakah* didn't drastically change over the centuries, we find a great deal of repetition among the three codes. Therefore, we've chosen excerpts from each code that treat a somewhat different aspect of the obligation to give *tzedakah*.

From Moses Maimonides (1135–1204), *Mishneh Torah* (A Recapitulation of Torah), *Hilkhot Matanot Aniyyim* (The Laws of Gifts to the Poor), Chapter 10

There are eight gradations in the giving of charity, each higher than the other. The highest of these, which has no superior, is to take the hand of a fellow Jew and offer him a gift, or a loan, or enter into a business partnership with him, or find him a job, so that he may become economically strong and no longer need to ask others for help. Scripture says about this, ". . . and you shall strengthen him, that is, the stranger or sojourner, so that he may live with you . . ." (Lev. 25:35). In other words, you shall strengthen him so that he does not fall into poverty and need charity. (Section 7)

We tend to think of charity as something we give to unfortunates to offset their calamities. There is much merit in that, as Maimonides will indicate (see below). But here this great Jewish conceptualist introduces a new and illuminating hierarchy to Jewish tradition. *Tzedakah,* he wants us to understand, involves more than merely alleviating symptoms. At its best, it is about eliminating causes. Don't scrimp on vision—think big, even if you must give little. Raise your *tzedakah* sights beyond tiding people over; instead, try to get them firmly back on their own two feet.

Less praiseworthy than this is giving charity to the poor so that the donor does not know to whom he gave and the recipient does not know who gave it. In this way the act of giving *tzedakah* is done *lishmah,* for its own sake. This is like the Chamber of the Discreet in the Jerusalem Temple. The righteous would secretly deposit funds and the decent poor, just as secretly, would enter and be sustained by what they took (Shek. 5.6). Another way of giving *tzedakah* in this fashion is to give to the community charity fund. However, one should only contribute to the community fund if its overseers are trustworthy and informed, and know how to manage its affairs according to proper standards, as R. Ḥananiah b. Teradion did according to the Talmud (B.B. 10b). (Section 8)

If our charity giving is meant to relieve truly awful conditions, then it ought to be done for its own sake. It is a true greatness of heart that responds to a commandment by performing it in a way that honors the sacred deed. We should not need to see those we help, and we should be mindful of assuring the recipients' dignity by preserving their anonymity.

Furthermore, Maimonides, like others before him, makes high demands on the trustees of the community *tzedakah* fund. They should be people of the highest integrity, for anyone can be tempted in the presence of money. Ensuring full disclosure of funds received and funds disbursed is part of our obligation to give charity. By safeguarding these controls, all of us who make our gifts through our community institutions come close to this level of Maimonidean praise.

> Less praiseworthy than this is the charity in which the donor knows the recipient, but the recipient does not know the donor. This is like the practice of our sages who would go about discreetly leaving money in the doorways of the needy. This is appropriate and especially critical if the custodians of communal charity funds don't conduct their affairs meticulously. (Section 9)

We all can tick off specific charities we once considered worthy but that, unfortunately, were administered by less-than-worthy persons. But these few problems don't justify our abandoning the whole *tzedakah* process; this excuse only serves our selfishness. Here Maimonides urges us to be more cautious and creative in our giving, recognizing that no completely foolproof, crook-detection mechanism exists. However, if we do choose to give *tzedakah* directly, the least we can do is not add to the indigent's indignity by forcing him or her to face us, thereby subjecting him or her to the physical and psychological shame that comes with directly accepting a handout. In preserving the poor's self-respect, we offer something more valuable than goods or money, for it preserves their humanity.

> Less praiseworthy than this is the situation when the needy knows the donor but the donor does not know the recipient. This is like the practice of the greatest of our sages, who would tie coins in their shawls which would trail behind them, so that the needy could come and take without any embarrassment (Ket. 67b). (Section 10)

We should try to avoid any sense of self-aggrandizement in our giving, remembering how we have felt when someone has done us a favor and then has diminished that generosity with the unspoken sense of "What a wonderful person I am for doing this." We must not try to derive pleasure, even secretly, from someone else's misfortune. Shielding ourselves from any direct knowledge of the person we have helped thus protects us against this wile of the Evil Urge.

> Less praiseworthy than this is personally giving a gift to someone before being asked. (Section 11)

Tzedakah requires us to be thoughtful of others. As the fall weather turns chilly and then downright nasty, we should notice children who shiver badly on the way to school and poor adults who have little protection against the biting wind. What warm clothing have we stuffed somewhere in our closets that we don't really wear or are about to replace? Many social service agencies will gladly take our warm clothes and give them to those who truly need them. And other seasons bring other needs. We should try to have the kind of heart that needs no prompting to feel and then do for others.

> Less praiseworthy than this is giving after being asked. (Section 12)

But our hearts sometimes do need prompting. Our spine often stiffens when we are continuously asked for money. We resent being bombarded on our city streets by panhandlers. What if they misuse what we give them? What if their needs are fraudulent? Francie often addresses this quandary by asking for a "doggie bag" for her uneaten restaurant meals and handing over its contents to the first person she meets who requests money for food. This way she knows she isn't feeding an alcohol or drug problem and can personally vouch for the food she offers. Thus, she gives after being asked—and knows that her *tzedakah* is helping, not hurting, those in need.

> Less praiseworthy than this is giving less than is appropriate, but doing so graciously. (Section 13)

Some time before April 15, conduct a little experiment: Compare your charitable deductions with what you recall spending on entertainment, vacations, or clothes, or whatever you do with your "disposable income," simply because you feel you're entitled to it. And if that still doesn't loosen up more *tzedakah,* then at least try to be gracious when you give however much you do give, whether in money, effort, or time. For example, if you serve food at a soup kitchen, be genuinely friendly with a person you have just served there. In so doing, you have given a gift of self, which also provides nourishment.

> Less praiseworthy than this is giving, but resenting having to do so. (Section 14)

How we marvel that some people volunteer year after year to solicit pledges to our Federations or synagogues. They will tell you that the only part of the job they dislike is dealing with donors who may in fact give, but seem perversely intent on making solicitors first feel miserable. And the ordeal is even worse when volunteers must endure this treatment from a major donor whose gift the charity cannot afford to lose. It is hard to accept that these insufferables still earn merit for their donation. Yet we cannot deprive the needy, simply to mollify our personal sensitivities. Such behavior is indeed baffling to most of us. Since these contributors actually intend to do good, why don't they enjoy showing or doing it?

From Jacob b. Asher (d. 1340), *Arbaah Turim* (The Four Pillars), "Yoreh Deah" (He Teaches Knowledge), Chapter 251

[Note: The Tur does not separate individual topics into distinct sections, as Maimonides does. We have done so to make our commentary easier to follow.]

We give charity to anyone who stretches out his hand in need. This includes gentiles as well as Jews, for the talmudic rule states that, for the sake of peace, we sustain the gentile needy along with the Jewish. (Git. 5.8 and Talmud ad loc.)

Jacob b. Asher shifts our attention from personal to communal aspects of *tzedakah*. During the fourteenth century, before Jews were required to live behind walled ghettos, they lived in mixed neighborhoods rather than exclusively Jewish ones. Since they were never entirely safe from sporadic persecutions, they knew that getting along with their non-Jewish neighbors was critical to the survival of every Jew in the area. So Jewish giving had a universal dimension, not only because it was idealistically the right thing to do, but because this quite practically helped secure the Jews' physical well-being, at least for a time.

> Eliezer b. Samuel of Mainz wrote that a Jew who transgresses any of the commandments should not be considered as included in the commandment: "So that your brother may live alongside you" [Lev. 25:36] and we are therefore not required to give him charity until it is clear that he has repented of his act.

While medieval Jewry often found it expedient to give *tzedakah* to their non-Jewish neighbors, the same was not true regarding their fellow Jews who strayed from a rather rigorous following of the commandments, which might seem paradoxical. The reasoning behind this policy was as follows: if some Jews refused to accept community discipline, why should the community feel bound to support them, if their actions showed they could not be relied on? In those days, when life was particularly precarious, these "free thinkers" were a threat to the group's security. Although one needn't be a saint to be accepted as a member of the Jewish community, there are limits to how much divergent behavior any group can tolerate, particularly an imperiled one.

> Anyone who gives money to his adult children, mature enough that the parent is no longer obligated to sustain them, in order that the adult males may study Torah and the females may live uprightly; so, too, anyone who gives gifts to his needy father and mother, may consider these gifts a fulfillment of the duty to give charity. Indeed, he

needs to give these relatives priority over others in his charity giving. He should give a similar priority to his relatives over all others. The Torah commands that the needy of his "household" come first, then the poor of his city, and they in turn have priority over the poor of another city.

Since the number of deserving causes vastly exceed our funds, how do we decide who should receive our charity? Just to gauge the extent of our problem in contemporary terms, we did an experiment: We saved all of the "junk mail" we received in one week. In this time, together we received a total of 60 separate charity solicitations! And that does not include the daily telephone solicitations, office or community requests, street or subway begging, or the charities that we give to without being asked. The priority system of the Tur can intelligently guide our *tzedakah* decision-making. It follows a familiar Jewish strategy—give the greatest attention to those near you, determined first by birth and then by physical proximity—and progressively less to those more distant. Today, we who are modestly affluent will want to add a place for causes that are particularly dear to us.

> Suppose that Reuven has a priority obligation to many poor relatives in his city and Shimon, his neighbor, does not have any. Reuven desires to establish a fixed community charity allowance for the poor of the city and to decently provide for them. At the same time he would decrease the allowance to the poor who come to the city from elsewhere, and bases himself on the Torah text: "The poor of your city get priority [Exod. 22:24]" (R. Joseph, B.M. 71a). Shimon is against this procedure. Rabbi Isaac b. Barukh wrote that we do not follow Reuven's proposal, for the text: "The poor of your city get priority" carries the intention that we do not dispatch our poor to another city to be cared for. However, when outsiders come to our city, we do not say to them, "Sorry, the poor of our city have priority" but, as best we can, we first decrease what we give our city's poor and give some to the outsiders. Thus far, his words.

Reality now intrudes. Imagine we are on our way to an Allocations Committee meeting for our favorite charity. Jacob b. Asher continues:

However, Rabbi Isaac's ruling does not convince me, for surely the poor of our city have a clear priority. Rabbi Saadiah [882–942, the famous Gaon of the Babylonian community] wrote that a person is required to put his own sustenance first, and is not duty bound to give charity to others until after providing for his own. The Torah says, "And your brother shall live with you" [Lev. 25:36], a verse which clearly establishes that your life comes first and only then, the other person. Also remember what the widow of Tzarefat said to the prophet Elijah [1 Kings 17:12], "And I have done this for me and my son," first for herself and afterward for her son, a comment he approved of since Elijah said [v. 13], "Do it for yourself," "and your son" only afterward. After one has seen to his own sustenance he may then give priority to the sustenance of his needy parents over that of his adult children, and then he should see to the sustenance of his adult children.

The Tur's ruling returns to the traditional hierarchy, almost equating our connection to parents and then to adult children with the obligation to first help ourselves. We are told to help others only after we have taken care of "our" own needs.

Should it happen that his parents and his children have been taken captive and he does not have the means to ransom them all, he should follow this priority: He should ransom his father and leave the sons, then ransom the sons, then his brothers, then his other relatives, then his neighbors, then other people from his city, and after these, [he should ransom] captives from other lands.

Even when lives are in danger, perhaps particularly when that is so, we should follow the classic *tzedakah* priority list. Though we may empathize with the downtrodden of the whole universe, we must first use our means to save those who gave us life and only then reach out to others with our remaining funds. We pray that God spares us from such heart-rending choices! But should they occur, the Tur gives us tradition to guide us.

Should anyone's extended household include poor orphans, it is a mitzvah and a good thing to employ them as servants; even though this means over-staffing his home, it will surely be "accounted to him as *tzedakah*" [Gen. 15:6].

Translated into English, the phrase "even if it means over-staffing" may be too literal. In fact, the Tur directs us to hire this needy person, even if we have little use of his services. So, for example, this holds if we have one domestic and don't need two. The hiring has little to do with household needs, but everything to do with the needs of the orphan, whom we thus help.

> One must give priority to feeding the starving over clothing the naked, for one can die of starvation. However, women must be given priority over men when it comes to feeding and providing clothes, for women will be too embarrassed to ask for either. And should both a man and a woman separately come seeking financial help to marry, the woman should receive preference.

Again, the priorities spell out survival over mere social niceties. Without calories, we soon sicken and may die; without proper clothing we are only self-conscious. Do women have special needs in this regard? The Tur suggests the answer is yes, due to women's more frail constitution and the reactionary nature of societies in general. The rule probably originated as a way to enhance modesty; in our egalitarian day, can it be considered defensible sexism?

The Tur continues:

> Maimonides wrote that if we find ourselves facing many needy people and we do not have enough in the communal *tzedakah* fund to sustain or clothe or ransom them all, then we assign the following priorities, which are derived from the ancient familial divisions among our people: Kohanim (priestly families), Levite families (associate priests), then ordinary Jews, then those descended from families whose lineage is clouded, and, finally, freed slaves. However, this ranking holds only when they are all equal in Torah knowledge. But should there be a High Priest who is an ignoramus, and a *mamzer,* a Jewish illegitimate, who is a Torah scholar, then the scholar has priority. The overriding rule is that anyone who is greater in Torah knowledge is given a higher priority. Nonetheless, should one of the needy be someone's teacher or his father, even though there may be someone far more knowledgeable, his teacher or his learned father takes priority over those whose Jewish social status is greater.

Now a new conflict in priorities appears, between standard communal status and the special dignity that Torah knowledge confers, with the latter receiving clear-cut preeminence. Even in the case of redeeming one's father, ordinarily the highest priority on anyone's list, we see that he must earn this ranking position through his learning. Life's choices can be quite complex.

> Here is a *teshuvah*, a formal legal response, to a question addressed to my father, Rabbenu Asher b. Yeḥiel, (the "Rosh"). A community that had supported a rabbi and a *sheliaḥ tzibbur*, a cantor, now found that it did not have sufficient funds for both. Which person should be retained? He responded: If the rabbi is quite able and an expert in Torah, legal decisions and the law, then we apply the rule *"Talmud Torah keneged kulam,"* Torah study takes precedence over everything. If he is not, it is better to keep the cantor, since he leads worship and thus enables the community to fulfill their obligations to pray.

The practical needs of the community—their daily worship—take precedence over even a supreme halakhic value like study. For all their worth, study and knowledge may remain theoretical. But living God's commandments persists every day.

The *teshuvah* continues:

> In the next issue you concede that it is permissible in special circumstances to expend restricted community endowments [on other necessary items], even if earmarked for the purpose of Talmud Torah, for study. You ask what should be done if this money is needed to meet the annual payment demanded of the Jewish community by the local ruler. It certainly should be used for this purpose, since this involves the commandment of saving lives. For if the ruler will not reduce the amount owed to him, there will be many poor people who will not be able to pay the minimum demanded. They will then be beaten and stripped of their possessions. Saving lives has priority over the sanctity of endowments.

Charity money is a sacred trust and must be treated as such. A restricted endowment must fulfill the donors' stated desires. Nonetheless, times change and priorities may therefore need adjustment. Organizations love to receive unrestricted gifts, since these let the group determine how the money may best be used in light of their shifting priorities. The longer an institution survives, the more leeway its trustees may reasonably require.

From Joseph Karo (1488–1575), *Shulḥan Arukh* (The Properly Set Table), "Yoreh Deah," (He Teaches Knowledge), Chapter 248: "Who Is Obligated to Give *Tzedakah* and Who May Appropriately Receive It"

[Note: The Ashkenazim resisted accepting the *Shulḥan Arukh* because it stressed Sephardi decisions, sometimes clashing with Ashkenazi custom. This resistance disappeared after "Rema," Moses Isserles (d. 1572), a leading authority among Polish Jews, wrote a series of comments, *Mappah* (The tablecloth), which were printed as insertions in the text. We include them here.]

> Everyone is required to give *tzedakah*. Even the indigent person sustained by charity must give from what has been given to him. The communal *beit din*, [the Jewish court,] may use coercion on anyone who has contributed less than what he should appropriately give. They may have him beaten as provided for in the laws concerning rebellious citizens, until he gives what the court estimates he should. The court may even seize his assets and use them as his required *tzedakah* obligation. (248.1)

Contemporary society grants rights to individuals, making personal choice an exalted value. But before the modern nation-state, Jewish life was quite different. Rights [charters] were dispensed to an entire group; individuals derived their personal privileges from the rules of their specific community. And should the community expel an individual, he or she forfeited the right even to live in that town. These laws, reflecting the dominance of the community over the individual, sound quite unreasonable to us. But is the institution of American individualism so superior to this early communitarian way of life? In all honesty, we must concede that social responsibility sometimes suffers by it. For example, few Americans today vote for their civic leaders. Finding ways to avoid our duty to the group, like serving on juries, is widespread. And despite the long-standing Jewish tradition of social conscience, fewer than half of American

Jews contribute to local Federation campaigns. We, therefore, have something to learn from this ancient law that commendably grants the community carefully chosen rights.

> It is permitted to make a formal pledge to give *tzedakah* even if the Sabbath is approaching. (248.2)

Nothing must stand in the way of saving a life, not even Shabbat's sacred prohibitions. Legitimate requests always outstrip our ability to help. Our law here bends—but does not break—the Sabbath law, expanding our allowable time to give *tzedakah*, bestowing a special status on our generosity.

> The community does not include money of orphans in levying its *tzedakah* contributions, even if used to ransom captives. This is the rule even if an orphan has a great deal of money. An exception is made when the community levies an amount on an orphan so that he may be honored and thus "earn" an appropriately worthy reputation. (Rema: This holds true in the case of charitable drives which have no fixed limit, or if there is a fixed amount levied on orphans' funds. We do permit orphans to delay their payment until they are somewhat older, as in the case of their having untithed produce and have no current need to eat from that harvest [thus they do not incur required contributions]. But if they do need to eat of that harvest now, the court takes the appropriate tithes and priestly dues, making the rest available for us. This is the law when there is a fixed limit to the amount of *tzedakah* sought, such as when an orphan has indigent relatives to help, but his father had set an annual limit on what he could spend. He might then have to go begging from door to door to accommodate his relatives. Since that would be degrading, his trustees should advance the necessary sum from their own assets so the relatives can be supported.) (248.3)

Of course, there are always special cases. Here the rule protecting orphans and their assets clashes with the extreme importance of everyone doing *tzedakah*. As always, the law tries to do justice to both claims, even as this example respects the father's decision to restrict the payout of his child's endowment. Once again, great faith is put in the trustees of the communal funds and their appropriate use of power. No wonder our ancestors considered the *gabbaei tzedakah*, those in charge of collecting and distributing charity, among the most distinguished people in their community. To serve in such an office is itself an act of *tzedakah*.

> The communal charity overseers may not receive gifts from women, slaves, and infants. They can accept a small sum, but should they take a large one, people would assume that, since they do not [legally] own anything, these donations were stolen or taken from others. How much is a "small sum"? It all depends on the wealth or poverty of the householder with whom they live. That is the general rule, but if the householder protests against their giving anything at all, then it is forbidden for the overseers to accept any contribution from them.
>
> If a wife hires a teacher for her son and the head of the household knows about this and is silent, this indicates that he agrees with what she has done. But if he objects to it at once, then her hiring has no legal validity. (Rema: Even if she carries on a business from her home, he has the right to invalidate her act.) (248.4–5)

Jewish communities have always reflected most of the social mores of the surrounding gentile society. Thus, from biblical times on, a woman took orders from a man, be it her father or husband or employer. This was especially true regarding financial matters, since even money she earned herself—Jewish women have often run successful businesses—legally belonged to either her father or husband and was administered by the ranking man of the family. This arrangement, which originally derived from a system that seeks to protect women from any suspicion, must today be superseded by the rule stating that independent means obligates giving *tzedakah*.

> A son who is still eating at his father's table, or a servant who eats with his master, may give a small portion of food to a poor person or the son of his good friend, and no one will think that this is a form of robbery, for that is the custom in most homes. (248.6)

Here we have an exception to a rule about people without assets giving charity, which then itself becomes the rule. If we can overlook its sexism, it provides that the moral customs of the society can obviate an old, rather restrictive law. It formally allows someone with no personal assets still to fulfill the *tzedakah* commandment by giving someone else's money as if it were his or her own. In a rough analogy, it once would have seemed uncouth to suggest making a charitable donation by credit card. But as plastic has significantly replaced money to accommodate our secular needs, it is commonplace in *tzedakah* drives, assuring the swift conversion of a pledge to hard cash.

> When a generous and well-to-do person is expected to give more charity than is really appropriate for him, or someone comes upon hard times but then is likely to give considerably to trustees to avoid embarrassment for not doing so, it is forbidden to ask these individuals for *tzedakah* directly or to raise funds through them. Any charitable trustee who thus shames them may count on God's punishment in the world to come. (248.7)

Jewish law instructs us that a successful charity drive is not, as is so often the case today, simply determined by the amount raised or the percentage gained over previous efforts. Not only recipients, but potential donors as well may require our attention. The fund administrators must exercise their Jewish hearts and heads to protect manic types from giving away so much that they soon need charity themselves. When we know that someone of means has fallen upon hard times, we must, most gingerly, preserve their dignity. Giving *tzedakah* may be structured by Jewish law, but we must never forget that it operates as an instrument of Jewish compassion.

> Anyone who wants to acquire some merit for himself should suppress his urge-to-do-evil and become open-handed, remembering that any act which is done for Heaven's sake should be both good and beautiful. If someone builds a synagogue, let it be more lovely than one's own home. If someone feeds the starving, let him feed him from the best and sweetest that is on his table. If he clothes the naked, let him clothe him with the most exquisite of his clothes. And if he dedicates something to God's service, then let it be among the most beautiful of his possessions, as the text says, "All the choicest is for *Adonai*" [Lev. 3:16]. (248.10)

Here is one of those laws that is an ideal we reach for, not an everyday regulation to be followed in detail. It rightly calls on us to strive for our highest goals. For a code of religious practice should set its sights higher than those social regulations associated with administering a secular group, which must focus on the least common denominator of acceptable custom. And this means a continual reaching, not just for the better, but for the best.

From Our Tradition

If a man gives his comrade all the good gifts in the world with a downcast face, Scripture accords it as if he gave nothing. However, if he receives his companion cheerfully, even if he gives him nothing, Scripture accords it as if he gave him all the good gifts in the world.

—A.R.N. 13

Benjamin the Tzaddik was the overseer of the communal fund. Once during years of famine, a woman came to him and said, "Rabbi, feed me!" He said to her, "I swear there is nothing in the *tzedakah* fund." She said to him, "If you do not feed me, a woman and her seven children will die." Rabbi Benjamin went and bought food for her using his personal funds.

—B.B. 11a

For an example of the sinfulness of the people of our generation, consider that when R. Joshua b. Levi went to Rome, he saw marble pillars that had been carefully covered with wrappings to keep them from cracking during the heat and from freezing during the cold. By contrast, he saw a poor wretch who had no more than a reed mat under him and a reed mat over him.

—P.R.K. 9

The wife of Rabbi Naftali of Ropshitz said to him, "Your prayer was lengthy today. Have you succeeded in bringing about that the rich should be more generous in their gifts to the poor?" The Rabbi replied, "Half of my prayer I have accomplished. The poor are willing to accept them."

—Newman, *The Hasidic Anthology*

PART IV

Refining the Inner Person

CHAPTER 11

Humility—*Anavah*

One Kol Nidre *Eve the rabbi was overcome as he recited the opening prayer that acknowledges the sins of the synagogue leaders, and asks for God's help to lead the congregation. He threw himself on the floor before the opened ark and cried out, "God, I am a nothing!" When the cantor heard the murmur of approval in the congregation, he also threw himself down and shouted, "God, I am a nothing!" As the congregational buzz grew even louder, the synagogue president followed suit, practically screaming as his body hit the carpet, "God, I am a nothing!" At which the cantor nudged the rabbi and whispered, "Look who wants to be a nothing now!"*

Our lives these days seem to be turning into one huge oxymoron. We pressure people to be more patient; we stress ourselves out perfecting our relaxation techniques. And we exalt humility extravagantly. Does our conscious striving to be humble threaten to make us like the Dickens character Uriah Heep, who continually approvingly proclaimed his "nothingness"?

Our tradition doesn't think so. On the contrary, Judaism enthusiastically promotes *anavah*, humility. R. Pinḥas b. Yair said that the greatest virtue of all is piety, but R. Joshua b. Levi said that it is humility (A.Z. 20b). The eleventh-century Spanish philosopher-poet Solomon ibn Gabirol found "humility a greater help to me than all of my friends" *(Mivḥar Hapeninim)*. What exactly is this *anavah* that our sages so esteem, and how can we avoid becoming arrogant for attaining it?

"The Greater the Noble, the Smaller He Acts When Alone" (Yiddish Proverb)

Many of the biblical figures that our Jewish teachers want us to emulate have a strong sense of their personal insignificance. Abraham, who lived more like a sheik than a poor nomadic herdsman, refers to himself as "but dust and ashes" (Gen. 18:27). Moses and Aaron, after negotiating with Pharaoh to bring the Jews out of Egypt, ask, "Who are we?" (Exod. 16:7). David poetically disparages himself, saying: "I am a worm, less than human, scorned by men, despised by people" (Ps. 22:7). Such putting oneself "in one's place" continues as a significant theme throughout Jewish literature.The early thirteenth-century Franco-German sage Judah the Pious counsels: "One should remember that snow begins pure white but soon turns into slush. So we, too, despite our great beauty, will one day become a small heap of worm-eaten matter" (Judah Hehasid, *Sefer Hasidim*, 305). The Spanish mystic-philosopher Nahmanides, living about the same time as Judah, gives this advice to his children: "Let your voice be low and your head bowed; let your eyes turn earthwards—every man should seem in your eyes as one greater than yourselves" (*Hebrew Ethical Wills*).

Maimonides explains this austere attitude: "Some believe that it is forbidden to take the middle way when it comes to humility. Rather, they think people should distance themselves as far as possible from the one extreme, pridefulness, and go to the other" (M.T., Hil. Deot, 2.3). For pride, says the Bible, is the great threat to Jewish character and deserves God's punishment: "God, see every proud man and bring him low" (Job 40:11). "God says, 'I cannot endure the haughty and proud man'" (Ps. 101:5). "*Adonai* abominates haughty people" (Prov. 16:5).

The antidote to pride is humility. For centuries, our teachers have sought ways to keep us from becoming people who "lie back on our beds, sigh, and say in our heart, 'How great I am'" (Maimon, *Sarei Meah* [The century's princes]).

The Golden Meaning of Humility

Back in the days when he still called himself Cassius Clay, the legendary boxer Mohammed Ali introduced the art of wild boastfulness as a form of self-promotion. He was unusual because he actually lived up to many of his claims. Many lesser lights who have taken the path of braggadocio earn only our contempt. Instead of acting like one of those braggarts, some of our ethicists have urged us to exaggerate our smallness; but this therapy, like so many others, can easily be overdone. Maimonides, assuming his role as physician to our spirits, reflects classic Jewish good sense in rejecting an extreme position. He finds an acceptable balance "half-way between pride and self-abnegation" (*Shemoneh Perakim* [Eight chapters], chap. 4). This echoes Hillel's famous challenge—"If I don't stand up for myself, who should? But if I'm only self-concerned, what good am I?" (Avot 1.4).

The medieval ethicist Baḥya b. Asher explains the religious reasons for this dialectic stand: "Humility as the intermediate quality between arrogance and self-effacement does not mean that we should disgrace ourselves, or allow others to tread upon us. We were created in God's image and are therefore precious. We need to care for our honor and the high status that possessing a rational soul gives us among God's creatures" *(Kad Hakemah).* Several hundred years later, the hasidic sage Rabbi Simḥa Bunim of Przysucha graphically teaches: "Every person should have two pockets so he can reach into one or the other, according to his needs. In his right pocket are to be the words: 'For my sake was the world created,' and in his left: 'I am earth and ashes'" (Buber, *Tales of the Hasidim,* bk. 2, *The Later Masters).* And his near contemporary, the Sephardic musarist Eliezer Papo agrees: "Be serious and humble; do not seek honor or take pride in your position or clothing. But don't overdo it, for excessive humility easily becomes presumption" *(Pele Yoetz).* As Yiddish folk wisdom realistically reminds us: "If you bend down too much, people walk on your head," and "Better to die upright than to live on your knees."

The Greatest Exemplar of Jewish Humility

Moses's daring achievements save the Jewish people. He is impulsive enough to kill an abusive Egyptian taskmaster who won't stop beating a Hebrew slave (Exod. 2:11–13). He is undaunted by the power of Pharaoh, as great a king as the world had known, and he is strong-willed enough to lead the rebellious Jewish people out of Egypt to freedom (Exod. 5–12). Even God's fierce anger does not stop Moses from trying to change God's "mind." How astonishing, then, is the Torah's description of him: "Moses was exceedingly humble, more so than any other man on earth" (Num. 12:3).

What specifically prompts the Torah's mention of Moses's humility is his response—more accurately, his lack of response—to Miriam and Aaron's personal attack on his wife (Num. 12:1). The narrative tells us that Moses says and does nothing to retaliate. He remains remarkably passive to his siblings' denunciations. For someone with his history of explosive outbursts, such behavior is completely unanticipated. Bahya b. Asher tells us that Moses's "exceeding" humility was caused by his unwavering focus on his goal, *shalom bayit,* the family harmony so esteemed by our tradition *(Kad Hakemah).* Of all the praiseworthy qualities he possesses, it is Moses as the model family man that the Bible chooses to honor for his personal code of *anavah.*

The Two Great *Musar* Interpreters of *Anavah*

The classic era of musar literature is framed by two books, each giving concentrated attention to the topic of humility. Bahya ibn Pakuda, an eleventh-century Spaniard, was the first Jew to specifically write about Jewish spirituality and its effect on Jewish character. He called his book *Hovot Halevavot* (Duties of the heart) because he wanted to show how a thoughtful relationship with God could inspire us to live by classic Jewish virtues. This widely studied and beloved text encouraged others to produce the many works of Jewish pietistic writings that we so often cite in this book. Some seven hundred years after Bahya, the Italian mystic Moses Hayyim Luzzatto wrote a treatise entitled *Mesillat Yesharim* (The path of the upright), the last great work in this genre. *Mesillat Yesharim* was so highly respected in certain nineteenth-century eastern European yeshivot that regular times were devoted to its study, and students were encouraged to memorize substantial portions of it. Modern readers sometimes see these volumes as early self-help guides because they seem to talk readers through the traits they discuss, offering medieval versions of checklists that we find so helpful. Reviewing their key points about Jewish humility will show us the constancy of Jewish thinking over this long period, helping us gain insight into the subtle Jewish dialectic of *anavah*.

Baḥya ibn Pakuda, The Pioneer of **Musar** Literature

Baḥya was the first sage to focus on the inner, everyday religiosity that ought to ground a Jew's outward behavior. What follows is a summary of Baḥya's seven means of acquiring Jewish humility and our commentary on it.

One: We Need to Remember Our Humble Origins

We all begin as a single cell that requires nine months of total dependency to grow into a fully formed being, able to take our first independent breath. And for a long time thereafter we must look to others for our most basic needs, only slowly learning to live on our own. A talmudic comment puts us bluntly in our place: "Why did God wait so long, not creating humankind until the sixth day of creation? So that if people became puffed up, they could be quickly deflated by pointing out, 'The gnat was created before you'" (San. 38a).

Gazing at the evening sky can give us the same feeling of smallness. We come to realize that our galaxy is not an especially grand one, amid countless others. So we ask, along with the Psalmist: "*Adonai,* what are people that You bother with us, human beings that You involve Yourself with us?" (Ps. 144:3). We really are "a nothing"—but God's involvement in our lives makes us quite "a something" indeed.

Two: But If We Are So Great, Why Aren't We Perfect?

Humility does not demand that we deny or ignore what we have achieved. But our accomplishments need to be mentally balanced by our failings. Thinking we are short on shortcomings is a sorry delusion. While our tradition doesn't encourage a morbid fixation on anxiety or guilt, it does demand we acknowledge our limitations. This way we can do something about them.

Three: Our Time on Earth Is Fleeting

Jewish teachers have always believed that thinking about death drives us to live with character. One may be as glamorous as Diana, Princess of Wales; as self-sacrificing as Mother Theresa; or as musically gifted as Sir George Solti. But death inflicted its finality upon all three within the same week. The grave mocks our boasts and posturing.

Four: We Need to Keep the Inventory of Our Blessings Current

How wonderful to be able to sit with eyes closed, contemplating the many good things in our lives! In gratitude, we recite the standard Jewish wake-up blessings, thanking God for a working body, awareness, freedom, vision, clothing, opportunity, ground to stand on, feet that work, personal dignity, respect from others, and strength to continue. That's a pretty impressive list! We can add all the things that specifically pertain to us. We learn to temper our pride in our accomplishments through our humble gratitude for all of the gifts we have received.

Five: We Need to Honor the Giver of Our Gifts

We don't need an airtight theology to occasionally feel a rush of thanks to God for the good that has come our way. It makes no difference whether we think of God as limited or unlimited, as personal or impersonal, as distant or near. Acknowledging God's reality reduces even the most self-confident to timidity. "For who in heaven can be compared to *Adonai,* and what so-called 'god' even comes close to the Divine reality?" (Ps. 89:7).

Six: We Need to Remember God's Judgment

Baḥya, like all premodern Jewish thinkers, is more certain than most of us today that God metes out reward and punishment. When we consider our historic and personal tragedies, we find the idea of Divine retribution problematic, even unbelievable. While we do have standards and values, we give more weight to the judgment of our peers—and our conscience. It is through them that we often hear an echo of God. This still, small voice of discernment, Baḥya teaches, keeps us from putting on airs.

Seven: We Need to Understand That the Unexpected Often Occurs

Computers keep getting faster, processing larger amounts of data, and connecting us more quickly with more people and information sources. Yet with all these technological marvels, we still cannot know for certain that, when we go to sleep at night, we will wake up the next morning. To our limited minds, events often seem random; existence, unpredictable. Unanticipated trauma makes a farce of our plans. But if we cultivate a strong streak of humility, life and its oddities become more gift than threat.

Moses Ḥayyim Luzzatto, Last of the Classic **Musarists**

Though he lived seven centuries later, Luzzatto mirrors Baḥya's understanding of humility as deferential action and submissive lifestyle. As Luzzatto himself summarizes: "The essence of humility is not thinking highly of yourself for any reason whatsoever" *(Mesillat Yesharim)*. True, Luzzatto tends toward preachiness. Yet his four guidelines for living with *anavah* help us prepare our response to those who would push us aside as they elbow their way to prominence.

One: Make Deference Part of Your Lifestyle

A certain submissiveness becomes all of us. As the rabbis note, God didn't choose the highest mountain as the place from which to give the Ten Commandments to Israel, but picked Sinai. Why? "Because it was so low" (Sot. 5a). And, by analogy, rather than making a fuss about not being invited to or not seated properly at that trend-setting dinner, we should follow the midrashic rule: "Never insist on the seat to which you believe you are entitled. Go occupy a seat in the academy two or three rows 'lower,' so that people ask you to 'come up' rather than, seeing where you put yourself, tell you, 'come down'" (Lev. R. 1.5). And don't "go about with pompous gait and head held high, but rather with your eyes down, like people who have tasks to perform" (San. 88b). "Always speak gently" (Yoma

86a), for as R. Abbahu said: "I had always thought I was humble, but when I saw how R. Abba of Acco refrained from anger when the academy's official interpreter cited his teaching incorrectly, I said to myself, 'I am not humble'" (Sot. 40a).

Two: Practice Forbearance

Our *musar* teachers agree that provocation is the classic test of humility. Judah the Pious states: "One can tell the truly humble by the way they handle their anger" (Judah Heḥasid, *Sefer Ḥasidim,* 184). A couple of generations later, the Roman sage Yeḥiel b. Yekutiel explains: "The truly humble do not return insult when insulted, but answer softly so as to turn back wrath" *(Sefer Maalot Hamiddot).* In this they are following the rabbis, who praise "those who endure insults without offering retaliation and those who listen to words of abuse without retort" (Shab. 88b). Humility includes not having to prove what intelligent, honorable people we are. It thus shields us against the stupidity of fools, and the temptation to respond to them in kind.

Three: Avoid Authority and Shun Applause

"R. Menaḥma said in the name of R. Tanḥum: Whoever assumes authority for the sake of the pleasure it affords is as bad as an adulterer" (*Yalkut* to Prov. 25:8). Our contemporary idiom, "ego trip," may be less hyperbolic than its rabbinic counterparts, but it conveys the same disdain. Few of us become arrogant from hearing an occasional "well done," or even a well-deserved round of applause; when sparingly employed, such praise will unlikely turn our heads. But appreciating being appreciated is quite different from gauging our personal worth by the number of offices we hold or the length of our resumes. We should consider the role of leadership as a mark of a good citizen rather than a reward to be vainly displayed. We see that R. Gamaliel spoke the truth when he castigated the disciples who refused to accept the offices he proposed to them: "Do you think I'm bestowing authority upon you? No, it is servitude that I impose on you" (Hor. 10a).

Four: Habitually Honor Others

Two motifs combine here: Recognizing the worth of others will lessen our infatuation with our own worth; concentrating our attention on others will limit our own self-absorption. Both call attention to our curious modern expression, the economy of praise, for many who demand a lot of appreciation are often quite stingy about bestowing it. They seem to believe that if they praise others, the pool of gratitude remaining for them will be depleted! This Ladino proverb proves much wiser: "Honor is more appropriate for those who share it than for those who hoard it."

"Too Much Humility Is Halfway to Pride" (Yiddish Proverb)

Against the prevailing principles of rabbinic teaching and Maimonides's insistence on the middle way, some Jewish teachers have insisted on interpreting *anavah* as self-abnegation. Thus Judah the Pious [as his followers called him], one of the pioneers of medieval ascetic German Hasidism, wrote: "People ought to keep track of what they do to keep from enjoying the doing" (Judah Hehasid, *Sefer Hasidim*, 8). And less than three hundred years ago, the hasidic Savraner rebbe taught: "In all traits of character it is best to walk in a middle path. The exception is pride. In getting as far away from pride as we can, we should become extremists" (Newman, *The Hasidic Anthology*).

Though it goes against the grain of modern life, the near-contemporary social philosopher Simone Weil defined herself through total self-denial. Weil could claim neither mystic or pietistic roots, having come from a typically middle-class, assimilated French Jewish family. But she was not willing to live a life of privilege, in which she would only imagine how the poor lived. To experience the grim reality of proletarian existence, she worked in a factory and later went to Spain to observe the suffering created by civil war. As her mystical, religious solidarity with the destitute intensified, she kept pushing herself beyond her physical limits despite her delicate health. After France fell to the Germans, Weil fled first to the unoccupied zone and eventually to England. Determined to subsist on only what her poverty-stricken French countrymen were eating, she became progressively weaker and died in 1943, not yet forty.

At the root of Weil's extremist view of ethical responsibility was the need to destroy pride utterly: "Without humility, all the virtues are finite. Only humility makes them infinite" (Paxichas, *The Simone Weil Reader*). "We possess nothing in this world other than the power to say I. This is what we should yield up to God, and that is what we should destroy" (Paxichas, *The Simone Weil Reader*). "The more I exist, the more God abdicates. So if I take God's side rather than my own, I ought to regard my existence as a diminution, a decrease. . . . Salvation is consenting to die" (Coles, *Simone Weil: A Modern Pilgrimage*).

Weil rejected her Jewish heritage as too worldly, believing that the crucifixion more aptly symbolized the perfection to be found in God. Though she thought herself a devout Christian, she refused to convert, believing that the Roman Catholic Church, the only one she took seriously, was too compromised by its involvement in this world. Weil was correct in saying that her ideas caused her estrangement from Judaism. More than a decade after Weil's death, the eminent philosopher Martin Buber sought to interpret her religious views through a psychological prism: ". . . Simone Weil turned away from a Judaism [she] did not know. . . . But even if [she] had known the true God of Israel, she would not have been satisfied. God turns toward nature, which He dominates, whereas Simone Weil sought flight from nature as well as from society; reality had become intolerable to her and for her, God was the power which led her away from it" ("The Silent Question," in *At the Turning*).

God's Humility

Jewish humility can never be as radical a denial of self or world as Weil desired. Our God, though unique and supreme, is humble enough to be involved with ordinary people. As R. Yoḥanan said: "Wherever Scripture mentions the transcendence of the Holy One, blessed be He, it also immediately makes reference to God's humility. . . . The Torah says, 'For the Lord your God, *Adonai* is the God of gods and the Lord of lords' [Deut. 10:17], and then immediately indicates, '*Adonai* executes justice for the fatherless and widow' [Deut. 10:18]. We also find this in the Prophets: 'For thus says the High and Lofty One that inhabits eternity . . .' [Isa. 57:15], only to say immediately afterward, 'I dwell with him that is of a contrite and humble spirit—refreshing the spirits of the lowly, reviving the hearts of the contrite' [Isa. 57:15]. It is stated a third time in the Writings: 'Extol him that rides upon the skies, whose name is *Adonai*' [Ps. 68:5], and immediately afterwards it is written, 'A father of the fatherless and a judge of the widows' [Ps. 68:6]" (Meg. 31a).

Jewish humility arises from the living relationship between an empathetic humanity and its involved God. "'The fear of God which is wisdom's crown is the heel of humility's sandal' (Yer. Shab. 1.3), for all the wisdom of the world cannot compare with humility" (Luzzatto, *Mesillat Yesharim*).

From Our Tradition

R. Abba b. Yudan said: We consider it disgraceful for someone to cook and eat from broken vessels. But God does not at all hesitate to use broken vessels, as it is said, "The Lord is near to the broken hearted" [Ps. 34:19].

—Lev. R. 7.2

The sacrifices of God are a broken spirit; a broken and contrite heart, O God, you will not despise.

—Ps. 51:19

Both the school of Shammai and the school of Hillel are "words of the living God," but the law agrees with the rulings of the school of Hillel. Why? Because the followers of Hillel were kindly and modest. They not only studied the rulings of the school of Shammai, they even mentioned these rulings before their own. . . . This teaches that whoever humbles oneself, God raises up, and whoever exalts oneself, God humbles. From the person who seeks greatness, greatness flees. But the person who flees from greatness, greatness follows.

—Er. 13b

Saul deserved to become the first king of Israel due to his humility. Protesting the prophet Samuel's efforts to crown him king, Saul said, "Am I not a son of Benjamin, the smallest of the tribes . . . and my family the least of all the families of Benjamin?" (1 Sam. 9:21).

—Yeḥiel b. Yekutiel, *Sefer Maalot Hamiddot*

Said the Baal Shem Tov: A king was told that a man of humility is endowed with long life. He attired himself in old garments, took up residence in a small hut, and forbade anyone to show reverence before him. But when he honestly examined himself, the king found himself to be prouder of his seeming humility than ever before. A philosopher then remarked to him: "Dress like a king— live like a king—allow the people to show due respect to you—but be humble in your innermost heart."

—Newman, *The Hasidic Anthology*

Modesty—*Tzeniyut*

We've all been similarly traumatized. We are at a large get-together where we don't know other people. Or we are stuck on a crowded airplane that seems to be interminably delayed in takeoff or landing. So there we are, and someone we've never seen before engages us in animated conversation. Before we know it, we're listening to the most intimate details of the other's life or are forced to hear about some obnoxiously precocious children, nieces, or grandkids. Or we find ourselves involved in the behind-the-scene details of an award this stranger just picked up and the ceremony that accompanied it. These bubbleheads have no idea how their exhibitionism makes us squirm, particularly since we are miserably captive to their prattle. We can only pray privately that they and others like them develop a little modesty—and fast. Its scarcity is the reason that the thirteenth-century Spanish poet Moses ibn Ezra's observation is still so appropriate today, "Man's finest virtue is that of which he is unaware" (*Shirat Yisrael* [Song of Israel]). From an earlier adage we are taught that just as a vine with large, heavy grape clusters hangs lower than one covered with smaller bunches, so our sages abhor those whose too-high opinion of themselves weighs them and us down (Mid. Sam. 16). The principle is simple: "A small act done modestly is a thousand-fold more acceptable to God than a big act done in pride" (*Orḥot Tzaddikim*).

So far, so good. But then we encounter those self-appointed zealots of religious correctness, the "*tzitzit* inspectors," who are constantly checking to see if others live up to their exalted sense of Jewish duty. Proud of their neuroses, they use the sin of immodesty as a weapon to punitively monitor the behavior of others. They claim legitimacy from our classic texts, all written by male authorities, who unhesitatingly prescribed rules for female Jewish modesty while also preaching their subservience. We find these attitudes so disheartening that we are sometimes tempted to abandon the entire category of modesty.

Yet we don't, because we believe that today's "tell-anything, show-almost-everything" culture could benefit from a corrective dose of restraint—though we are unlikely to find it by accepting these two-thousand-year-old injunctions: "Don't go perfumed into the marketplace [compensation for that society's infrequent bathing]. . . . Do not speak with a woman in a public place [dispensing with the usual segregation makes proximity erotic]. . . . One should not take overly long strides [do you think you own the place?]. . . . One should not walk with an erect carriage [are you trying to lord it over everyone?]" (Ber. 43b). To reclaim the Jewish wisdom of our ancestors, we must take a closer look at all of the virtues they cherished, *tzeniyut* included. In this quest we take as our guide the deceptively simple statement of the medieval philosopher-poet Solomon ibn Gabirol: "Modesty is meekness and wisdom combined" *(Mivḥar Hapeninim)*.

The Primacy of Privacy

The Hebrew root *tz-n-[ayin]*, usually translated as "modesty," actually means "to be private, to do something in seclusion." For example, the Talmud records that R. Ḥiyya b. Abba uses the term when he wishes to differentiate between solitary and communal prayer (Taan. 16a). R. Yoḥanan of Anatot, opposing the free-for-all atmosphere of the talmudic academy, claims that private study enables us to retain more (Yer. Ber. 5.1) and cites this verse to prove it: "With the secluded is wisdom" (Prov. 11:12). In his discussion of Jewish mourning customs, R. Yoḥanan rules that, while outward displays of grieving should cease on Shabbat, private sorrowing may continue even on this sacred day (M.K. 24a). We read a striking example of *tzeniyut* in a comment that a woman tells her daughter: "Why are you not more secretive when carrying on your sexual affairs?" (B.B. 58a). More than a millennium later, the hasidic sage Naḥman of Bratzlav, describing how he prays, uses the same Hebrew terminology: "When everyone is around me, that is when I seclude myself with God" (Mykoff, *The Empty Chair*).

Privacy played a role in some of the most important events in the lives of our biblical patriarchs. Before Abraham made his heart-breaking climb up Mount Moriah to sacrifice Isaac, he told his two servants to wait below with the donkeys so he and his son could be alone (Gen. 22:5). During the mysterious night before Jacob's reunion with his brother Esau, "he was left alone, and a 'man' wrestled with him until the coming of dawn" (Gen. 32:25). As we all know, the "man" was really an angel who changed Jacob's name to Israel. Ever since that secluded hour, our entire people has been called Israel.

"Privacy Is a Beautiful Thing" (Num. R. 1.3)

The most famous use of the root *tz-n-[ayin]* occurs in the third phrase of Micah's prophetic injunction, so often translated as: "It has been told you, O man, what is good, and what *Adonai* requires of you; only to do justly, to love mercy, and to walk humbly (*hatzne'a*) with your God" (6:8). The editors of the Jewish Publication Society's 1985 *Tanakh: The Holy Scriptures* chose a more accurate translation: "walk modestly with your God." Commenting on this verse, the eighteenth-century Bible commentator David Altschuler (*Metzudat David* [David's Fortress]) connects "*hatzne'a*" with "*hester*," meaning "concealment, privacy." Altschuler interprets Micah's statement as "walk privately with your God," reminding us that in God's presence, self-promotion is usually self-defeating. Instead we walk in God's ways by maintaining a certain reserve, rejecting human arrogance. One talmudic text on the Micah phrase provides a social implication. It suggests that a simple meaning of the verse refers to the mitzvah of attending funerals and giving brides a dowry. But it then goes on to state: "If 'walking modestly' requires our attention to matters normally done in public, how much the more does it apply to matters normally done in private?" (Suk. 49b).

Long before our current heyday of individualism, the sages taught that human dignity demands a certain measure of privacy in those moments that we share only with God. We can understand this more clearly if we look at the blending of the collective and the individual that informs Jewish prayer. The Bible and the Talmud stress the importance of communal liturgy. Yet traditionally, the central prayer of our group worship, the *Tefillah*, is said quietly by each individual, whispered to God for God's "ears" alone. The rabbis felt so strongly that this should be a private time that they said: "One who says the *Tefillah* so that it can be heard by those standing nearby is small of faith [because he implies that without heightened volume, God will not hear him]" (Ber. 24b). And after we recite the required parts of this prayer, we are encouraged to conclude with whatever words we find to say to God from our heart, another example of individual, inward piety.

King David, the Second Book of Samuel (chap. 6) tells us, exuberantly dances half-naked in front of the public procession that brought the Ark of the Covenant to its final home in Jerusalem. Oblivious to the almost delirious passions brought on by this historic action, his wife Michal upbraids him for behaving shamelessly. A midrash says she contrasted her husband's vulgarity to her father Saul's household, where, in appropriate royal dignity, "no one had ever seen the naked heel or toe of any of them" (Num. R. 4.20). Obviously the author of this ancient midrash commends Michal's standards, suggesting that *tzeniyut* means keeping part of ourselves to ourselves, hidden from the prying, gossip-seeking eyes of others. It is a standard that our own generation, notorious for its self-promoters and shameless flaunters, needs to take to heart.

Tzeniyut as a Commended Category

The rabbis referred to various groups in their society as the *tzenu'im,* "the pious" or "the virtuous," since they considered modesty to be a good indicator of religiosity. Only the priests who were *tzenu'im* were permitted to speak God's sacrosanct names: "Our rabbis taught: At first everyone could say God's twelve-letter name. When they perceived that indecency was becoming commonplace, uttering this name was restricted to priests who were *tzenu'im*, and even when they pronounced it they 'swallowed it' [they said it indistinctly to keep it from immodest others]. . . . R. Judah said in Rav's name: The forty-two-letter name of God may be spoken only by those who are *tzenu'im*, meek, middle-aged, even-tempered, sober, and not insistent on their rights" (Kid. 71a).

Scholars were encouraged to be exemplars of *tzeniyut:* "A scholar should be reserved about his deeds and recognized only by his seemly ways" (D.E.Z. 7.3). "R. Huna and R. Ḥalafta said in the name of R. Simeon b. Lakish: Just as modesty becomes a bride, so it is fitting for a disciple of the wise" (S. of S. R. 4.11, 1). Maimonides expands this theme to include the whole Jewish people: "A scholar's garment should be unsoiled and presentable. . . . He should not wear flimsy garments that reveal his body. . . . His cloak should not drag on the ground. . . . Wearing patched shoes is simply unacceptable" (M.T., Hil. Deot, 5.9).

"The Body Is the Palace of the Soul" (Baḥya b. Asher, *Kad Hakemaḥ*)

Jewish teachers have realized that, though we humans are only one more creature created by God, our unique likeness to God requires us to hold our bodies in special regard. After all, before the expulsion from the Garden of Eden it was God, no less, who made the first clothes for Adam and Eve (Gen. 3:21). The rabbis so prize modesty that they imaginatively find it in the conduct of our "cousins," the animals. "The dove is modest in its conduct and graceful in its movements" (S. of S. R. 1.15, 2), and reputedly, "camels are modest [private] about their copulation" (Gen. R. 76.7). Nonetheless, our sages teach that we humans should display more *tzeniyut* than other animals. "Standing around naked inevitably decreases a person's dignity" (T. Ber. 2.14). The medieval Roman commentator Yeḥiel b. Yekutiel agrees: "It is great immodesty in a man to go about naked, even in his own home. He thereby demeans himself by behaving like an animal" *(Sefer Maalot Hamiddot)*. So most of us put clothes on even if we don't expect visitors. However, in an example of rabbinic exaggeration gone too far, the Talmud approvingly records this story: "Our rabbis taught that once a certain man married a woman with a stumped hand, yet did not notice it until the day of her death. Rabbi observed, 'How modest this woman must have been in covering herself that her husband never saw this!' Said R. Ḥiyya, 'But that is precisely what she should have done. Rather say, how modest was this man, that he didn't look much at his wife!'" (Shab. 53b).

How odd that sounds to us today! We crusade with almost religious zeal, promoting the legal right of consenting adults to do just about anything in private. Fortunately the Talmud also gives us two other examples of *tzeniyut* that we moderns may find more appropriate. R. Judah was so modest that he would not take off his outer cloak all day (Men. 43a). And it was Rabbi Akiba's modesty, we are told, not a more cerebral characteristic, that made the daughter of his rich master fall in love with him, a lowly shepherd (Ket. 62b).

Since the rabbis were so concerned about the body and privacy, it comes as no surprise that elimination and proper outhouse behavior were critical indicators of a person's dignity. "R. Tanḥum b. Hanilai said: Whoever behaves modestly in a privy is delivered from three things: from snakes, from scorpions, and from evil spirits. . . . There was a certain privy in Tiberias where, if two persons entered together, even by day, unpleasantness would follow. R. Ammi and R. Assi used to enter it separately, and they suffered no harm. The rabbis said to them, 'Are you not afraid?' They replied, 'The tradition is that one avoids harm in the privy by one's modesty and silence'" (Ber. 62a). We who have grown up in modern, western cultures are accustomed to private, clean, decent-smelling bathrooms and fervently hope to find such public facilities when we need them. It would be interesting to know what our contemporary teachers would consider appropriate bathroom modesty today.

Modesty and Sexual Intercourse

If *tzeniyut* stems from a concern for human dignity, particularly as it relates to our bodies, it will certainly be concerned with sexual intercourse. Our sages would have been appalled that anyone would consider having intercourse in the presence of onlookers. From the time of the Talmud, they opposed having sexual intercourse during the day or with a light on in the room (S.A., E.H. 25.5). Nearly a thousand years after the Talmud, Eliezer b. Samuel of Mainz summed up this teaching: "Marital intercourse should be modest and holy, carried on in a spirit of restraint and delicacy, in reverence and silence" *(Hebrew Ethical Wills)*. Our sages voiced this same spirit when they railed against abusive sex: "R. Meir used to say that one who marries his daughter to an ignoramus might just as well have bound her and set her before a lion. Just as a lion tears his prey and shamelessly eats it, so an ignorant man will shamelessly beat his wife and then have intercourse with her" (Pes. 49b). "Citing R. Assi, Rami b. Ḥama ruled: A man is forbidden to force his wife to have intercourse, for Scripture says, 'One who rushes around will sin' [Prov. 19:2]" (Er. 100b). Rabbi Assi's ruling became the standard demanded by Jewish law.

The sexual urge has the potential for such cruelty and violence that we have always sought means of controlling it. Perhaps the most terrifying biblical story of sex gone amok is the "acquaintance rape" that took place between King David's children, Tamar and her half-brother Amnon: "'No brother, don't force me. . . . Such things are not done in Israel!' . . . But he would not listen to her; he overpowered her and had sex with her by force" (2 Sam. 13:12–14). The rabbis know the great injustice committed against Tamar, and though they do not vociferously condemn the crime, they at least call attention to it as the heinous act that it was: "It was taught in the name of R. Joshua b. Korḥa: In that hour Tamar demonstrated how great a need we have for a 'fence' to guard against impulsive sexual acts. Hearing what happened to her, all the other women in the kingdom said, 'If this could happen to kings' daughters, how much more might it happen to the daughters of ordinary men; if this could happen to the chaste, how much more might it happen to the wanton?'" (San. 21a).

"Men Must Be Modest, But Women Even More So" (Papo, *Pele Yoetz*)

All of us need to exercise special control over our libidos. The difficulties rise up when people take it upon themselves to create appropriate methods to guard against untoward sexual practices. True, our tradition has long taught that some modesty must be legislated. But premodern societies in general and some people today still self-righteously assume that women's immodesty somehow causes men's wanton and even violent sexual acts. The victim thus becomes responsible for the aggressor's actions. Blaming the victim violates both individual male and female dignity. If generally condoned, it shows the moral bankruptcy of the greater society as well.

Yet the Talmud was a product of its times, echoing the other male-dominated cultures of the Middle East. So its teachings prescribed the segregation of women as the fundamental antidote for womanly provocation. Its standard biblical justification was the verse, "The chief glory of the king's daughter is that she remains deep within the palace" [Ps. 45:14–15]. Thus Sarah, the first matriarch, serves as a model for all women to follow: "When the visiting angels asked Abraham, 'Where is Sarah your wife?' he answered, 'Behold, she is in the tent.' [Gen. 18:9]. This is to inform us that Sarah was modest" (B.M. 87a). A text from the Jerusalem Talmud at least gives those females who practice seclusion a reward—a prominent spouse and male children [*sic*]: "A woman who remains at home merits marrying a high priest and being the mother of a line of high priests" (Yer. Yoma 4.2). Several hundred years later, the German sage Eliezer b. Samuel of Mainz counsels: "My daughters ought always to be at home, and should not even stand at the door so as to watch whatever passes by" (*Hebrew Ethical Wills*).

Yeḥiel b. Yekutiel also follows this talmudic theme when he blames physically malformed children on the fact that their mother "weaves in the marketplace, speaking and gazing at all men. Weaving in a public place exposes her arms; men who see her might desire her and be brought to transgression. Because of her misdeeds, one of her children is lame, another blind, another a fool and evil doer" *(Sefer Maalot Hamiddot)*. True, Maimonides does grudgingly say about a man's wife: "She is not in prison where she cannot come and go. . . ." But he then glaringly affirms his patriarchal mentality by stating: ". . . It is unseemly for a woman to be constantly in the streets. Her husband should not let her go out except once or twice a month, as the need may arise" (M.T., Hil. Ishut, 13.11). Even the realm of Jewish folk literature concedes that the appropriate place for women is a private one: "The good woman knows that her kingdom is behind the house door" (Ladino proverb).

Women's Actions: Traditional *Tzeniyut* Gauges

How women stand, how they walk, what they show of themselves, and what they keep concealed are all part of the tireless rabbinic policing of proper female behavior. We offer the following texts despite our aversion to them, to honestly share with you the mindset of our sages: "He who closes his eyes against gazing upon evil is saintly" (B.B. 57b). Yeḥiel b. Yekutiel uses this text to prove that "one should not gaze at women when they stand over their washing" *(Sefer Maalot Hamiddot)*. "A man should not walk behind a woman on the road, even if that woman is his wife" (Ber. 61a). "Why are the words of the Torah compared to the thigh? To teach that, just as the thigh is hidden, so the words of the Torah should be hidden [taught in privacy, not in the marketplace]" (Suk. 49b). And one of the classically hyperbolic rabbinic statements: "R. Sheshet said: If one gazes at even the little finger of a woman, it is as if he gazed at her genitals" (Ber. 24a).

Ruth, we are told, first came to her husband-to-be Boaz's attention because of her modest behavior as she worked in the field: "The standing ears of corn she gleaned standing, but when it came time to gather what had fallen, she gleaned sitting on the ground" (Shab. 113b). Elsewhere the following words are put in Boaz's mouth: "All the other women act provocatively, bending over to pick up the ears of corn, but Ruth sits down to gather the fallen gleanings. All the other women hitch up their skirts as they move around, but she keeps hers down. All the other women joke with the male harvesters, while Ruth is reserved with them" (Ruth R. 4.6). Though a convert to Judaism, Ruth was so exemplary a model of *tzeniyut* that she became the great-great-grandmother of King David and thus eventually an ancestor of the Messiah.

Our Problems with Traditional Female *Tzeniyut*

Two provisions of the modesty laws with regard to women are so troubling that they divide Orthodox Jews even today. The first teaches that a woman's hair is powerfully erotic; therefore, no one but her husband should ever see it. For "Never even letting the beams of my house see my hair'" (Yer. Meg. 1.12), the modest Kimḥit merited having seven sons, who all served as high priests in the Temple. A sermon derived from the bitter water ritual during Temple times tests a woman [but never a man] suspected of adultery (Num. 5:11–31). It allowed the priest to violate *tzeniyut* when judging her: "When the priest uncovers the head of a suspected adulteress he says to her: 'You have departed from the ways of the daughters of Israel, whose habit it is to have their heads covered, and you have behaved like the idolatrous women who walk about with their heads uncovered. Here then, be as you wanted to be!'" (Num. R. 9.16).

This rule about covering a woman's hair has led many Orthodox women to wear wigs in public. Recently Ovadiah Yossef, the former Sephardic chief rabbi of Israel and that community's halakhic authority, reacted to the fashionable wigs that some women wear by condemning this practice as extreme immodesty; it draws attention to women in public places. He predicted that both the wig and its wearer would burn in hell and that, should a woman dare come to synagogue so "coifed," both she and her husband should be excommunicated.

The other rule applies to men and says that merely listening to a woman's voice is a grave sexual violation. "Samuel taught: A woman's voice is a gross sexual provocation, as it is written, 'For your voice is sweet and your appearance comely' [S. of S. 2:14]" (Ber. 24a). Thus those who observe this ruling may not attend the opera or theater, or even listen to women on radio, television, or recordings.

Of course, you don't need us to tell you that modern women find these rabbinic attitudes regarding women's modesty reprehensible. The rabbis' promised reward for following the laws of *tzeniyut,* that women would bear prominent male offspring, insults the feminine sensibility even further. How different is the preferred notion of privacy, with respect for the dignity of women as its benchmark. A comprehensive reworking of Jewish modesty is clearly overdue. But this time the leadership must come from our feminist thinkers, who have already demonstrated their creative sensitivity in other areas traditionally restricted to male points of view. We look to them for guidance, to help us refigure reasonable standards of Jewish modesty in demeanor, in speech, in dress, and in general behavior of both sexes.

"Nothing Is More Precious to God Than Modesty" (Pes. R.)

We suggest that our feminist scholars ground their efforts in the notion that God, too, practices *tzeniyut.* "Before the *mishkan* [the wilderness tent of meeting] was set up, God spoke with Moses publicly—from a bush, in Midian, or on Mount Sinai. However, as soon as the *mishkan* was erected, God thought, 'Privacy is a beautiful thing,' and so from then on God spoke to Moses only inside it" (Num. R. 1.3). This is not to say that God's modesty precludes a divine presence in the community. For even as God's indwelling presence in the world is conceptualized by the Shekhinah, a feminine figure, so too, *tzeniyut* does not require that we isolate ourselves from our neighbors, male or female. We can also infer that, even for God, seclusion has its limits. Our prophetic command only states that as we do justly, love mercy, and walk *hatzne'a* (privately) with God, we remember that it is God's image we seek to reflect.

From Our Tradition

*R*aba said: Three requests have I made from Heaven. Two were fulfilled, and the third evaded me. I prayed for R. Huna's learning and R. Ḥisda's wealth, and I was granted both. But Rabbah b. Huna's modest disposition was not granted me.

—M.K. 28a

R. Samuel b. Naḥman said in the name of R. Jonathan: Every bride who is modest in the house of her father-in-law is rewarded by having kings and prophets among her descendants. How do we prove this? From Tamar, as it is written, "And Judah saw her and thought her to be a harlot; for she covered her face" [Gen. 38:15]. Because she covered her face in the house of her father-in-law and he did not know her, she was rewarded by having among her descendants kings and prophets.

—Meg. 10b

Our mother Sarah was extremely modest. When Isaac was born and the neighbors began to gossip that he couldn't possible be hers, since she was so old, Abraham said to her, "This is not a time for modesty. Uncover your breasts so that all may know the Holy One, blessed be He, has begun to perform miracles." She uncovered her breasts and the milk gushed forth as from two fountains, and noble ladies came and had their children suckled by her.

—Gen. R. 53.9

CHAPTER 13

Contentedness—
Histapkut

Tsu feel iz umgezunt—that is the theme of this chapter. If Yiddish has infiltrated American English as pervasively as some Yiddish lovers insist, we'd do our best to have this phrase made into everyone's favorite bumper sticker. We can see it now—cars zipping by, teaching *musar* as they go: *"Tsu feel iz umgezunt!*—Too much ain't healthy!" What a revolution we'd witness in our society if a measure of self-restraint, of being content with what we have, suddenly became an honored American character trait.

But we are getting ahead of ourselves. The truth is, needing to set our own limits is as old as the human appetite. Our conflicting primal drives of animal need and social acceptance have always spurred moralists to teach us to say to ourselves, "Enough already." So it should come as no surprise to hear that wise Jews, from our rabbis to our bubbes, have made food the classic Jewish example of the importance of *histapkut*. And surely compulsive calorie counters are not excused from what follows, for they should see the same validity. With thinness, too, *tsu feel iz umgezunt*.

Food, Glorious Food

The Bible indicates the standard for self-restraint with edibles when describing how God fed the 600,000 people who wandered in the desert for forty years. The miraculous foodstuff God provided every morning of that journey, the manna—a honey-like, sticky substance—was just enough for each person: "The one who gathered much had nothing left over, and the one who gathered little did not lack" (Exod. 16:18). To this day, in one of the recent, short versions of the *Amidah,* our prayer composed of eighteen petitions, we entreat God to give us "enough to live on and . . . what we need," neither a sumptuous banquet nor bread-and-water rations. Anticipating modern nutritionists, our rabbis urge us to curb our cravings for fatty, sweet morsels by "eating salad and more salad, rather than developing an appetite for goose and chicken" (Pes. 114).

Maimonides, the medieval philosopher, was also a hard-working physician. He prescribed: "Eat that you may live, and lay a ban on excess. By taking the little food one can easily digest, a person's vigor and health increase and one's mind becomes clear and calm" *(Hebrew Ethical Wills).* Showing a somewhat greater ascetic bent, Solomon b. Isaac, a fifteenth-century Spanish sage, hoped to teach his children *histapkut:* "In order to restrain myself from enjoying in this world more than is necessary to maintain my body, I do not eat at one meal more than one course of meat, nor drink more than two cups of wine" *(Hebrew Ethical Wills).*

Our Roman musarist Yeḥiel b. Yekutiel gave this theme more graphic form, stating that our throat, like our eyes, is "small in size but vast in capacity. Give it only what it needs. If you give it sweets, a small quantity will not suffice, for it will desire more. But if you accustom it to light fare, this will become natural to you and you will not lust for fat foods and sweet delights" *(Sefer Maalot Hamiddot).* Near chocoholics like Gene and Francie know the truth of that teaching, for while we try to restrain ourselves, our *histapkut* doesn't always come through. We admire that young rabbi—name withheld to protect the still struggling—who seeks to control her chocolate passion by limiting its eating to a special Shabbat treat. One doesn't need a psychoanalyst expounding about oral fixations to inform us of the power of the taste buds, since most of us readily admit to succumbing—too often! So food psychologists have cautioned us not to buy groceries near mealtime, because it is nearly impossible not to impulsively throw stuff into the cart that would never otherwise make the shopping list.

Our Classic Counsel: Learn to be Content

Sefer Ḥasidim, the medieval text attributed to the Franco-German Judah the Pious, reminds us that food-lust isn't the only craving that overcomes us. It cautions us not to be contentious, jealous, sensuous, or relentless in seeking honor, for these dispositions "drive us from the world" (51). To the best of our knowledge, we are not born with these dispositions; rather, they result from our response to living with others. It just bothers us that some people have things that we don't have. We want them, too—maybe only because they have them. Nearly two thousand years ago, Pirke Avot voiced similar sentiments: "Don't seek greatness for yourself, and don't lust after honor. Do more than study. Don't lust to sit at the tables of the mighty, for your (study) table is more significant than theirs, and your crown is greater than theirs. And the One for whom you work is totally trustworthy and may be counted on to give you your proper recompense" (6.5).

How often do we find it hard to react calmly when we see others' names in the papers, on everyone's tongues, and then seated at the dais, while we go unnoticed? We are overwhelmed by a rush of longing that demands satisfaction. Dramatically put, we become the slaves of our passions. Maybe it's too messianic to hope, mere mortals that we are, that we can consistently dominate our baser side, but it would be absolutely unworthy of us—and certainly a blot on our Judaism—not to try. Maybe we should start by a stiff regimen of impulse control and then revert to the obvious good sense of "Enough already!"

"If You Stay at Home, You Won't Wear Out Your Shoes" (Yiddish Proverb)

Jacob, like his grandfather Abraham and son Joseph, also doesn't stay at home. Yet he may well be the greatest biblical exemplar of *histapkut.* A fugitive, he sets out on the perilous journey to Haran with a prayer requesting God to guard him in his travels and give him just "bread to eat and a garment to wear" (Gen. 28:20). After Jacob finally gets to his uncle's home, the wily Laban defrauds him of his chosen bride after seven years' labor and tricks him into marrying Leah. Jacob must serve another seven years to wed her sister, his beloved Rachel (Gen. 29–30). Only once does he complain about this to Laban. He accepts the inevitable and gets past it, glorying in what he finally acquires. Other biblical authors offer a similar philosophy. Proverbs tells us: "A contented heart makes a cheerful countenance" (15:13) and adds: "Better a little with the fear of the Lord than great wealth and much trouble (15:16). Ecclesiastes chimes in: "Better is a handful of gratification than two fistfuls which come from unworthy work" (4:6).

There has been no lack of Jewish teachers reiterating this theme. Ben Zoma gave the classic talmudic epitome in his rhetorical "Q & A": "Who is rich? One who is happy with what he has" (Avot 4.1). The eleventh-century Spanish poet-philosopher Solomon ibn Gabirol said: "Who seeks more than he needs, hinders himself from enjoying what he has. Seek what you need and give up what you need not. For in giving up what you don't need, you'll learn what you really do need" (*Mivḥar Hapeninim* 155, 161). Two centuries later, Yeḥiel b. Yekutiel added a touch of realism to the instruction without changing the ideal: "True contentment is found only among those saintly souls who are satisfied with little, just as most people are content only with a lot" *(Sefer Maalot Hamiddot)*. About a hundred years ago Judah Steinberg, an early Hebrew *littérateur,* poetically wrote: "If there is no light from the sun, then let the light of the moon delight your eye" (*Mishle Yehoshua* [Proverbs of Joshua]). This was also the time that our seriously impoverished Yiddish-speaking ancestors wryly commented, "With only one pair of feet, you can't dance at two weddings, and with one behind you can't ride two horses." They knew they didn't have much, but they sensed: "Even a temporary satisfaction is worth cherishing," or, putting it negatively, "It's better to lose your hat than your head."

But surely the most famous defense of appreciating what one has is this often-told folk story: "Once a poor Hasid became so distraught because of the crowding in his hovel that he appealed to his Rebbe, 'We have so many people living with us that we can't turn around in the house.' The Rebbe counseled the man to first move his goat, then his chickens, and finally even his cow into the house.

He returned, half crazed, to the Rebbe. 'It's the end of the world,' cried the man. The Rebbe responded, 'Now go home, turn out the goat, chickens and cow, and report to me tomorrow.' The following day the Hasid showed up beaming. 'Rebbe! My hut seems like a palace now!'" (Browne, *The Wisdom of Israel*).

"A Penny at Hand Is Worth a Dollar at a Distance" (Yiddish Proverb)

Like our many examples of self-restraint, frugality has also been commended by our teachers as a mode of *histapkut*. While "delayed gratification," "making do," and "settling" often sound strange to members of the "X" generation, they were staples of wisdom for those who grew up in the aftermath of the Great Depression. Money was truly scarce, though not as limited as in many a shtetl home, where one learned to cope with only two changes of clothing, an "everyday" and a *"yom tov,"* special occasion, outfit. No wonder our Sephardic folk wisdom said: "Bread for two will also satisfy three" and "When you eat and leave some on your plate, it's like setting a table for two meals" (Ladino proverbs). We like the Yiddish proverb: "Be frugal and you won't need loans," which we update as ". . . and you won't max out your credit cards."

Yet for all of the explicit wisdom we may reap from our tradition, we feel more than a tad uneasy about transmitting all this inspirational *musar* of extreme self-restraint and penny-watching. We sit in our plush studies, using computers costing several thousand dollars. We drive cars not only heated and air-conditioned, but often equipped with multiple speakers, CD players, and portable telephones. Even when sending off our children on their "European experience," with only a backpack to see them through many weeks of travel, we make sure that they carry a credit card, "just in case." We may momentarily be warmed by the ideal of *histapkut* when we hear that our frightfully poor ancestors tried hard to be happy with their lot. But we know that it won't be long before we are again dreaming about owning our own sun bathed island (or wherever your dream finds you). After all, isn't Judaism life-affirming and this-worldly? Aren't there plenty of texts that urge us to enjoy life?

After all, Jacob received his blessing from Isaac, his father, only after bringing him a pot full of savory food (Gen. 27:25). And Esther saved her people from certain death at the hands of Haman after throwing not one, but two banquets and lulling the villain into a wine-soaked, food-satiated smugness (Est. 5:4–8).

"Better Has No Limits" (Yiddish Proverb)

The simple truth is that contemporary American affluence has radically altered our notion of *tsu feel iz umgezunt*. We take pride in our own "disposable income," and we consider it an important learning tool to give our children regular allowances, part of which they may spend at their discretion. Perhaps if we followed the notion of spending only to satisfy our needs, we might become like those benefactors we hear about who live in radical self-denial and then give millions to a particular school's scholarship fund or double a museum's already splendiferous collection of paintings. But as numerous commentators have pointed out, only if we show a little self-love can we genuinely love our neighbor as ourselves.

But by accepting our somewhat well-to-do status, we have made the problem of living with reasonable self-restraint more complicated. We tend to blame a good part of this problem on the mythic powers of advertising. Of course we gladly acknowledge its beneficial aspect, its capacity for making us more aware. People can't take advantage of what they don't know about, and advertising, as an information-disseminating service, clues us in to new products that might improve our lives. Many first learn of the latest pain medication or cholesterol-reducing drug from a print or television ad. And, thanks to the immediacy of home pregnancy tests so widely touted by advertising, hopeful couples and anxious teens alike don't have to wait. But we cannot say that this proliferation of information, so clever and well-designed that we often like watching the commercials more than the programs they interrupt, has created a less stressful, more relaxed ambiance. The other function of advertising is to make us want things we hadn't before desired. So we get bombarded with ads not-so-seductively suggesting that we throw out the old, yet serviceable, to make room for the very latest, most powerful thingamajig.

Add to this continual importuning, the American notion that we were born to improve ourselves, indeed, must fulfill ourselves—a goal that must make us perpetually dissatisfied—and one can understand why the characteristic American figure these days is the "mall rat" and the favorite current American pastime is cruising what the more mature of us remember calling a "shopping center." We are consumed with consuming, not only doing it but talking about it and demonstrating our expertise in it. Thus people spend fortunes decorating their homes and then soon come down with cabin fever inside them. Having mastered one encompassing challenge, they then need a new buy-and-be-special focus. Give us the chance and we fill our walk-in closets until they overflow and then build additions to our homes to accommodate our still never-ending "stuff." The more affluent add a second dwelling, separating their workday from their weekend/vacation possessions.

Never Enough

Francie calls this the "gift shop syndrome." Craving a little culture herself, she occasionally attempted to introduce her then-small children to the wonders of a museum. But the outings became ordeals, because it regularly took at least half an hour to make it past the entrance, where savvy marketers strategically placed their store. You know the plaintive cries that then ensued: "Mommy, buy this; Daddy, please, can I get that?; I really need it for science (art, music, English) at school." It goes without saying that rooms full of comparable toys and games remained untouched back home. Something similar happened in supermarket aisles—and when Grandma came to visit, her loving grandchildren's first words were inevitably, "What did you bring me?"

We quickly admit that opportunity and means do not refute old wisdom—they just increase temptation and make the need for strength of Jewish character all the more important. Isaiah sounds like he's addressing the beneficiaries of a bull market when he says: "On a high and lofty hill you have set up your couch. There, too, you have gone to perform idolatrous sacrifices. . . . Though weary by much travel you have never said, 'I've had it.' You keep finding gratification for your lust and just never care" (57:7–10). It's also hard to call this observation of Ecclesiastes dated: "A money-lover never has his fill, nor a lover of wealth, enough income" (5:9). A Hasid once asked Rabbi Abraham Yaakov of Sadagora about social ethics: "Since our sages say there's no thing that does not have a place, then each person must have his own place. Then why do people sometimes feel so crowded?" The master replied: "Because each wants to occupy the place of the other" (Buber, *Tales of the Hasidim,* bk. 2, *The Later Masters*). *The Union Prayer Book* poetically chided its users for their discontent: "The eye is never satisfied with seeing, endless are the desires of the heart . . . discontent abides in the palace and the hut, rankling alike in the breast of the prince and the pauper."

And while we may protest that we can control our itch for continuous self-gratification, human nature may outwit us with tragic results. As the sages said, "[A spender] exhausts his parents' possessions. When he then seeks his accustomed fare and doesn't find it, he goes to the crossroads [today we would read, "the nearest mall"] and robs people [or runs a scam or cheats the government]" (San. 70a). Every week brings another story that turns the stomach, like that of the teacher who lost her life because she stopped for a slice of pizza on her way to an evening class and was killed by a young man who wanted the car she was driving.

Worthy Discontent

There are times, we readily acknowledge, when resigning ourselves to reality is sinful. In the face of any human suffering that we, alone or with others, could rectify, *histapkut,* for all its usual virtue, shows its darker face. The beauty and limit of this virtue are brilliantly illuminated by the great Yiddish storyteller I. L. Peretz, in his story, "Bontshe the Silent." We apologize for desecrating Peretz's artistry by our pedestrian abstract of his tale, and we hope our synopsis prompts you to read the full version. Bontshe was a downtrodden porter who would have considered himself rich if he had ever held two pennies in his hand at one time. His life was a journey in suffering, which began, symbolically enough, with a botched circumcision. And he died in such lonely insignificance that no one erected a tombstone to mark his grave. Yet, paragon of *histapkut* that he was, Bontshe never complained, but praised God for every slight good that came his way. After death his condition reversed, and he was greeted effusively in Heaven. His judgment before the Heavenly Court was swift and deferential. Finding his character exemplary, the Court told Bontshe that his heavenly reward was to have anything he desired. After much disbelief and hesitation, Bontshe finally, haltingly asked for a hot roll with fresh butter every morning. Saintly indeed! But the story does not end with Bontshe's heartwarming self-effacement. For Peretz's last words indicate that in response to Bontshe's request, the Prosecuting Angel let out a bitter—perhaps triumphant—laugh. Is *histapkut* a plan for training people to such minimal expectations that they accept misery even when they might take action to rise above it?

Many of our Jewish role models didn't think so. Rebecca didn't sit back and resign herself to accepting that her unsuitable older child, Esau, would receive her husband Isaac's main blessing; Esther did more than fast and pray for her people's survival. Modernity has taught us that contentment in the face of injustice and indecency is morally decadent. Rabbi Ḥanokh of Alexandrow said, "The real exile of Israel in Egypt began when they learned to endure it" (Buber, *Tales of the Hasidim*, bk. 2, *The Later Masters*). And the hasidic sage Rabbi Naḥman of Bratzlav mused: "If we are not better tomorrow than we are today, why have a tomorrow?" (Elkins, *Melodies from My Father's House*). Today Americans honor Thomas Paine for being so disgusted with Britain's overbearing colonialism that he wrote, "These are the times that try men's souls" *(Common Sense);* we applaud Samuel Adams's deeds as a patriot for organizing the first scruffy band of rebels to battle against the well-trained British redcoats.

The practice of contentment must never degenerate into moral complacency. Had we been diligent early on, Hitler could have been stopped. We may not be able to do much personally about genocide in Bosnia and Rwanda, but we must be grateful for the spiritually heroic few whose discontent is so powerful that they make the rest of us squirm, rousing us from our mind-numbing state of premature *histapkut*. Two twentieth-century examples quickly come to mind in which a dynamism of change overtook a lethargic status quo. The first, in the 1930s, gave the elderly back their dignity; the second, more recent one has seen how a change in individual mind-set as well as national law began to give women equality in our society.

Before the advent of social security, living past retirement was tough. The limited opportunity to save meant one's final years might be spent as a burden on family members or subsisting in what was then regularly called "the poorhouse." Finally, despite enormous opposition, our country corrected that injustice, so that those who paid social security when they were younger and working receive an automatic monthly check for the rest of their lives. Several decades later the elderly stated that they were "entitled" to basic health care, which became the basis for what we know today as Medicare. Yes, financing all this has its difficulties. But the human gains have been so great, our moral will demands that we find ways to continue to do so.

Similar changes are moving forward more grudgingly in giving women effective equality. Francie remembers that, as a new college graduate, she nearly accepted a job as a "newsman" in a small Midwestern city, after being told outright that, of course, a male getting the job would earn one hundred dollars more a month! Some courageous women, defying the contentment that was supposed to be one of the preeminent feminine graces, misbehaved and demanded that their sex be emancipated from tokenism and paternalism. Similarly, we cannot commend *histapkut* to African-Americans, gays and lesbians, and the disabled, among others, as the most significant Jewish virtue they should exemplify.

Knowing When to "Say When"

But there are many things we cannot change. One of these is the past—no amount of discontent about what once happened will change the record, though harping on it is likely to make us miserable and prevent us from living with an eye to the future. Maimonides said: "Only the ignorant sorrowfully mourn what's past. So worrying over the money you've lost is about as useful as worrying that you were created a human being and not an angel" *(The Preservation of Youth)*. To some extent, that also holds true for those of us in a perpetual stew about the future. The Talmud counsels: "Don't panic about tomorrow's trouble, for you don't know what the day will bring. In fact, tomorrow may come but you may not be around to see it and so you will have worried about nothing" (Yev. 63b).

And though we find it useful to focus on the changes we can make, much of life involves what we can't change, like our date of birth, our DNA endowment, even our place in the political-economic orbit. Our situation is certainly not as restricted as that of eastern European Jews in the eighteenth and nineteenth century. Yet there is something about their overwhelming acceptance of their lot that still speaks to us. "Rabbi Moshe of Kobryn told his followers, who found their abject poverty an obstacle to piety, 'In this awful day and age, the greatest devotion, greater than learning and praying, consists of accepting the world exactly as it happens to be'" (Buber, *Tales from the Hasidim,* bk. 2, *The Later Masters*). His older colleague, Rabbi Bunim, advised: "To stop being bent double with worry, bend yourself rather to bear complacently whatever may happen, and be satisfied no matter what the outcome" (Newman, *The Hasidic Anthology*). And Rabbi Mordechai of Lechovitz proposed that we clear the mind by realizing: "All worrying is forbidden, except to worry that one is worried" (Elkins, *Melodies from My Father's House*).

So many virtues resurface as we search for family values and nostalgically remember simpler, easier times. Thus, as against infantile discontent, traditional *histapkut* may also experience a rebirth, accompanied by modest resurgences of self-restraint and frugality. While we disavow his sexism, we commend the balanced sense of *histapkut* expounded by R. Avira: "A man should always drink and eat less than his means, clothe himself according to his means, and honor his wife and children more than his means, since they are dependent on him and he is dependent on *Adonai*" (Ḥul. 84b).

From Our Tradition

Rabbi Yehiel Mihal of Zlotchov said: There are two things it is forbidden to worry about. That which it is possible to fix and that which it is impossible to fix. What is possible to fix, fix it and why worry? What is impossible to fix, how will worrying help?
—Elkins, *Melodies from My Father's House*

Rabbi Shmelke of Nikolsburg and his brother asked the Maggid of Mezritch how to understand the rabbinic command to bless God for the evil as well as the good. He sent them to the Study House to find Zusya who, he indicated, would give them the explanation. They found Zusya there smoking his pipe, and they put their query to him. He laughed: "Sorry, you've come to the wrong man. You'd better ask someone else since I've never experienced suffering." But the two knew that, from the day he was born, Rabbi Zusya's life had been a web of need and anguish. Then they knew what the answer was: to accept suffering with love.
—Buber, *Tales of the Hasidim*, bk. 1, *The Early Masters*

Rabbi Hanokh of Alexandrow said: People are always enjoying themselves—some days it's one person and other days it's another. No person is happy all the time.
—Klagsbrun, *Voices of Wisdom*

A greedy person yearns to get his mother's dowry.
If you live well and still want more, don't complain when trouble comes.
If you keep pressing your demands, you'll drill holes in your gut.
Those without patience have paper eyes.

—Ladino proverbs

CHAPTER 14

Inclining toward Good—*Yetzer ha-Tov*

God said to Cain, after rejecting his sacrifice: "Why are you so upset? And why is your face fallen? Isn't this the way things are: If you do good, you'll be elevated, and if you don't do what's good, remember that sin is always lying in wait for you at your door and eager to get you. But you, you can rule over it."

—Gen. 4:6–7

Why do human beings, uniquely equipped to do good, also do so much and such awful evil? We are badly conflicted: our angelic good impulse, our *yetzer ha-tov*, is constantly tempted by a lusty urge to do evil, *yetzer ha-ra*. Our spiritual sages reject a make-believe, everything-is-beautiful faith, insisting on a realistic understanding of human nature when they discuss the real traumas that people face. Yet as our hopeful opening text teaches, Jewish realism convinces us that God's help makes our good inclination supreme.

Historically, few themes in Jewish belief have seen such extreme shifts of emphasis as this notion of the two inner urges. In some eras Jewish teachers verged on total pessimism; in others they enthusiastically embraced an optimistic view of human potential. In our time, with its terrible examples of social and individual perversity, we struggle to comprehend why some of our "best and brightest" also show a clear talent for malevolence. Some of us despair of the future, while others remain hopeful. Let us survey historical Jewish highlights that explore how our two *yetzarim* have influenced Jewish character.

The Critical, Biblical Insights

The early chapters of Genesis deal with humanity's formative experiences, laying the background for later biblical texts presenting the same theological viewpoint. Cain discovers that merely offering a sacrifice will not assure him of God's favor: ". . . if you do not do right, sin couches at the door; its urge is toward you . . ." (Gen. 4:7). We might think that this somewhat stern admonition from God would resolve the good-versus-evil struggle so blatant in Cain. But what does Adam and Eve's oldest child do next? He suggests to his brother Abel that they go into the fields together, where "Cain rose up against his brother and killed Abel" (4:8). At first Cain's conscience must bother him, since he tries to evade God's inquiry about Abel's whereabouts. Yet his evil urge immediately reasserts itself, so that he actually "sasses" the Eternal through his infamous taunt: "Am I my brother's keeper?" (4:9). Thus sin triumphantly drives human history after Eden.

God does not punish Cain with death, but holds open the possibility that he may yet freely learn to control "that beast crouching at the door." What surprises us in this and other Genesis texts is that God, as well as humanity, needs to learn about freedom. The Torah dramatizes what God "discovers": how we, God's last created beings, will use our extraordinary potentials of self-consciousness and free will. Here are the "divine musings" imagined by biblical authors to explain the story of the flood: "*Adonai* saw how great was man's wickedness on the earth and how every plan he devised . . . was nothing but evil all the time. So *Adonai* regretted creating humankind on the earth, and was sad at heart" (Gen. 6:5–6). When the flood is over, God promises there will be no more catastrophes that destroy almost everyone and everything on earth. For what would be the point, since "from a man's youth all he does is think up evil" (Gen. 8:21)?

An Introduction to Rabbinic Psychology

Building on this biblical background, the rabbis provide a graphic parable of our inner struggle between good and evil: "The Bible tells us, 'Better is a poor and a wise child than an old and foolish king who cannot accept correction' [Eccles. 4:13]. The phrase 'a poor and wise child' refers to the *yetzer ha-tov,* the good urge. Why is it called 'wise'? Because it directs people onto the right paths. Why is it called 'poor'? Because not everyone pays attention to it. Why is it called a 'child'? Because the good urge doesn't emerge until a person becomes thirteen. The phrase 'an old and foolish king' refers to the *yetzer ha-ra,* the evil urge. Why is it called 'king'? Because all parts of the body heed it. Why is it called 'old'? Because it is part of a person from his youth through his old age, as the Torah says, 'For the disposition of a person's heart is evil from his youth' [Gen. 8:21], that is, from the time that he was expelled from his mother's womb. Why is it called 'foolish'? Because it directs people into evil ways" (Mid. Pss. 9.5).

Although our current studies of human development demand that we refine our understanding of such rabbinic generalizations, it is, nonetheless, sometimes unnerving to meet ourselves in their description of human behavior. Kids still "do the darndest things" without worrying about the consequences. And we adults often seem afflicted with a similar moral amnesia. Why else do we get flustered and agitated right before we do something we know we shouldn't?

"Heaven and Hell Can Both Be Had in This World" (Yiddish Proverb)

Our very humanness means we sometimes behave badly. Our teachers cared mightily that we live up to the high standards set by Jewish law and communal ideals. They couldn't easily rationalize how little good most of us actually do and how easily and regularly we fall into sin. Yet despite their unblinking look at how we actually behave, the rabbis remained optimistic, knowing that the Torah's positive influence upon our moral choices cannot be disputed: "I have put before you life and death, blessing and curse. Choose life—that you and your descendants may live!" (Deut. 30:19). They attributed our chronic sinning to the powerful nature of the evil urge, a foe so wily and untiring that it can never be permanently defeated. Nonetheless, the Torah's teaching is plain: with God's help we can ally ourselves with God's goodness and rule humanity's evil streak. One of our sages actually pictured us as schizoid, with the two *yetzarim* evenly split in their ability to dictate our actions: "As R. Levi taught: There are six parts of the body that serve a person; three are under his control and three are not. The eyes, the ears, and the nose are not under a person's control; he sees what he doesn't want to see, hears what he doesn't want to hear, and smells what he doesn't want to smell. The mouth, the hand, and the foot are under a person's control. If he wants he can use his mouth to study Torah or speak gossip and blasphemy. He can use his hand to give charity or steal and kill. He can use his feet to walk to synagogue or houses of study, or to brothels" (Gen. R. 67.3).

"When an Evildoer Looks in the Water, the Fish Die" (Yiddish Proverb)

As the age of the rabbis gave way to the medieval period in Jewish history, rabbinic hopefulness yielded to a more pessimistic view. Also true of much of western civilization at this time, a general darkening arose from the universally harsh lives most people lived. As Jewish history repeatedly testifies, dire economic and social circumstances result in tragic consequences. Searching for a scapegoat to vent their frustrations, Christian and Muslim majorities soon found all-too-familiar victims, the Jews. Informal segregation became legally sanctioned discrimination, then walled ghettos or isolating shtetls; occasional riots became expulsions lasting for decades, if not centuries. Life was hard in ways that we scarcely comprehend. Like others living at the same period, Jews began to see the natural world as more hostile than the rabbis had envisioned. Now demons lurked everywhere, seeking to tempt and destroy us; Gehenna waited for the sinner with such fearful torments that piety was often pursued with a sense of desperation.

For example, the Kabbalah, the esoteric teaching of the Zohar and later mystical texts, gave evil a cosmic status it had hardly known among the rabbis. In the kabbalistic view, God's reality in our world must be understood as operating on two levels. On one level, God is *Ein Sof,* the One with no limits, hence the One about which nothing at all can properly be said. Fortunately, on the other level, we *can* talk about God, as the Bible already indicates, with an extraordinary profusion of metaphors. The most abstract envisions the Divine as a dynamic system of ten emanations, the *sefirot* (literally, "the spheres"). In one major strand of kabbalistic teaching, these ten positive *sefirot* are matched by ten negative attributes of divine potency, conceptualized as the "Other Side," the *Sitra Aḥra*. The *Sitra Aḥra* employs demons and shades as its agents, bringing chaos and disorder into the world, making sinners of even the well intentioned. This doctrine explains why life is so full of dark experiences. But it also encouraged a certain religious passivity and dependency, for now evil was not merely an inner urge or a menacing external force, but a cosmically effective part of existence itself, an energy nearly as great as that of God and the holy *sefirot*.

Even sages whose ideas were not mainly kabbalistic reflected this sense of evil as nearly overpowering. Judah Loew, the sixteenth-century Prague rabbi known as the Maharal, is famous as the legendary creator of a golem, a Frankenstein-type creature whose sole purpose was to protect the Jews from their enemies. But Rabbi Loew was also an intellectual of the period, a major thinker and writer. This is what he said about the *yetzer ha-ra:* "The Evil Urge in people is the emptiness and absence which clings to all existing things. This nothingness strives to totally nullify a person. The Evil Urge is a negation which is Satan and the Angel of Death, for these cling to all things which exist" (*Tiferet Yisrael* [The book of divine power]). Toward the end of the eighteenth century, the Vilna sage Zevi Hirsch Kaidanover wrote a *musar* book filled with monstrous descriptions of the *yetzer ha-ra:* "O mortal man, if you knew how many demons of the *Sitra Aḥra* lurk for every drop of blood in man's heart, you would at once devote yourself to the service of God . . . (*Kav Hayashar* [An honest measure]).

Yet so strong was their faith in God's goodness and power that the sages of this era, despite their fearsome depiction of evil, still did not lose all hope. As the Vilna Gaon, the late-eighteenth-century Lithuanian teacher, wrote: "It is not in people's power to do more than begin the work. Its conclusion is brought by the help of God, who accompanies each person in fully completing the work" (*Kol Eliyahu* [Elijah's voice], Sukkah). Dark though life might be, most

Jews never totally surrendered to fatalism. Instead, they continued to find ways to believe that doing commandments would counteract evil forces. One of the Vilna Gaon's best known disciples was Rabbi Hayyim of Volozhin. Though usually a staunch advocate of the primacy of study, Rabbi Hayyim considered prayer the best weapon in the battle against the evil *yetzer.* "On rising every morning, one should say: 'Master of the Universe, I walk in the valley of darkness; save me from the Evil Impulse and save me from these sins'" *(Sefer Tosefet Ma'aseh Rav* [An additional book of the master's practices], She'iltot, 35, 36).

Yet anxiety over the power of evil in the world did not vanish with the dawning of modernity. While the charismatic nineteenth-century sage Israel Salanter was willing to learn the latest enlightened ideas of western civilization, the dark Jewish view of existence persisted in his writings. Though the Musar movement he founded linked modern psychological insight to classic Jewish teaching about human nature, he cautioned his followers: "A person's imagination leads him wildly in the direction of his heart's sinful desires, fearing not the inevitable future when God will hold him accountable for all his deeds" (*Iggeret Hamusar* [A letter about musar]).

Jewish Freedom Begets Jewish Optimism

With the French Revolution at the end of the eighteenth century, the emancipation of the Jews of western and central Europe began. Equality and citizenship came slowly and grudgingly, but the fact that they took place at all seemed almost miraculous to the Jews of the period. Wherever freedom was made available, Jews avidly took advantage of it. In the process, Jews radically transformed their view of human nature and its battle between good and evil.

. The society in which Jews enthusiastically immersed themselves was one of extraordinary economic expansion and cultural creativity, of scientific and technological triumph, and thus, of apparently well-founded optimism. Human initiative, not tradition or revelation, was credited for making all this possible and promised yet more. Human reason was viewed as the engine that empowered longer, fuller lives; if applied to great social problems, it was believed that reason would soon eliminate many of humankind's ancient ills. This certainly affected society's understanding of the evil that people did to each other. The problems we for so long blamed on the devil were really our own inability to shake our outmoded, self-imposed superstition and dimwittedness. Now that human progress had finally begun to show its genius, we saw evidence of its benefits everywhere.

Modern Jewry had special reasons to espouse the optimism embraced by the general society. In this new freedom we personally experienced the benefits of reason; we perceived our emancipation as a modern-day reenactment of that classic redemptive experience of the Jewish people, the Exodus from Egypt. Only this time the mighty hand and the outstretched arm were not God's but humanity's, acting through the new political and social order. Disproportionately, Jews became the prophets of education, culture, and social betterment. The *yetzer ha-ra* now seemed a nightmare of an impoverished premodern imagination; the *yetzer ha-tov* was seen as a primal aspect of modern rationality, as championed by the philosopher Immanuel Kant.

From early in the nineteenth century until the second half of the twentieth century, Jewish teachers proclaimed the essential goodness of human nature and the beneficent power of human reason. They seized whatever rabbinic evidence they could find to convince those few who still doubted that we ourselves had the means to overcome the evil urge. For instance, "R. Samuel b. Naḥman said: The words 'Behold, it was good' refer to the impulse to good, and the words 'Behold, it was very good' [Gen. 1:31] refer to the impulse to evil. But how can the impulse to evil be termed 'very good'? Extraordinary! However, were it not for the impulse to evil, a man would not build a house, take a wife, or beget children. As Solomon said, 'Again I considered all the labor and excellent work and found them to be the result of man's rivalry with his neighbor' [Eccles. 4:4]" (Gen. R. 9.5–11). Judaism now taught that by using our God-given human intelligence, we could harness even the evil urge in the service of the good.

Two Jewish Thinkers Capture This Optimism

The first internationally renowned Jewish philosopher, the German professor Hermann Cohen, gave this interpretation of Judaism academic respectability. His major treatise on Judaism, *Religion of Reason out of the Sources of Judaism,* indicates by its very name that modern thought should now determine what remained viable in Jewish faith. Radically departing from the late medieval Jewish view and trusting fully in what humanity could itself accomplish, Cohen wrote: "All human sin is error; it is wavering and vacillation. This is the basic meaning of the Hebrew word ḥet" (*Religion of Reason,* "Atonement"). No longer chained to an all-powerful evil beyond our control, we could rationally assess our shortcomings, admit our errors, and thus learn how to do better. Optimistically, we could look to each new day as yet more evidence that activism can overcome adversity.

In the United States, Mordecai Kaplan, the mid-twentieth-century advocate of reason and human initiative, similarly argued that sin is "the abuse of human freedom by the attempt of men to make their own interests and passions the sole determinants of their behavior" (*The Future of the American Jew*). Kaplan maintained that a significant exposure to education and culture, both American and Jewish, enabled people to fulfill their full potential for good. In this human-centered thinking, God should be imagined as everything in nature that aids individual and social improvement. Forsaking supernatural notions, we should become our own source of messianic aspiration, bringing salvation to this world.

The Loss of Optimism and the Return to Rabbinic Realism

This enthusiasm for the human ability to overcome evil, shared by most modern religious thinkers, was finally betrayed by the events of the middle decades of the twentieth century. Yet we should not be too hasty to condemn the surging optimism of a prior generation; we must not overlook the great good that was achieved. As a result of our "can-do" attitude, much of the world has enough to eat, and democracy and justice embrace ever more people. Free societies now increasingly recognize the genuine human dignity of their minorities, formerly considered outsiders. But we cannot ignore the fact that we still face complex and intractable problems. For even as we acknowledge the great good that we can do, we must also allow for the great evil that often accompanies radical progress unrestrained by morality.

The Jewish teaching that best explains our mixed character comes from the Talmud. Its sages demonstrate an uncanny prescience in insisting that the path toward doing good begins with admitting our genuine urge to do evil. For example, they affirm the insidious nature of the *yetzer ha-ra* by listing derogatory terms the Bible uses to describe this vice: "The evil one, the unclean one, the uncircumcised one, the enemy, the stumbling block, the stone, and the ambusher" (Suk. 52a). As R. Joshua b. Levi asserts, "We never outgrow the *yetzer ha-ra:* The evil inclination stays with a person from youth to old age. Day by day it seeks to overthrow him. Even if it must wait eighty years to find an opportunity to do so, it will not cease trying" (Tan. B. Beshallaḥ).

The *Yetzer ha-Ra*'s Strategies

Are these descriptions of the tenacity of the *yetzer ha-ra* foreign to us? We think not. Compare your own experiences to this observation of the sages: "The rabbis say: it desires only what is forbidden. On Yom Kippur, R. Mena went to visit R. Ḥaggai, who was ill. R. Ḥaggai said, 'I am thirsty.' R. Mena said, 'Drink.' Then he left. After an hour he returned and asked R. Ḥaggai, 'Are you still thirsty?' He replied, 'No sooner had you permitted me to drink than the desire left me'" (Yer. Yoma 6.4). Or consider the "wisdom" of this Yiddish proverb: "If it weren't for all the pretty girls, one could laugh at the Evil Urge," and this Ladino adage: "Don't trust strangers with either your store or your daughter."

Jewish tradition cautions us never to underestimate the wiles of the evil inclination: "Today he tells us, 'Do this.' Tomorrow he tells us, 'Worship idols,' and we do" (Shab. 105b). "In the beginning the evil inclination is as delicate as a spider web; later it becomes as sturdy as a cart rope" (Suk. 52a). Few of our rationalizations are as ineffective as "a little bit never hurt anyone" and "I can handle this"—

just ask any drug user. The rabbis warn us: "If the evil inclination says to you, 'Sin and God will forgive you,' don't believe it" (Ḥag. 16a). And adding cynicism to sinful action only increases the evil. Flirting with the limits of decency practically invites the *yetzer ha-ra* to take over: "Evil doesn't lurk at the margin of things, but walks around, right in the middle of the bustle. When it sees someone giving others the once-over, or continually preening, or strutting around, he says, 'You're mine now!'" (Gen. R. 22.12).

God, Our Partner in Fighting the *Yetzer ha-Ra*

Should such sobering realism about our evil tendencies threaten to deflate us, let us remember that the sages' optimism did not come from overreaching confidence in our *yetzer ha-tov;* they admitted its serious limitations. Rather, they knew that God, the source of our inner ambivalence, is also our ally in combating the evil inclination. The thirteenth-century mystic Judah the Pious spoke for generations of Jewish commentators when he offered the following comfort to his disciples: "Whenever a temptation to sin comes our way, we should reason: If they required me to convert, I would accept martyrdom. But if I can carry out so hard a commandment as that, how much the more so should I be able to not do this lesser act . . . and when we do this, God in heaven helps us" (Judah Heḥasid, *Sefer Ḥasidim,* 28). If we have learned anything from the "choiceless choices" our people faced during the Holocaust, it is that the human spirit is indeed limited in what it can do on its own to overcome evil.

Thus it is a comfort and a spur to action to remember that we are *not* alone in this struggle we call life. "R. Sinai said, the evil inclination may be compared to a rock standing at the crossroads. First people stumble over it. Then the King commands: chip it down, little by little, and when the time comes, I will remove it altogether" (P.R.K. 165a). God is our Maker and the source of our urges, for good and for ill. God accepts our honest defeats—sometimes more easily than we do. With the same mercy God showed in fashioning creation, God makes our fragmented selves whole once again. Judaism celebrates this partnership; God's help completes our humanity. As the prophet said: "Seek good and not evil that you may truly live and that *Adonai,* the God of hosts, may truly be with you . . ." (Amos 5:14).

From Our Tradition

Rabbi Dov Baer of Mezritch said: This is how our good inclination should rule over our character traits: We need to learn how to be proud—and not be proud; how to be angry—and not be angry; how to speak—and to remain quiet; how to be quiet—and to speak.

—Elkins, *Melodies from My Father's House*

Rava said: Though God created the evil inclination, God created the Torah as its antidote.

—B.B. 16a

In the world to come, *Adonai* will bring the evil inclination and slaughter it before the righteous and before the wicked. To the righteous it will appear as a great mountain; to the wicked it will appear as a strand of hair. The righteous will cry, and the wicked will cry. The righteous will say: How could we have conquered this great mountain? The wicked will say: How could we have not overcome this strand of hair?

—Suk. 52a

Why did Cain survive Abel? The Bible says, "'The Lord tries the righteous' [Ps. 11:5]. R. Elazar commented: 'A man had two cows, one strong and one weak. Upon which will he lay the yoke? Surely upon the strong.'"

—Gen. R. 32.3

Rabbi Yaakov Yosef of Polnoye warns: It is impossible that the good we do should ever be totally free of our self-interest.

—Jacob Joseph of Polnoye, *Toldot Yaakov Yosef*

All of history is a sphere where good is mixed with evil. The supreme task of man, his share in redeeming the work of creation, consists [of] . . . separating good from evil and evil from good.
      —Abraham Joshua Heschel, "Confusion of Good and Evil,"
                              in *The Insecurity of Freedom*

PART V

Facing the World

CHAPTER 15

Shamefacedness—*Boshet*

*P*raise can be as fleeting as a kind look, or as lasting as the engraving on a gold plaque. We smile with a certain interior satisfaction and stand a little straighter when we think of times when we've been honored. But human nature being what it is, we are far more likely to remember being chided for doing something wrong. Anyone who has ever been publicly dressed down—stripped naked of dignity and worth—can still feel the sting of that humiliation. Worse yet are wordless condemnations by someone we love—a parent, a spouse, or a friend. While those looks may not really kill, we certainly feel that something has died within us, perhaps just for now, perhaps for good.

Fortunately, reprimands often have their desired effect. They powerfully move us not to repeat the behavior that will inflict them. Since conscience and a sense of shame are closely linked in all societies, we all have found ways to avoid the awful sinking sense that comes with violating group standards. The Hebrew word for this psychic avoidance mechanism is *boshet*, whose English counterpart is the awkward "shamefacedness." Sadly, these days it is not a highly esteemed virtue. Indeed, many people believe that cultivating *boshet* inhibits them, laying the groundwork for neuroses or worse. Despite a measure of truth to this view, we are not ashamed to say up front that this chapter is our attempt—and Judaism's—to make a judicious amount of shamefacedness (hereafter, simply *boshet*) an integral part of our character.

187

Our Parents Teach Us *Boshet*

One needn't be a child psychologist to recognize that we get our fundamental sense of values from our parents. Even if they are wonderfully loving types, they still manage to inculcate a sense of shame in us—simply put, we love them, so we want to please them. And long before words shape our communication with them, we feel rotten if we fail to meet their standards. Since we don't want to feel ashamed before our parents, we usually try to resist temptation and do the good.

This lifelong desire lies behind *kever avot,* the custom of visiting our parents' graves during the month before Rosh Hashanah. Standing there, we remember all that they expected of us, so we keep their memories alive by rendering an account of what we have done in the past year. No matter how long they have been gone, they still share God's role in judging us. Even now, when we can no longer claim youth or inexperience as an excuse, we still don't want to appear unworthy before them. So we more or less intuit their familiar prodding and promise to do better. The rabbis tell us that this was the reason Moses declined God's offer to make a great Jewish nation from only his family. They sense Moses explaining: "I would be ashamed before my ancestors who would then complain, 'See what a leader God set over them. He only sought greatness for himself'" (Ber. 32a).

Boshet in the Classroom

If our parents are the primary source of our *boshet,* surely the next most significant influences upon us are our teachers and classmates. The Greek philosopher Aristotle, who tutored Alexander the Great in the fourth century B.C.E., taught that the people before whom we feel shame are those whose opinion is important to us *(On Rhetoric).* Since going to school means being judged, our teachers and our peers figure prominently in shaping our value systems. Most of us can easily recall the memory of at least one teacher who served as our role model, thus significantly influencing the kind of person we were determined to be. As medieval *musar* put it: "If you would acquire *boshet,* study with a rav in whose mere presence you are already a bit ashamed" *(Orḥot Tzaddikim)*. However, other Jewish sages are more sensitive to our feelings. Maimonides interprets the adage from Pirke Avot that "A bashful person cannot learn" [2.6] as urging us not to let brilliant classmates make us feel inferior. He counsels us not to feel ashamed if we need to hear a lesson several times before we truly understand it, while the class stars seem to grasp it almost before the words leave the teacher's mouth (M.T., Sefer Hamada, 4.5). And though our teachers (like our parents) may be very wise, they are not infallible. So what should students do if they catch the teacher saying something contrary to the Torah? Judah the Pious, the thirteenth-century Franco-German sage, suggests that students not challenge their teacher directly because, in an unhappy reversal of roles, it would likely cause the teacher intense embarrassment. Instead, they should quietly inform the teacher's best friend, who can be trusted to discreetly convey the information to the teacher (Judah Heḥasid, *Sefer Ḥasidim*, 139).

Communal *Boshet*

As we grow and our horizons expand, so do the groups whose judgment we seek for approval. What once was largely a matter of family and school extends to include community, nation, and humanity as a whole. We would be unhappy if "they"—any of these groups with which we identify—find our behavior repellent. This explains why those who become part of a deviant group seem defiantly proud of behavior that the rest of us find appalling. Today's hoodlums are in this respect no different from these shameless souls: "People who get together to steal a beam and feel no shame in the presence of one another" (Kid. 80b). Hundreds of years later, the folk wisdom of the Sephardic community gave us this pithy maxim, describing similar ne'er-do-wells as those shameless thieves in the Talmud: "Dirt doesn't acquire stains" (Ladino proverb). Living in communities whose high standards reflect our own thus becomes an important part of creating Jewish character. Of course Jewish values, shaped by biblical and rabbinic traditions, have been refined by centuries of diverse experiences. Yet the ethos of the traditional Jewish community always meant a good deal to individual Jews.

Various biblical texts have taught that, while societies may set the standard for their members, they themselves stand under the judgment of God. The prophets regularly indicted their community for failing to live up to its responsibilities under the covenant. They taught that with the proper amount of *boshet* we can turn from evil and do good, a message with almost no parallels in the history of world religion. A wave of recrimination was set off in 70 C.E., when Jerusalem was conquered and the Temple destroyed, not so much against the Roman oppressors as against the Jewish people as a whole for its wickedness: "R. Ulla said, Jerusalem was destroyed only because its inhabitants had no shame before one another: 'They shall be put to shame because they have committed abomination. They are not at all ashamed, neither know they how to blush, therefore shall they fall among the casualties' [Jer. 6:15]" (Shab. 119b). This lesson has total relevance in our time, in which shamelessly proclaiming one's innocence often is an automatic first pleading, merely a prelude to being found guilty.

What Does a Jewish Sense of Shame Look Like?

While significant to the moral shaping of groups, *boshet*—a sensitivity to the judgment of worthy others—has long been a defining quality of the Jewish self. Yeḥiel b. Yekutiel, the thirteenth-century Roman ethicist, characterizes *boshet*'s essence as an ability to conduct ourselves in an unpretentious, introspective manner *(Sefer Maalot Hamiddot)*. It reflects our continued concern with how others view our behavior. Since we are determined to avoid being shamed, we find that a major consequence of *boshet* involves treating others with respect, even if we disagree with them on critical issues. It teaches us that any public shaming of our neighbor is a horrendous evil. To guide us in this regard, the rabbis point to the Torah's stories about Tamar and Joseph in which both characters refuse to put others to shame.

Condemned to death for apparent harlotry, Tamar will not identify her father-in-law Judah as the man who made her pregnant. This is the rabbinic interpretation of Tamar's reasoning: "If he confesses, well and good, but if not, I would rather die than put him to shame by publicly acknowledging him as the father of my unborn child." Judah soon admits Tamar's innocence, declaring: "She is more righteous than I"—a stunning praise of her character [Gen. 38:25–26]. At the end of the story of Joseph and his brothers, we read that when Joseph finally has them in his power, he tells his servants: "All of you leave my presence" [Gen. 45:1]. Only then does Joseph reveal his identity. True, he had just accused the brothers of both robbery and espionage. But these accusations pale when compared to the public shame Joseph would have caused his siblings if he publicly revealed that they once sold him into slavery. Joseph risks their fright and possible retaliation rather than publicly humiliating them (Tan. Vayiggash 5).

Yet in their realism, the rabbis demanded that we balance these examples of idealized action with the Torah's commandment to reprove our neighbor who has behaved unacceptably. It would be shameless of us, and imply that we do not really care about certain values, were we to say nothing and let the other person continue acting badly. Since giving and hearing criticism are not easy for either party, the author of *Orḥot Tzaddikim* sensitively suggests that we reprove our friend in private, very gently. And should these best-intended remarks evoke shame, and our friend responds defensively by verbally attacking us, we should not answer back in kind. People being what they are, reproof has always been one of the hardest disciplines to accept. Even today, when we are supposed to be open to people's "different strokes," relationships require very delicate maneuvering, for shame is a supremely powerful force.

The Anguish of Being Shamed

The rabbis tell us that the mental torment of shame is worse than physical pain (Sot. 8b). Physical pain generally diminishes as, in its own way, does its memory—otherwise few women would bear more than one child. Nonetheless, it is remarkable how long our public humiliations continue erupting into our consciousness; some people can never put these incidents fully behind them. Thus the rabbis never belittled the physical displays of shame. It is an uncontrollable part of a person's physiology to blush when embarrassed and wonder if our face resembles a tomato. If truly mortified we blanch, turning "pale as a ghost." Indeed, among the hopes that the prophet Isaiah extended to our people was the coming of a day when "Jacob shall no longer be ashamed, neither shall his face go pale" (29:22).

The rabbis saw in this sudden loss of blood a type of public death, the person who inflicts public humiliation is, metaphorically, a murderer. "R. Naḥman b. Isaac said: 'I have seen how public shaming can cause even a ruddy complexion to give way to a pale, white face.' Abaye asked R. Dimi (who often traveled from the Land of Israel to Babylonia and back), 'What do people in the West most carefully seek to avoid?' R. Dimi replied, 'Saying anything that would cause the blood to rush from someone's face'" (B.M. 58b). Later in the same tractate we read: "One who shames his fellow in public is guilty of a sin so terrible that he will not be among those whom God eventually takes up out of Gehenna" (B.M. 59a).

One Jewish teacher has suggested that the Hebrew word *"ḥasid,"* one who is pious, comes from a root whose meaning is the color white *(Orḥot Tzaddikim)*. In the hyperbolic writings of our commentators, someone who is especially devoted to fulfilling the Torah actually has a measure of whiteness, or pallor in his face, a sign that he is always worried about inadvertently sinning and thereby being ashamed before God. Even if the Hasid has done nothing wrong, he will take a measure of shame on himself, reminding him not to do anything that might bring on a true physical change.

Boshet Includes the Sensitivity Not to Embarrass Others

Because of the cruel psychological wounds inflicted by thoughtless words, the rabbis warn us that certain topics should be off-limits if they cause people shame. One talmudic discussion specifies the issues that wound: "If a man has repented his former sins, don't talk about what he once did. If he is the son of a convert, he must not be taunted with: 'Remember the deeds of your ancestors.' If a convert comes to study the Torah, one must not say to him, 'Shall the mouth that ate unclean and forbidden food, abominable and creeping things, come to study Torah, which came from the mouth of

God?' If someone is afflicted with suffering, or taken ill, or has buried a child, don't speak to him as his companions thoughtlessly spoke to Job, 'Remember, no one ever perished who was innocent' [Job 4:7]" (B.M. 58b).

Though everyone is born with the dignity of being created in God's image, when we put to shame the socially or politically prominent, we doubly betray this divine spark and dishonor God. Our rabbis felt so keenly that they specifically addressed this type of degradation when assessing the financial penalty for this offense. "All of the compensation is to be estimated in accordance with the status of the offender and the offended. . . . If, along with whatever else happened, a person of great honor and dignity is shamed by the event, then his resulting shame is greater than that of the average person in the same situation" (B.K. 86a–b). Spitting in someone's face is embarrassing enough, particularly if done in public. But if you do it to a dignitary, you insult the office as well as the person occupying it, causing a public outcry.

Here are two stories of people our tradition esteemed for going out of their way to avoid humiliating others: "Once R. Gamaliel II said: 'Send seven scholars to the upper chamber early in the morning and we will set up the calendar of the year.' When he got there he found eight. 'Whoever came without permission must leave,' he announced. Samuel the Little stood and said, 'I am the one who came without permission, not to fix the calendar but to learn the law.' 'Sit down, my son,' said Rabban Gamaliel. 'You may stay . . . but the law is that only those specifically appointed for determining the calendar at a given time may participate.' In reality, it was not Samuel the Little who had not been invited, but another scholar. Samuel had taken the blame upon himself to save the other from embarrassment" (San. 11a).

"A hasid entered the synagogue of Rabbi Wolf Zbarrazer one Sabbath afternoon, took his seat, and began to eat radishes, loudly smacking his lips. Other hasidim whispered to him to stop, fearing that the noise might disturb the Rabbi's meditations. Nevertheless, he continued his uncouth eating. Rabbi Wolf heard the whispering and observed that the hasid's face was turning red. So he said, 'I feel a craving for radishes. Has anyone got any radishes?'" (Newman, *The Hasidic Anthology*).

Because shame is so powerful an emotion, prior generations regularly made it their chief means of discipline, particularly when they stopped using physical punishment. Teachers would put naughty children in the corner and make them wear "dunce caps"; their vengeful classmates often made the punishment worse by inflicting additional torments. While today's youth have devised more contemporary but similarly cruel ways to inflict pain on their victims, they continue to hurt not only those who actually suffer it, but those who watch in their own silent misery. For shame is a poor teacher; reward and repetition are far more effective teaching tools than simply punishing a wrongdoer. Then, too, the accompanying trauma may so encumber us that it stifles our initiative and denies us life's normal pleasures. And when we think about downright silly consequences of misplaced shame—the embarrassment people feel for not having the right body shape, for example—*boshet* would seem to have no place in the life of a healthy-minded, mature person.

The Decline of *Boshet* in Our Time

One result has been a real effort by some people to rid us of any sense of shame at all. Many parents seem obsessed with giving their children a life without stress, doing whatever it takes to keep their children "happy." Others seem willing to endure just about any behavior in the name of tolerance. And, as we often learn these days, there are those who feel that a certain amount of money, power, or prestige entitles them to live by their own rules. In recent years, many public figures accused of breaking the law have paraded before television cameras without a trace of shame, assuring huge viewing audiences (and themselves) that they will be found innocent.

Surely the classic case is that of real estate zillionaire Leona Helmsley, who didn't pay a couple of million dollars of federal income tax since, as she demurred, "Taxes are for little people." What made her case so egregious was the repeated testimony of former employees. They described her arrogant combination of cheap chiseling and brazen shamelessness, as she screamed obscenities at them for not doing her bidding. After being found guilty and serving a reduced jail term, Helmsley was released with the condition that she perform several hundred hours of community service; however, she soon found ways to avoid even this punishment by ordering her employees to do it in her stead. She has never shown the slightest indication of remorse, but is one of many who confirm Jeremiah's observation about those who flout the law: "They have acted shamefully and have done abhorrent things, yet they cannot even be made to blush" (6:15).

Reclaiming *Boshet*

Psychotherapists have now identified a major psychic ill that Freud's uptight Vienna could not have imagined: people lacking moral boundaries, delighting in behavior totally devoid of standards. Today, those who seek therapy are far more likely to suffer from a lack of limits, thus depriving themselves of a solid sense of self, than from a guilt so punishing that they cannot "get a life." We need organizations such as Tough Love to assist parents in facing their child's shameless behavior. These groups help parents establish rules that a child must accept or no longer find a welcome in the family home. We see something similar in our tougher public attitude toward people who brazenly continue to break the law. Many states now require offenders to serve automatic jail sentences if they are found guilty of repeating the same crime.

Yet neither a self-punishing shamefacedness nor a libertine shamelessness can give us the lives and social order our tradition has taught us to demand. So we are not ashamed to say that a good measure of *boshet* must once again find a place in the worthy Jewish life. The possibility of being ashamed may keep us honest and worthy: "Love that friend who clearly shows that he cannot do without your help, even though you need his help more than he needs yours; the one who forgives you if you wrong him in such a manner that it would appear that he was in the wrong; and the one who asks of you things he does not need, in order that you will not be embarrassed to ask for things that you truly need" *(Orḥot Tzaddikim)*.

From Our Tradition

Once Rabbi Zusya came to an inn, and on the forehead of the innkeeper he saw long years of sin. For a while he neither spoke or moved. But when he was alone in the room which had been assigned to him, the shuddering of vicarious experience overcame him in the midst of singing psalms and he cried aloud: "Zusya, Zusya, you wicked man! What have you done! There is no lie that failed to tempt you, and no crime you have not committed. Zusya, foolish, erring man, what will be the end of this?" Then he recited the sins of the innkeeper, giving the time and place of each as his own, and sobbed. The innkeeper had quietly followed Zusya, and heard his strange outbursts. First the innkeeper was seized with dismay, but then penitence and grace were lit within him, and he woke to God.

—Buber, *Tales of the Hasidim,* bk. 1, *The Early Masters*

The sign of good children is discernible on their faces.

—Yev. 79a

People eat up the bashful without bothering to say a *berakhah.*

—Iraqi Jewish proverb

A person who studies midrash, halakhah, and aggadah, but has no fear of sin, is left with empty hands. It can be compared to a man who said to his friend, "I have a thousand measures of grain, a thousand of oil, and a thousand of wine." His friend asked, "Have you store-chambers in which to keep them? If you have, all those things are yours; but if you have not, then you have nothing."

—Exod. R. 30.14

When R. Yohanan b. Zakkai fell mortally ill, his disciples came to visit him. . . . They said to him: "Master, bless us." He said to them: "May it be God's will that the fear of Heaven shall be upon you as is the fear of flesh and blood." His disciples said to him: "Is that all?"

He said to them: "Would that you could attain this level of piety. You can see how important is this fear of people. When someone prepares to commit a sin he says, 'I hope no one will see me.'"

—Ber. 28b

Ratzon

*W*hy is this chapter different from all other chapters? In all other chapters we are "up front" about the English equivalent of the virtue we're discussing. But in this case, we admit we're stumped. All the English translations we've considered seem woefully inadequate, giving truth to the Italian proverb, "Traduttore, traditore" (all translators are traitors). With *ratzon,* as with many other Hebrew words, we're not referring to one idea but to a whole group. For example, does the word *barukh* mean "blessed" or "praised," or both at once? Is *tzedakah* "righteousness" or "charity," or a mix of them, with all sorts of overtones? *Ratzon* seems to us an even more complicated case. So we're simply going to leave it in Hebrew and take you on a tour of its fourteen implications. Fortunately we can bunch these in three categories: *ratzon* as manner; *ratzon* as defense; and *ratzon* as strategy. But first we'll try to explain the basic problem that *ratzon* addresses.

Life after Eden: "I Never Promised You a Rose Garden"

Rodney King's cry during the Los Angeles riots some years back plaintively states the problem: "Why can't we all get along?" That question is a plea for more *ratzon* in our society. Nice people that most of us are—and are trained to be—we try to face the world with good will and expect everyone else to be similarly nurturing. So we are badly shaken when we encounter massive indifference, niggling pettiness, or downright nastiness from others, not to mention from ourselves. Freud explained the problem we have living together in simple terms. Analyzing what drives people, he saw that not just love, but aggression powers everything we do.

If that seems too pessimistic a view of human nature, let us test this theory in that great psychology laboratory, the American highway. Even normally calm people can get a little crazy when they drive. Let some hotshot cut them off, or steal their parking space, or suddenly make a left turn from the far-right lane, and as the Yiddish proverb puts it, "they become the color of plums and red meat." If they manage to remain rational, they merely mutter, usually not softly, "What is that #$&x*! doing?" Some people totally lose control, causing fender-benders climaxing in two livid people screaming at each other. In the most tragic cases, one driver grabs a gun and shoots his antagonist. Alas, ours is an age in which people kill each other for even a jacket or a pair of sneakers.

When Anger Overcomes *Ratzon*

The Bible knows the dangers of hostility well. "My eyes dimmed with anger," Job says (17:7), and the Psalmist goes further, saying, "My eyes are wasted by vexation" (6:8). As we all know, it is possible to get so angry that we can't even see straight. The rabbis conclude logically: "Consider one who tears his clothing, or breaks his vessels, or scatters his money in his anger an idolater" (Shab. 105b). "R. Yohanan said in the name of R. Yose: From what verse in the Torah did R. Simeon b. Eleazar derive his teaching that we must not try to placate a man in the time of his anger? [Avot 4.23]. From Exodus 33:14, where it is written: 'My wrathful face will go and then I will give you rest'" (Ber. 7a). Today children are taught that when they find themselves "losing it," they need to take some "time out" and retreat to a quiet place to calm down. If not, as Yehiel b. Yekutiel says, irritability leaves its residue everywhere: "Whatever a woman weaves, falls on her spindle; whatever the pot boils, spills on its sides; whatever one spits on high, comes down on his face" *(Sefer Maalot Hamiddot)*. Trying to find security in the growing turbulence of twelfth-century Spain, Judah ibn Tibbon wrote to his son: "Contend not with men, and meddle not in strife not your own. Enter into no dispute with the obstinate, not even on matters of Torah interpretation. Even when you are convinced you are in the right, never try to make your case by subterfuge" *(Hebrew Ethical Wills)*.

What anger does to individuals it also does to societies. An uneasy truce can degenerate into ghastly war. Maimonides notes, "I have seen the white become black, families smitten sorely, great cities destroyed . . . all because of contention. Prophets have prophesied, sages have spoken wise words, all have expanded on the evils of factionalism without exhausting the subject" *(Hebrew Ethical Wills)*. In the former Yugoslavia, ethnically and religiously diverse peoples lived together in peace for centuries. Then, for reasons still unclear, they turned against each other with unchecked fury. Our sages have compared such strife to "a kettle on coals. So long as it is not boiling, no one knows what it contains. Once it starts boiling, it spills its contents and everyone knows what is in it" (Yehiel b. Yekutiel, *Sefer Maalot Hamiddot)*. Perhaps we Jews, like many minority peoples, have a heightened sensitivity for the destruction that political chaos can cause. Too often in the past, we have been the victims of national disorder and violence.

Freud was right: the world quivers with animosity! Therefore, it is simple self-preservation to learn how to encourage the good will of others as we go about our everyday routines. *Ratzon* is the Jewish art of living defensively. And now, we are ready to begin our tour.

Ratzon as Manner: "In General, Be Acceptable to People" (*Torah Lishmah*)

Living in close proximity to one another, as Jews did until recent times, Rabbi Ḥayyim of Volozhin, the late-eighteenth-century author of *Torah Lishmah* (Torah for its own sake), knew the importance of making the irksome routine of life more bearable. He would agree with our first characteristic: someone who embodies *ratzon* works hard at being congenial. Second, *ratzon* implies cultivating an easy-going nature. Rabbi Ḥayyim offers specific examples: "Always be the first to extend greetings to others, and respond to them calmly." Perhaps he had this maxim from Ecclesiastes in mind: "The words of the wise can be heard in calm" (9:17). Living in the

New York area as we both do, we are often told by friends who have moved elsewhere that people "there" are so pleasant. If the reputation of New Yorkers carries any truth, those of us still "here" could all use a major dose of such *ratzon!*

This leads us to a third characteristic of *ratzon*, showing good will to others. Instead of being quick with a rebuke, the person of *ratzon* knows when to "sit on his indignation and conciliate the other person with soft, sweet words spoken with care" (Yeḥiel b. Yekutiel, *Sefer Maalot Hamiddot*). Two Yiddish proverbs vividly capture this idea: "A kind word is better than a stick" and "A wicked tongue is worse than an evil hand." We are to be friendly, even when trying to change someone's behavior. The hasidic master Rabbi Mordechai of Lechovitz teaches: "Friendship is like a stone. A stone has no value, but when you rub two stones together properly, sparks of fire emerge" (Elkins, *Melodies from My Father's House*).

This takes us to *ratzon*'s fourth meaning, being amiable, which involves more than being pleasant or merely doing the acceptable thing. For while a Ladino proverb rather glibly announces: "If you want to make people happy, show them a happy face," a Yiddish proverb reminds us that "One hand washes the other (and both wash the face)." Our fifth aspect of *ratzon* involves having a soft tongue and speaking gently to others. As the Book of Proverbs advises: "A healing tongue is a tree of life, but a devious one makes for a broken spirit" (Prov. 15:4). Where Yiddish maxims say: "A kind word is better than alms" and "A gentle word can break a bone," Americans say, "Honey is more effective than vinegar." Naḥmanides, the thirteenth-century philosopher-sage, states our goal plainly: "Accustom yourself to speak gently to all men, at all times" *(Hebrew Ethical Wills)*.

Meaning number six, be obliging, finds its echo in Yeḥiel b. Yekutiel's idealistic vision: "If one has an obliging mind, his life is good, his joy is constant, and he is not bowed down by adversity" *(Sefer Maalot Hamiddot)*. He also quotes a non-Jewish adage with approval: "One who willingly undertakes responsibility will be obliging when carrying it through." Not surprisingly, *ratzon* as manner thus includes being available to other people. The eighteenth-century sage Elijah, the famous Gaon of Vilna, interprets the rabbinic statement: "Be humble and affable to all persons, particularly to your household" (D.E.Z. 3.5) as counseling us to combine authority with approachability: "The aim of the Torah, in large part, is to induce us to want to cause happiness. Let there be no dissension in our households, men and women, but let love and brotherliness reign. Be lowly of spirit with everyone, but with members of your household even more than with others. If you grumble and fight with your family, your end is for Gehenna" *(Hebrew Ethical Wills)*. A good dose of *ratzon* can keep a silly family squabble from becoming an unbreachable lifetime rift.

Ratzon as a Defense: "You Won't Get Far with Anger" (Yiddish Proverb)

Emotions act something like a Newtonian law of motion: every display of anger against us incites an equal and opposing urge to be angry back. And since there is so much hostility around, one can live one's life as a continual series of indignant explosions. Learning to control anger after being provoked thus becomes a major component of *ratzon*. At its simplest, we should be even-tempered in the face of anger or disdain. Obviously, human nature has changed little since the rabbis included these descriptions of character in Pirke Avot: "There are four types of human temperament: (1) one is quick to anger but easy to appease—here the gain overrides the loss; (2) one is slow to anger and hard to appease—now the loss overrides the gain; (3) one is slow to anger and easy to appease—that's saintly; (4) one is quick to anger but hard to appease—which is downright wicked" (Avot 5.11).

One needn't be a sage to realize that it takes quite an effort to persevere after being insulted. Once again, we look to Rabbi Ḥayyim for sound, if rigorous advice: "Never allow enmity toward another to enter your heart, and by all means never answer someone with impatience. For tolerance enables one to accomplish far more than all the harshness in the world" *(Torah Lishmah)*. As Yiddish folk wisdom knows: "With patience you can even bore through granite," and the Ladino adage concurs: "Nothing can withstand good will."

The third aspect of *ratzon* in this category, being conciliatory to others who are hostile, seems more difficult to acquire than patience, for it asks us to go beyond passive forbearance. The platitude, "mountains cannot meet, but people can" seems unrealistic. It urges us to take the initiative in conciliating those who really mean to hurt and insult us. But if we are trying to bring even a touch of redemption into the ordinary, this is precisely what we need to do: "The Gastiner Rabbi made it a rule never to express his displeasure with anyone on the day when that person had offended him. On the next day he would more calmly say, 'You know, I was displeased with you yesterday'" (Newman, *The Hasidic Anthology*). The comparable Ladino adage suggests a less saintly pattern of delay: "Before getting angry, count to one hundred."

Our fourth and last entry for this section, be easily appeased, often is simply beyond us. We find ourselves saying, with more than a tinge of venom in our voice, "I'll forgive, but I won't forget!" Yet this unwillingness to let go of memory can easily turn into hard-heartedness, and a little self-pity. The rabbis are quite firm about our need to genuinely forgive: "One should be as soft as a reed and not as hard as a cedar" (Taan. 20b). R. Neḥunya b. Hakanah is commended for never going to bed without reconciling with his business associates (Meg. 28a). Yeḥiel b. Yekutiel wants us to go a step further, asking us to "apologize to our friends even before they ask forgiveness of us" *(Sefer Maalot Hamiddot)*. Granted, our sages are demanding a lot. Nonetheless, by finding the *ratzon* to end the build-up of anger and hostility, perhaps we can bring a redemptive touch to our everyday lives.

Ratzon as Strategy: "Many Smiles, Few Wiles" (Yiddish Proverb)

Our first pattern of *ratzon* discussed manner, living with everyday pleasantness, and the second was defensive, being conciliatory despite the slights of social existence. The third is strategic, acting to win the favor of others. Here, the biblical hero Mordecai and his cousin Esther can serve as our models, since each knew the value of being deferential. Mordecai advises his beautiful ward how to practice *ratzon* in her dealings with the Persian nobility. First, he tells Esther to enter King Ahashuerus's "New Queen Beauty Pageant."

Then, after she wins, Mordecai counsels her to avoid the ever-present prejudice at the court by not telling anyone she is Jewish. When he overhears a plot on the king's life, Mordecai tells Esther to warn Ahashuerus, thereby becoming known as a trusted subject. And Mordecai knows when it is time to change to bolder tactics, thwarting Haman's plan to annihilate the Jews. Now Esther must go to Ahashuerus, though he has not summoned her to the throne room for thirty days. Entering unbidden is a serious breach of court etiquette, punishable by death. Fortunately, the king is happy to see his beautiful queen and eager to attend the dinners she has planned. Her double-banquet strategy makes her even more beloved by the king, who lovingly listens to Esther, indignantly kills Haman, and righteously saves the Jews. Mordecai then is made a noble himself. He is described in a way not used anywhere else in the Bible: "For Mordecai the Jew ranked next to King Ahashuerus. He was highly regarded by the Jews and *ratzui* to the multitude of his people [they liked Mordecai, or as recent translators have it, he was 'popular' with many of them (*sic*)]" (Est. 10:3).

Few means of winning others' favor are as effective as simply listening to them. So God, the Bible tells us, wishes we would pay more attention to what God says. No other biblical command packs the sustained power of "Hear, O Israel . . ." A recurrent complaint of our prophets is that our biblical ancestors consistently failed to do so. The midrashic collection Exodus Rabbah uses medicine as a metaphor to restate this theme. "When someone falls from a roof and bruises himself, the doctor puts bandages all over him. But God can heal the whole body with only one bandage. And what is it? Listening carefully. The prophet Isaiah says: 'Incline your ear and come to me. Hear and your soul shall live' [Isa. 55:3]" (Exod. R. 27.9). As the anonymous author of the sixteenth-century work *Orḥot Tzaddikim* writes, "There is nothing as good in all the world as listening."

This ancient focus on ingratiating ourselves to God by attending to God's truth has been transformed in our own time; today's more human-centered society emphasizes the value of serious listening to encourage relationships. One of life's continual annoyances is that others simply don't listen to what we say to them. Since what we say is important to us, we find this failure deeply disturbing. And when people protest that we aren't paying attention to them—spouses and teen-agers being the most common sufferers—it doesn't seem to help when we simply repeat what they said to us. They don't want us just to hear their words; they want us to pay attention to the person saying them, the one whose life gives those words their special meaning. Martin Buber's famous theory of the I/Thou relationship explains the crucial difference between surface listening and genuine attention. What Buber calls for is even deeper and more comprehensive. Few things make us feel so understood as when people open up to us and hear the full dimensions of all we are trying to express.

But Should We Go as Far as Flattery?

Many people believe that if we want people to think well of us, we must practice the art of flattery, for the truth is that most people don't feel properly appreciated. The skillful flatterer—and some people are so needy that we can just about eliminate the finesse of subtlety—helps to convince them that's not so. However, buttering up people usually means moving beyond honesty. How far should we go to win the favor of others? Should we lie? Suddenly we face two conflicting rabbinic values: ingratiating oneself with others and telling the truth. What should the caring Jew do?

In matters of *musar,* our sages don't offer clear-cut guidelines that help us choose correctly in specific cases. Individual temperament and the human situation vary too greatly for that. Instead, our ethical teachers have left us a maze of differing opinions; we acquire wisdom in learning how to find our way through them. In the case of flattery, however, a specific path is mandated. We read in Numbers 35:33: "Don't profane or (spiritually) pollute, *taḥanifu,* the land in which you live." Since the word for flattery, *ḥanufah,* comes from the same root, *ḥ-n-f,* as *taḥanifu,* the rabbis rule that this biblical commandment prohibits verbal insincerity as well as profane actions.

The midrash to the Book of Psalms demonstrates further the rabbis' revulsion at verbal deception. "R. Ḥiyya taught: Hypocrites may be exposed publicly to prevent a profanation of God's name. . . . But why does God allow people to sin publicly? In order that, when a misfortune occurs to the flatterer due to his wickedness, people should not blame God" (Mid. Pss. 52.3). "Four kinds of people do not see the face of the Shekhinah: the mockers, the hypocrites, the slanderers, and the liars" (Mid. Pss. 101.3). Thus *aggadah,* non-legal rabbinic lore, backs up *halakhah,* talmudic law, in its condemnation of flattery.

Life's Practicalities: When Flattery Is Permitted

So much for idealism. But realism, then as now, demands that we occasionally kowtow to important people. Certainly in a day when rulers held the power of life and death over their subjects, flattery was regarded as permissible, even reasonable. Consider the classic case recounted in the Mishnah. Agrippa, whom the Romans appointed king of Judea in the first century C.E., was the grandson of Herod the Idumean (a nation forcibly converted to Judaism) and his Jewish wife, Mariamne. Once during Sukkot, Agrippa read from the Torah to the people assembled in the Temple courtyard. "When he reached the words: 'As king, you must appoint one of your Jewish kin,' Agrippa's eyes overflowed with tears. The people then shouted to him, 'Fear not, Agrippa, you are our brother, you are our brother.' But because of this flattery, certain talmudic sages said, Jerusalem was later destroyed" (Sot. 41a).

The Bible recounts another story about acceptable flattery: the patriarch Jacob's return to Canaan. After working for his father-in-law Laban for more than 20 years, Jacob finally is coming home. As he comes near to where he was raised, his scouts tell him that his brother Esau approaches with a retinue of 400 armed men. Jacob has not seen Esau since robbing him of his proper blessing. He so fears this reunion that he worries for his children's lives, taking elaborate measures to safeguard them. Yet when the brothers finally meet, Jacob unblushingly tells Esau, "To see your face is like seeing the face of God" (Gen. 32:8–9, 33:10).

In other words, if we perceive a situation to be life-threatening, then flattery—like almost everything else prohibited in Jewish law—is momentarily permitted. Over the centuries, various halakhists have posed more scenarios that permit flattery, including threats to one's body or one's assets. At the same time, they have suggested strategies to avoid lying: For instance, if you perceive a wrongdoing but decide not to protest, then try to say nothing at all. Or if you must speak up, limit yourself to the truth, even if that involves some exaggeration. Furthermore, if it is customary in your society to honor powerful people, follow the usual rites of homage, such as inquiring solicitously about their well-being. One authority goes so far as to say that necessary flattery is permitted in *this* world, since the Bible states only that it is eliminated in the world to come (*Entziklopediyah Talmudit*, s.v. "Ḥanufah").

Thus with regard to flattery, even Jewish law doesn't try to give us ironclad, inflexible rules. The rabbis who formed our legal tradition knew that some areas must be left to personal discretion. Today, our congregational rabbi is available to give us counsel. So, too, is the literature of guidance created by our musarists. And we can also look to oral folk wisdom, like the Ladino adage that warns us: "Everyone's friend is no one's friend."

Models for Our Behavior

Is there any public figure who has mastered the precarious tightrope walk between unstinting truth-telling and insincere ingratiation? In our culture we seem fated to choose between two extremes—between one whose lips seem sculpted into a perpetual smile, whose words are always upbeat and "have-a-nice-dayish," on the one hand, and on the other, the "boss," the street-smart, hardboiled survivor who is political in the worst sense of the term.

However, we can offer an unambiguous example of what a person of *ratzon* should not be—Oscar the Grouch, the famous trash can "resident" of "Sesame Street"! Nothing is ever right for him. He can turn anything pleasant into a new reason to be miserable. As our own tradition predicts: "One who doesn't know how to be happy when young won't even find the world to come satisfying" (Ladino proverb). When we look for a responsible balance between getting along well with others and standing up for our ideals, perhaps the best strategy is to think of what Oscar the Grouch would say, and then say the opposite!

Jews of medieval times (and even some in our own day) sought to guide their children by writing ethical wills. In these documents, the authors share their wisdom with those who will follow, teaching how Jews ought to behave. So we share their *ratzon* with you, to pass on to your own loved ones *(Hebrew Ethical Wills):*

> To be at peace with all the world, with Jew and Gentile, must be your foremost aim in life. Contend with no one. Your home must be the abode of quietude and happiness; no harsh word must be heard there. (Joel, son of Abraham Shemariah, d. 1799, Vilna)

> Elijah, the Vilna Gaon, said: Train your daughters to avoid scolding, oaths, lies, or contention. Let their whole conversation be conducted in peace, love, affability, and gentleness. (Eighteenth-century Poland)

> Should cause for dissension present itself, be slow to accept the quarrel; seek peace and pursue it with all the vigor at your command. Even if you suffer loss thereby, forbear and forgive. . . . As you speak no scandal, so listen to none. The less you say, the less cause you give for animosity, while "Where there is much talk, there is no lack of transgressing [Prov. 10:19]." (Eliezer b. Samuel of Mainz, fourteenth-century Germany)

> Raise not your hand against your neighbor. . . . Never be weary of making friends; consider a single enemy as one too many. If you have a faithful friend, hold fast to him. Let him not go, for he is a precious possession. (Asher b. Yehiel, thirteenth-century Germany and Spain)

From Our Tradition

R. Judah ha-Nasi made a feast for his disciples, serving them tongues that were tender as well as tongues that were tough. The disciples selected the tender tongues and passed up the tough ones. So he said to them: Take heed of what you are doing! Even as you select the tender and pass up the tough, so let your tongues be tender and not tough toward one another.

—Lev. R. 33.1

When Moses was angry with Israel, God used *ratzon* to diffuse Moses's wrath. Then when God was angry with Israel, Moses at first became angry at Israel as well. But then God said to Moses: "Shall two angry people put hot water into the drink, each adding to the other's anger instead of placating it? Have I not told you that when I am angry, you must use *ratzon* with Me, and when you are angry I will use *ratzon* with you? . . . Go and become reconciled with the people."

—Exod. R. 45.2

Rabbi Gedaliah of Lintz taught: It is ordained that the *mezzuzah* shall be nailed to every Jewish door. . . . When we enter our home, it reminds us to avoid anger and quarrelsomeness. When we leave our home, the *mezzuzah* again reminds us to curb our egotism in dealing with our fellow creatures.

—Newman, *The Hasidic Anthology*

R. Yose taught in Sepphoris: "Abba Elijah is an irascible man." After that Abba Elijah, who used to visit him regularly, absented himself for three days. When he finally did come, R. Yose asked him, "Why did my master not come?" Elijah replied angrily, "Because you called me irascible." Said R. Yose, "You see, you have just proved me right."

—San. 113b

Rabbi Pinḥas of Koretz said: If a man wishes to guide the people in his house the right way, he must not grow angry at them. For anger not only makes one's soul impure, it transfers impurity to the souls of those with whom one is angry.

Another time he said: Since I tamed my anger, I keep it in my pocket. When I need it, I take it out.

—Buber, *Tales of the Hasidim,* bk. 1, *The Early Masters*

Pure-Heartedness—
Temimut

Life is like a box of chocolates. . . . You never know what you're gonna get.

—Forrest Gump

*A*mericans once told tall tales about Paul Bunyan the logger and sang the praise of John Henry the railroad builder. In those days our national mythology celebrated hard physical labor. Today, when inwardness and personal search abound, Americans have found a new folk hero—Forrest Gump, the pure-hearted. Many other cultures have told similar tales of innocent, naive souls who live without guile and turn out to be wiser than the sophisticates who ridicule their simplicity. Often these have been religious figures, the "holy fools" common to many traditions, so struck by certain basic tenets of their faith that they live by these and little else.

Today, most of us take religion far less seriously. Nonetheless, highly talented filmmakers chose to portray a modern-day "holy fool" in the character of Forrest Gump, a young man whose limited reasoning powers remind us that we are sometimes too smart for our own good. Forrest's innocence and simple faith make him so admirable that we're almost willing to swap a score of IQ points with him in exchange for some of his unblemished decency, what Jewish teaching calls *temimut*.

Christians who yearn for such pure-heartedness can model themselves after their well-known medieval saint, Francis of Assisi, who saw nothing odd about preaching to his "brothers," the animals. Hasidic lore has provided us with our own unique Jewish model of *temimut,* Zusya of Hanipol, the late-eighteenth-century sage. Zusya is such a favorite of ours that we'd like to share some anecdotes about him. We know that these tales embroider history, but we who can take the Forrest Gump saga to heart should have little difficulty permitting these Zusya fables to instruct us.

Here, first, are some of the few facts that are known about Zusya. He was born about 250 years ago in Galicia, what is now southern Poland. As a young man he became a disciple of the famous hasidic rabbi Dov Baer, known popularly as the Maggid, the Preacher of Mezritch. Zusya, however, spent much of his time wandering the countryside in a manner reminiscent of the Baal Shem Tov, the founder of Hasidism. Although Zusya soon gained a reputation as a holy innocent, his surviving writings show him to be an accomplished scholar. That much is biography, but generations remember him as a blameless soul whose greatness stems from his personal integrity, his *temimut.* What now follows is legend, our abridged version of stories more elegantly retold in Martin Buber's *Tales of the Hasidim: The Early Masters.*

Presence

> Zusya learned his pure ways from his mother Mirl, who couldn't read but knew the important Jewish blessings. Zusya claimed that wherever she said the morning prayers, God's Presence remained the rest of the day.

The Hasidim thought enough of Mirl to recall her by name in this story. Like so many men and women who lived during those difficult times, she hardly seemed the Jewish ideal, since she was unschooled and had only the most rudimentary, practical knowledge. Still, Mirl followed the Bible's counsel: "Be pure-hearted with the Lord your God" (Deut. 18:13). Mirl did what she could with a full heart. Thus, her piety overshadowed her ignorance.

Not a Lot, Just the Most Important Thing

> Zusya, like other classic fools, was thought to be an ignoramus. The Rizhyner Rebbe, who studied with Zusya, tried to explain his companion's apparent lack of fundamental book learning. He said that

whenever their teacher would recite a biblical verse that began with the words, "And God said . . ." this was enough to drive Zusya into a fit of ecstasy. His screams and wild manner so disturbed the other yeshivah students that poor Zusya had to be taken outside until he quieted down. And that is why he missed hearing the substance of most lessons.

Our tradition usually cannot say enough about the virtues of study and the value of learning with a sage. But in the marvelous, self-correcting manner of our teaching, we also come across the sayings: "For as wisdom grows, vexation grows; to increase learning is to increase heartache" (Eccles. 1:18). How much more must a person know after learning the precious few things that truly matter? Consider, for example, the simple task of buying a new computer or even an upgrade of a software program we think we understand. For many (both of us certainly include ourselves in this category), merely glancing at the reference manual's table of contents is enough to plunge us into deep depression! All those extraneous bells and whistles get in the way of the few simple things we had hoped to master.

We moderns have devised an often unconscious strategy for simplifying our lives and gaining some *temimut:* psychologists call it denial. In the face of frequent intellectual or emotional overload we say, "I can't handle this," and try to put the irritant out of our lives by burying it in our unconscious. But though this technique often works, it always exacts a price. If what we've secreted away is quite traumatic, we will suffer its effects until we are able to find a release. Zusya had a more positive approach to life, one that came with not trying to handle so much. When he heard that the one God of the universe "talked" to us, he knew this to be the most important, the only thing he needed to know. He had no need to practice denial, since he didn't feel himself overwhelmed by life. Though the world may have thought him a fool, Zusya didn't spend his life tortured by slights he couldn't forget and troubled by pains he had stuffed deep inside himself. Rather, he exemplified the rule: "Happy are the simple of heart who follow *Adonai*'s way" (Ps. 119:1).

Love's Fool

Zusya became a disciple of the great Maggid, Rabbi Dov Baer of Mezritch. But instead of learning from the Maggid in his yeshivah, Zusya preferred walking in the forests, singing blessings to God. He was so simple-minded about this that people applied to him the lover's confession in Song of Songs: "My love, you have ravished my heart" (4:9).

Lovers are so taken with their beloved that they often do foolish things. Who can forget watching (and aching for) Forrest Gump as he ran back and forth across the country, trying to numb his pain after his sweetheart left? As he ran, he slowly healed, enabling him to spread his commonsense gospel of hope—and that, despite knowing that the opposite, too, "can happen." It's easy to be cynical, and we smugly poke fun at the lover's single-minded obsession. But the lover knows who is the real fool. Temimut means knowing what you truly love.

The Torah describes the patriarch Jacob as an *ish tam,* a pure-hearted soul. The rabbis interpret this unexpected phrase as a description of his extraordinary love for learning: "No one ever labored at studying Torah as did Jacob. As it is written in Genesis 25:27: 'Jacob was a pure-hearted man, dwelling in tents.' Not 'dwelling in a tent,' but 'dwelling in tents.' That implied that, having learned much, he would leave the academy of Shem and enter the academy of Eber, then leave that school and enter the academy of Abraham" (Tan. B. Vayishlaḥ, 8.9). And, of course, loving Rachel as he did, Jacob willingly served her father Laban for fourteen years in order to win her hand.

Jacob loved Rachel enough to slave for her, wasting his youth tending the flocks of her father, Laban, a man he grew to despise. May we now ask, whom do you so long for, "with all your heart, with all your soul, and with all your might" (Deut. 6:5), sacrificing everything, dedicating yourself to this aspect of *temimut?*

Affirming Single-Mindedness

Zusya worried lest, loving God so much, he did not hold God in sufficient awe. He decided to pray for full reverence of God. But when his prayer was granted, he was overwhelmed by the fear of God and crawled under his bed, howling like a dog. Zusya then begged that his single-minded love of God return, and it did.

Of course, there are limits to a simple-minded approach to life. One misses a lot. The holy fool is not so foolish that he doesn't know that. If anything, gaining as much as he does from his special encounter with existence, he would like to respond to the world more broadly. But he learns that even to hope to expand his breath of understanding to every aspect of his being is doomed to failure. As the rabbis say: "Try grabbing too much and you'll end up holding nothing. But lay hold of a little and you can manage very nicely indeed" (R.H. 4b). Even Zusya had to learn about the limits imposed by *temimut*.

Finding Our Way

Zusya once came to a crossroads, but being simple, he couldn't figure out which way to go to continue his journey. When he looked up he saw God's Presence leading him toward the right path.

We all like to think of ourselves as activists who do not cringe from life's challenges. As we set our goals progressively higher, our strategies to fulfill them become more complex. Some decisions, like whom to trust and whom to doubt, when to hold back and when to take a risk, have always required considerable wisdom. And now we face new decisions forced upon us by a constantly changing technology, expanding the range of what we may decide, from the fetus we carry to the plug we pull. Even our basic coping techniques often become inadequate. We stand at a crossroads and don't know which way to go. Expert opinions and our understanding of what worked for others only increase our options. This increased knowledge can paralyze us, and we find ourselves incapable of making even a simple decision. Then the best advice is to look deep within ourselves to see what we care about most. Some call this intuition; others refer to it as our "gut reaction." Judaism calls it God. We hope that our Jewish observance over the years has made our personal relationship with God so strong that it will show us the way now. As the Bible says: "God is a shield for the wholehearted and provides sound wisdom to the upright" (Prov. 2:7).

The Evil All around Us

Zusya once overheard someone confess to following an amoral lifestyle. Being so pure-minded himself, he bitterly condemned the sinner. But afterward, Zusya reproached himself for being so mean. Dov Baer, Zusya's teacher, saw how miserable this made him, and he blessed his disciple with the gift of seeing only the good in people. Although Zusya continued to see evil in the world, he now took the sins everyone else committed and heaped them on himself.

Innocence can blind us to the evil of others, an idea that no amount of holy naiveté can justify after Auschwitz. For to live only by *temimut* sets us up as prime victims for the bullies of this world. Yet Zusya's saintliness reminds us how awful it would be if we lived in perpetual wariness, always preparing ourselves for the next attack. Then paranoia replaces guilelessness, an unhappy shift that sounds suspiciously like the mood of our time. Although we who live without Zusya's heroic piety cannot afford his simple pure-heartedness, we also cannot live totally without it. When we begin to lose faith in the decency of others, we should recognize that *temimut* is also a survival skill, particularly if we want to give goodness the chance to make its power felt in our lives.

The World Can Hurt Us

Zusya, the all-embracing lover of the world, was once so charmed by a flame that he stretched out his hand to touch it—and was astonished when the fire hurt him.

Concentrating our life on the sacred can't wipe out all pain. Being innocent can make us so unsuspecting that when we inevitably encounter evil, we are surprised. Such unpretentiousness makes us a little like the child described in the Pesah Haggadah, the *tam,* to whom things seem so simple there's no reason to ask a question. But naiveté can be dangerous. Nature, so often nurturing and supportive, can be utterly indifferent to piety. As the rabbis say of fire, which they treat as a metaphor of Torah: "Get too close and it burns you, but move too far away and you freeze" (Sifre Deut. 343). We need to learn to come only close enough to be gently warmed by its heat. And many of us follow a similar disposition in our relations with people.

The Child of Nature

Zusya thought that even the ground beneath his feet merited his respect. Yet obviously he was forced to tramp on it as he moved about. One day he was overheard apologizing to the earth for his behavior, reminding it that he knew, while he now stood above it, it would not be long before he would be underneath the ground forever.

Psalm 85:12 says cryptically, "Truth springs out of the earth." The Slonimer Rebbe interpreted this to mean that truth is located near us, on the very ground at our feet. But he wondered why so few of us make the effort to bend down and pick it up (Newman, *The Hasidic Anthology*). The nineteenth-century American thinker Henry David Thoreau wrote his book *Walden* to remind his rapidly urbanizing fellow-citizens that they would benefit by returning to nature and re-learning her ways. Today, Thoreau's maxim, "simplify, simplify" speaks even more strongly to a generation that complains it is maximally stressed and overburdened. Our modern anti-hero Forrest Gump found spiritual pleasure by working as a gardener in his hometown even after he made his fortune. A certain innocence about existence carries with it a rich sense that we are deeply rooted in creation. Having this awareness, we are more ready to accept the ecological *musar* teachings of our time.

When Etiquette Is Improper

Rabbi Nathan Adler of Frankfort related the following mystical experience. He once fasted for a long time, hoping to gain a visit to heaven. After waiting patiently for the gates to open, he was permitted to enter and was astonished to find Zusya there ahead of him. Zusya was so simple-minded that it never occurred to him to follow usual etiquette and wait for official approval to enter. He just barged on in!

Much of our formality gets in the way of doing what we should. Or worse, our reluctance to get involved has tragic consequences. We may sense, or even see, that something is wrong and someone needs our assistance. But a too delicate understanding of good manners stops us from calling the authorities, much less volunteering our help until it is too late. Those of pure heart know when to dispense with ceremony; they jump in and do whatever has to be done. They know what is important and don't need to ponder the pros and cons before taking action. Sometimes we think—how foolish; but at the same time, we realize—how admirable. Our sages understood that people cannot be commanded to be heroes. Yet those who know the difference between what's truly important and what isn't transform even routine existence.

Greeting the New Day

> When Zusya would wake up, he did not immediately say the traditional prayer of thanks to God, *modeḥ ani:* "I thank you, O real and effective Sovereign, for restoring my soul to me . . ." Instead, he first called out a hearty "good morning" to Jews everywhere and only then did he thank his Creator.

The effortless innocence of those who are single-minded enhances their congeniality. *Temimut* does not mean isolation, just as withdrawing from others will not bring us closer to God. Mid-twentieth-century anthropologists discovered the same truths when they studied former shtetl dwellers. Mark Zborowsky and Elizabeth Herzog were so impressed by the faith expressed by those who came from these small eastern European villages that they called their report *Life Is with People.* Like them, Zusya found divine guidance rooted in the history, tradition, and observance of the Jewish people, grounding *temimut* not in individual genius but in covenant, our ageless communal relationship with God. We who specialize in self-invention and self-development could benefit from a simple appreciation of where we all must start—from our traditions, both secular and religious, that have formed each of us into a person-in-particular.

The Saint as Failure?

> Every weekday Zusya would keep a diary, writing down all the things that he did. But when he went to bed each night and read that day's entry, he would cry over his sins.

No aura of conceit can accompany a pure-hearted connection to God. As Proverbs tells us: "Who can say: 'I have made my heart clean, I am pure, without sin?'" (20:9). No Jewish saint has been without sin; what makes them our models is that they don't hide this fact, but face it. We all need some higher simplicity to keep us from creating elaborate rationalizations for what we do or don't do, encouraging us to face our responsibilities. We call this maturity.

On Not Being a Star

> When it came to mystic experience, Zusya considered himself a "nobody," for he did not often have a sense of nearness to God. But he wasn't bitter that other people, the "somebodies," claimed easier access to the "King." Rather, he considered himself like a palace menial whose labor exalted him because he was occasionally permitted to glimpse the Heavenly Ruler.

We might think that Zusya, a famous hasidic rebbe, basked in God's intimacy all the time. But Zusya knew that he was one of those people whose life was spent in everyday routine, only occasionally rising to heightened religious awareness. Being pure of heart, Zusya didn't consider his lot demeaning, and he didn't rebel at such indignities. But then he didn't grow up, as some of us have, with a remote control in hand, able to switch off a program that doesn't quickly grab our attention. We often similarly surf through our lives, trying a little of this, a little of that, imagining that we can happen upon experiences that will make us "somebodies." *Temimut* doesn't direct us to spend our lives in single-minded, simple-acting drudgery. Rather, it gives us a way to remedy our incessant, numerous dissatisfactions. As the Lubliner Rebbe taught: "When people know their worth and keep honest accounts with their souls, then truth, the seal of God, is set on them" (Buber, *Tales of the Hasidim,* bk. 1, *The Early Masters*).

At the End

> Zusya was sick for seven years before his death. Once a well-intentioned rebbe, visiting Zusya, complained to another, more renowned master who was also there that the latter was not doing all

he could to heal Zusya. The master replied that Zusya really could have cured himself, but he was so pure of heart that he accepted whatever God sent his way.

Imagine our anger if a loved one confessed that she or he had been aware of a health problem for some time, but did not go to a physician to have it checked out—or actually saw a doctor, but refused to allow a simple surgical procedure that would determine its seriousness. At first we'd be much too livid to be sad. We would probably curse the naive faith that made the one we care for so complacent. If there is one trait that we moderns detest, it is passivity. We fault those who don't take an aggressive approach.

Yet as we grow older, we begin to understand that we can fight for only so long. At a certain point the effort becomes counterproductive. Elizabeth Kubler-Ross discovered in her studies of the dying that those who can resign themselves to letting go seem to acquire a certain peace that is both natural and yet quite special. But why wait so long? Some of us have been fortunate to know a saintly Zusya, who early on learned the virtue of simple acceptance and whose quiet serenity caused us to marvel. Consciously modeling our lives on theirs would be our greatest tribute to these enchanting individuals, and a gift to ourselves that just might transform us.

The Ultimate Question

Before his death, Zusya said, "In the world to come, they will not ask me: 'Why were you not Moses?' They will ask me: 'Why were you not Zusya?'"

As we respond to life's challenges, we gain a fleeting sense of who we truly are, the self we ought to be. Sadly we discover that this ideal self will always elude us. The gap that separates even the best we have been from our full potential can plunge us into a melancholy that would undermine even saintly beings. Yet our ideals lure us on, encouraging us to try once more to find and to be "ourselves."

Zusya's Epitaph

These words were written on Zusya's tombstone: "He served God with love; he rejoiced in suffering; he wrested many from their sins."

A Jewish tombstone usually includes certain ritual phrases, words that must apply to so many that they say very little that is particular to the one buried beneath it. But what if our family decided that they would like our stone to say something quite specific about us? Since they wouldn't have a lot of space, they'd have to keep it brief and simple. Our life would come down to just those things, summing up what really mattered. What simple testimonies are we now writing with our lives?

A Realist's Guide to Idealism

The Zusya of legend and the Forrest Gump of the screen are not people like us. They could live guilelessly. The rest of us, however, must survive by relying on what our immigrant forebears called a *"Yiddishe kop,"* the analytic street-smarts that help us sniff out deception. Every time we answer the phone, open our mail, or even look out the small peephole so carefully drilled through our front door, we may find someone trying to take advantage of our last bit of innocence. Is there anyone who hasn't been victimized, who hasn't worn the fool's cap labeled "sucker" or "patsy"? And even after we've become defensive about defending ourselves, we know that for our own well-being, we mustn't let down our barriers for very long. But this can make us so watchful and suspicious that there's little left of the pure souls we were born with. We become something like Gertrude Stein's observation about Los Angeles, "There's no there, there."

We seem to specialize in being complicated. We hide behind elaborate psychological defenses and work hard to project the image we want others to see. Few of us learn Zusya's lesson that maturity means stripping away, not adding to. For all of its continued acclaim, Thoreau's injunction to "simplify, simplify" is not the way most of us live. Seven hundred years ago, the Roman scribe and ethicist Yeḥiel b. Yekutiel defined the person with *temimut* as someone who "speaks without deceit, who does business without scheming, and whose mouth and heart are one" *(Sefer Maalot Hamiddot)*. We need to build our lives on this simple wisdom. For when we get to heaven, they will not ask us if we had Zusya's *temimut,* they will ask us . . .

From Our Tradition

Rabbi Naḥman of Bratzlav said:

Better to be a fool who believes everything than a skeptic who believes nothing—not even the truth.

Steer clear of sophistication and cleverness. They add nothing to coming closer to God. All you need is simplicity, security, and faith.

Did you ever notice that the further people are from truth, the more they consider someone who turns away from evil to be a fool? When there is no truth in the world, anyone who wants to turn away from evil has no choice but to play the fool.

—Mykoff, *The Empty Chair*

R. Simlai said: Six hundred and thirteen commandments were given to Moses, 365 negative commandments answering to the number of the days of the year, and 248 positive commandments answering to the number of a person's members.

Then David came and reduced them to eleven: "Lord, who shall dwell in Your tabernacle? Who shall sojourn in Your holy mountain? He that walks uprightly, works righteousness, speaks truth in his heart; has no slander upon his tongue, nor does evil to his fellow, nor reproaches his neighbor; in whose eyes a vile person is despised, but honors those who fear the Lord. He swears to his own heart and doesn't change. He does not lend his money on interest, nor take a bribe against the innocent. He that does these things shall never be moved" [Ps. 15].

Then came Isaiah, and reduced them to six: "He that walks right-eously, and speaks uprightly, he that despises oppressors, who shakes his hand from bribes, who stops his ear from hearing about bloodshed, and shuts his eyes so as not to see evil—he shall dwell on high" [Isa. 33:15–16].

Then came Micah, and reduced them to three: "It has been told you, O man, what is good, and what the Lord requires of you: only to do justly, and to love mercy, and to walk humbly before your God" [Mic. 6:8].

Then Isaiah came again, and reduced them to two: "Thus says the Lord: keep justice and do righteousness" [Isa. 56:1].

Then came Amos, and reduced them to one: "Seek the Lord and live" [Amos 5:4]. Or one may say, then came Habakkuk, and reduced them to one, "The righteous shall live by their faith" [Hab. 2:4].

—Mak. 24a

Achieving Our *Musar* Goals

CHAPTER 18

A Good Name—
Shem Tov

Everyone has a name,
one given by God
and one given by parents,
one given by stature and a way of smiling
and one given by attire,
one given by the mountains
and one given by the walls,
one given by the planets
and one given by neighbors,
one given by sins
and one given by longing,
one given by enemies
and one given by love,
one given by feast days
and one given by one's job,
one given by the seasons of the year
and one given by blindness,
one given by the sea
and one given by
death.

—Zelda, "Everyone Has a Name"

lone among God's creatures, we humans underline our individuality by naming each other and ourselves. Each of us has a multitude of names. Some change with our age and status, so we start out as "baby" or "little one;" progress to "sissy" or "bro;" then answer to "sweetheart," "darling," "mommy," "auntie," or "dada;" and, if we are truly blessed, make it to "nana" or "grandpa." But we bristle if we hear the cruel "Uncle Tom" or "kike"—for these names foster an evil stereotyping, perpetuating ignorance and hatred, defaming the speaker as much as the person at whom they are hurled.

More than two hundred years ago, Jews living in Europe's sprawling Hapsburg Empire were forced to take surnames by governmental fiat. Obviously the easiest thing to do was to maintain the Jewish custom of being known by the name of one's father, so Isaac ben Abraham became Isaac Abrahamson or Abramson. Jews could also take names that are common descriptives, which is why so many of us are named for the German words for black ("Schwartz"), white ("Weiss"), small ("Klein"), or large ("Gross"). Or our great-great-great-great-grandfathers took their craft as their last name—hence "Silver," "Gold," or "Diamond;" or more humbly "Schneider" (tailor), "Schuster" (shoemaker), or "Schachter" (shohet—ritual slaughterer). Or they simply adapted the name of the town that they lived in, so many of us answer to "Frankfurter" or "Warshow."

All these names tell us little about the character of those who hold them. A name becomes a "good name," a *shem tov*, in the Jewish community when good deeds accompany it. Thus our first names or our Hebrew names may honor the memory of a well-loved relation, conveying the hope that we, as namesakes, will similarly live honorably. Jews by choice often take "Abraham" or "Sarah" as their Hebrew name, understanding that our first patriarch and matriarch were the first persons to heed God's calling. Because of this, they became the ancestral fathers and mothers of all Jews. Many Hebrew proper names recall an event. For example, the Torah tells us that "Israel" means "wrestling with God" and was the new name Jacob won from the angel he fought all night (Gen. 32:23–33). But it is our deeds that ultimately "name" us, for good or for ill. As R. Yose b. Hanina noted: People's names fall into four classifications: Some have fair names but have done foul deeds; others have ugly names but have done good deeds; some have ugly names to which their deeds correspond; and others have the good deeds to match their lovely names" (Gen. R. 71.3).

"Make Yourself a Good Name and You Can Lie Down in Peace" (Ladino Proverb)

When we strive to achieve a *shem tov*, we seek a good reputation among people whose standards are high and whose character we respect. Only our actions toward others, not the actions of our prominent ancestors, can influence their judgment. As Hillel said: "If you have acquired a good name, you had to do it yourself" (Avot 2.7), and Akabya b. Mahalalel gave the same advice to his son, seeking the sages' good opinion: "Your own deeds will bring you near, and your own deeds will remove you far" (Ed. 5.7). "A person gets three names—one that his parents call him, one that his friends pin on him, and one that he acquires by the way he acts. But the one that he acquires for himself is better than all the others" (Tan. Vayak'hel 1).

"Dress Up a Broom and It Will Also Look Nice" (Yiddish Proverb)

Since we are social animals and care about the opinion of others: "A good name is more desirable than great wealth, more even than silver or gold" (Prov. 22:1). The corollary of that maxim tells us that we can't buy our way into owning a good name, as one can with British titles or, apparently, American ambassadorships. Yes, money does open doors, encouraging people to speak well of you to your face, particularly when they want something. But we should never confuse cachet with honest respect, or mistake the status associated with dressing or living well with the regard that comes from an interior goodness that our actions reflect. Rabbi Eliezer Papo, a nineteenth-century Sephardic musarist, comments: "A good name means people praise you for your good deeds and character" *(Pele Yoetz)*. Certain Native Americans made this a part of their tradition. They waited until adulthood and then chose a name they believed best captured their essence, like the Kevin Costner character who derived his odd name, "Dances with Wolves," from his exuberant playing with his pet. Less literally, the Jewish *shem tov* is the reputation that accompanies our name. As Ben Azzai remarked: "People will call you by the name that rightly belongs to you" (Yoma 38a).

Our contemporary American culture turns this rabbinic adage on its head, insisting that a "good" name is one that sells the current "hot" product. Celebrity has become all, as the high esteem for character slinks into the background. When the two are joined we are pleasantly surprised, thankful that the power that enables actors and athletes to influence people's lives is not universally corrupted. A prurient notoriety may transform someone into a media darling for a short time, but it taints this name with a smell of sin that is not soon forgotten. No one so labeled may qualify for the blessing of the prophet Zephaniah, who promised that God "will gather the strayed, and will exchange their disgrace for fame and renown in all the earth" (3:19).

"A Person Is What He Is, Not What He Was" (Yiddish Proverb)

Sometimes decent souls believe that something they have done not only destroys their personal *shem tov*, but also fouls the name of the community they represent. Their sense of duty may drive them into a deep depression or even an act of violent expiation. Adm. Jeremy M. Boorda, the late United States Chief of Naval Operations, apparently wore among his many well-deserved decorations two combat medals that he may not have legitimately earned. When he discovered that some journalists were about to expose his deceit, Boorda committed suicide. He believed that he had polluted the good name of the Navy, the institution that honored him with a professional distinction he felt he no longer deserved. Did he also feel that he had betrayed his Jewish roots and the high standards of its religious community? He is unlikely to have known the specific teaching that generations of Jews have passed down to their children, though he undoubtedly based his life upon its message: "There are those who are mentioned and blessed, not only as a source of praise both for themselves and their parents, but also for their family and the tribe from which they are descended . . . and there are those who are a source of shame to themselves and their parents, their family and the tribe from which they are descended" (Exod. R. 48.2).

For our reputation depends upon our deeds, regardless of our education or our *"yihus"*: "R. Simeon said: There are three crowns— the crown of the law, the crown of the priesthood, and the crown of kingship. But the crown of a good name, to which anyone can aspire, is better than any of them" (Avot 4.17). To put it directly: "To acquire a name like that of Moses is better than uncounted wealth." Certainly: "To acquire a good name like that of Mordecai is better than all the riches of Haman" (Exod. R. 33.5).

"Happy Is He Who Grew Up with a Good Name and Died with a Good Name" (Ber. 17a)

Andy Warhol shrewdly commented that all of us are entitled to fifteen minutes of fame. Yet a brief, questionable notoriety is surely not what our tradition had in mind. Judaism emphasizes the lasting durability of a *shem tov*, opposing the fickle judgment of a bread-and-circus-loving public. "R. Simeon b. Yoḥai said: More beloved is a good name than the Ark of the Covenant, because the ark went before the Israelites for only a distance of three days [Num. 10:33], while a good name goes from one end of the world to the other" (Eccles. R. 7.1, 3). Jews think in terms of lifetimes. Thus a midrash explains Ecclesiastes's puzzling statement: "The day of death is better than the day of birth" (Eccles. 7:1). "R. Pinḥas said: When a person is born, all rejoice; when he dies, all weep. It should not be so. But when a person is born there should be no rejoicing over him, because it is not known whether by his actions he will be righteous or wicked, good or bad. However, when he dies, there is cause for rejoicing if he departs with a good name and leaves the world in peace. It is as if there were two ocean-going ships, one leaving the harbor and the other entering it. As the one sailed out of the harbor, all rejoiced, but none displayed any joy over the one that was entering. A shrewd man was there and he said to the people, 'There is no cause to rejoice over the ship that is leaving the harbor, because nobody knows what will be its plight. . . . But when it returns to the harbor all have reason to rejoice, since it has come in safely'" (Eccles. R. 7.1, 4).

As the years go by, we find ourselves perusing the obituaries more intensely than we ever used to. Perhaps it is to keep better abreast of the day's events, or to see if we have lost any old friends. But we think that other motives are also at work here. We readily admit to having a more than passing interest in the biographies of important people, to discover if they left with their good name still intact. As R. Pinhas's teaching continues: "We can say that when the righteous are born, nobody feels any difference, but when they die, everybody feels it. When Miriam was born, nobody felt it, but when she died all felt her loss because her well, [that miraculous source of water] that accompanied the Jews through the wilderness stopped appearing, and all felt [her loss]. When her brother Aaron the High Priest was born, nobody felt it, but when he died and the clouds of glory that had accompanied the Jews in the Exodus departed, all felt his loss. When Moses our teacher was born, nobody felt it, but when he died all felt it, because the manna made his death known by ceasing to fall" (Eccles. R. 7.1, 4).

If you have earned a good name, your deeds have had an admirable effect on others; they will sorely miss you after you die. The Book of Psalms poetically proclaims: "May his name last eternally; as long as the sun shines, may his name endure; let people invoke his blessings upon themselves and let all nations count him happy" (Ps. 72:17). A biblical proverb echoes the sentiment: "The name of the righteous is invoked in blessing, but the fame of the wicked rots" (10:7). This verse is said to be the source of the custom that when we speak of someone we remember as virtuous, we say of them: *Zekher tzaddik livrakhah,* may the memory of the righteous serve as a blessing. No wonder our tradition esteems a *shem tov,* valuing it even more than the ancient treasured commodity, precious oil (Eccles. 7:1). "Good oil is temporary, while a good name endures forever. Good oil is bought with money, while a good name is free. Good oil can be used only by the living, while a good name is valued by the living and, for their anointing, by the dead" (Eccles. R. 7.1, 1).

The Classic Jewish Curse: *Yimakh Shmo,* May His Name Be Blotted Out

The opposite is true of those mean souls who die seemingly without a single redeeming quality. Of these bad seeds it is difficult not to agree with the Psalmist: "May *Adonai* always be mindful of them and cause their names to be cut off from the earth, because they were not minded to act kindly, but hounded the poor and the needy, and squeezed the life out of those crushed in spirit" (Ps. 109:15–16).

Three classic villains summon special revulsion in our tradition; two plagued us in biblical times, the third in recent years. Each year on Shabbat Zakhor, the Sabbath of Remembrance occurring right before Purim, the Torah reminds us of the Amalekite treachery. Personifying that nation, the Book of Deuteronomy demands: "Remember what Amalek did when he ambushed you on the Exodus march and massacred all the stragglers in your rear" (Deut. 25:17). So we are told: "The Lord said to Moses . . . I will utterly blot out the memory of Amalek from under heaven. . . . I will be at war with Amalek throughout the ages" (Exod. 17:14, 16). We read these lines before Purim because the other classical biblical villain, Haman, is described as a descendant of Agag, king of Amalek (Est. 3:1). Long ago folk custom developed an annual practice of blotting out the name of Amalek, by having us whirl our Purim *gragers* wildly every time we hear the name of Haman read in the Megillah of Esther.

There is no contest for the third exemplar of the infamously wicked. Well into the twentieth century, German Jews would consider "Adolph" as a respectable name to call their infant sons. Even out of family loyalty, no Jew would do so now. "R. Eleazar said: What is the meaning of the verse, 'but the name of the wicked shall rot'? [Prov. 10:7]. Rottenness enters their names, as you can tell from the fact that no one names their children after them" (Yoma 38b).

In Judaism, Bad-Mouthing a Person Is a Sin

A good name is so important that giving someone a bad name is a vile Jewish offense: "R. Eleazar b. Perata said: Come and see how great is the power of an evil tongue! The ten spies who brought back an evil report against the wood and stones of the land of Israel received a severe punishment; how much the more so will this happen to one who bad-mouths his neighbor!" (Ar. 15a). A similar story is told in a legal context. Under Jewish law, one witness is not enough to convict someone of a crime. "It once happened that Tobias sinned and Zigud alone came and testified against him before R. Papa. Since one witness does not constitute definitive proof, R. Papa had the witness Zigud punished. R. Papa explained, the Torah says: 'One witness shall not rise up against a man' [Deut. 19:15], so by testifying against him, you have brought him into ill repute" (Pes. 113b).

As children, we proved how self-righteous we were if we responded to someone who called us something awful by screeching out: "Sticks and stones will break my bones but names will never hurt me." Today we know how false that is, for a "bad name" can be hurtful indeed. Our rabbis obviously knew this; when they wanted to identify an evil practice, they would deliver a string of unpleasant names. Thus, a scholar "who feasts much in every place . . . profanes God's name, the name of his teacher, and the name of his father, bringing an evil name upon himself, his children, and his children's children until the end of all generations. . . . Said Abaye: He is called a heater of ovens. Raba said: A tavern dancer! R. Papa said: A plate licker! R. Shemaiah said: A gutter-sleeping drunk!" (Pes. 49a).

Giving your new wife a bad name is a particularly heinous act. The Torah describes the sin quite explicitly: "A man marries a woman and has intercourse with her. Taking an aversion to her, he gives her an evil name, saying, 'I married this woman, but when I cohabited with her, I found that she was not a virgin.' In such a case, the girl's parents should produce the sheet that shows the evidence of the girl's virginity and display it to the elders of the town. . . . Finding the man's report false, they will then flog him and fine him one hundred shekels, to be given to the girl's father, for the man defamed a virgin" (Deut. 22:13–19). Today we wince at the obvious sexism of awarding payment to the father when the daughter's reputation was impugned. But we should also be mindful of the historical treatment of women and look with favor at the Jewish law that prohibits the defamation of the innocent female as male prerogative.

Superstitious? No—But Give Our Children the Names of Good People

Few sentiments are as widespread among us as ensuring that the name of a loved one lives on in our community. Its roots go back to the Bible. When Boaz married Ruth, his kinsman's widow, he acquired not only a wife but the ancestral property of her deceased husband Maḥlon. The text gives the following reason for Boaz's act: "To perpetuate the name of the deceased upon his estate, so his name would not disappear from among his kinfolk and from the gate of his home town" (Ruth 4:5–10). Today we try to convey the same custom by reading the names of those we memorialize in our synagogues and by lighting a memorial candle for them in our homes.

In 1953 the Israeli government established a national institution to honor the memories of all those Jews who died in the *Shoah* and called it Yad Vashem, from the text of the prophet Isaiah: "I will give them in My house and within My walls, 'a hand and a name' better than sons or daughters. I will give them an everlasting name which shall not perish" (56:5). At first glance this biblical idiom seems an unusual way to advance continuity. But in the Bible, "hand" is the standard metaphor for power or agency. Thus when the Bible speaks of something being done by "the hand of God," it simply means "by God's power." To give the dead a "hand" is to give them continuing power among us. A "name," as we have seen, is our way of invoking the memory of the dead for a blessing. That is exactly what Yad Vashem seeks to do, giving the dead an eternal, sacred role in the lives of those who seek their *shem tov.*

May we, whose opportunities are many and whose means are great, live so that those who come after us will invoke our names in love, and find in them a continuing blessing.

From Our Tradition

One day the Tzanzer Rebbe passed through the marketplace and noticed a weeping woman seated before a fruit stand. She told the Rebbe that no one was buying her apples and she faced ruin. The kindhearted *tzaddik* immediately began to shout: "Buy fine apples, a dozen for a gulden." The news that the holy man was selling fruit soon spread, and the wealthiest residents came to buy. They considered it an honor to make a purchase from this famous teacher. The apples were quickly transformed into a pile of guldens, to the delight of the poor widow.

—Newman, *The Hasidic Anthology*

If a man places his wife under a vow that she is to neither borrow nor lend a winnow, a sieve, a mill, or an oven, he must divorce her and pay the amount stipulated in her marriage settlement, because, were she to follow that vow, he would give her a bad name among the neighbors.

—Ket. 72a

Why are disciples of the wise in Babylon so meticulous about their clothing? Because they are not so well learned. R. Yoḥanan said: Because they are not in their own country—they are in Palestine. As people say, "In my own town my name is what matters; away from home, my attire."

—Shab. 145b

If one dreams that he is sitting in a small boat, he will acquire a good name. If in a large boat, both he and all his family will acquire good names, but only if the boat is on the high sea.

—Ber. 57a

You alone are *Adonai*. . . . You performed signs and wonders against Pharaoh, all his servants, and all the people of his land, for You knew that they acted presumptuously toward them. You made a name for Yourself that endures to this day.

—Neh. 9:6, 10

CHAPTER 19

Peace—*Shalom*

Come, my children, and listen to me,
and I will teach you what it is to respect Adonai.
Are you eager to truly live?
Do you yearn to have rewarding years?
Then keep evil off your tongue,
deceitful speech away from your lips.
Shun evil, do good,
love shalom *and pursue it.*

—Ps. 34:12–15

R. Simeon b. Gamaliel, used to say: The world rests on three
things: justice, truth, and shalom. *As it is said: "Judge*
each other truthfully, and in your gates, render a judgment
of peace" [Zech. 8:16].

—Avot 1.18

Shalom—what a beautiful word. We use it when we greet one another, as if to say, "Come in peace." It always carries Sabbath overtones, for our doubly meaningful greeting on the day of rest is "Shabbat Shalom." We use it when we leave one another, as if to say, "Go in peace until we meet again." But this is no simplistic, passive statement. The root *sh-l-m* conveys the meanings "complete," "whole," or even "perfect." So to say *"shalom"* is to breathe the air of Jewish hope and human aspiration, wishing that the day will come soon when we are all fulfilled. No wonder, then, that loving peace, as the Psalmist puts it, or living to create peace, as the rabbis glorify it, is a climactic Jewish ideal, the outcome of worthy living, the chief virtue of Jewish character.

237

The talmudic sages share this view and give *shalom* important mention in Jewish observance. Insisting that the whole purpose of the Torah is to create peace, they have directed that each time we complete our Torah reading, we return this precious scroll to the ark and chant: "Its ways are ways of pleasantness, and all its paths are *shalom*" (Prov. 3:17). We learn from those who compiled our traditional liturgy: "What was their reason for calling the morning petition for peace, *sim shalom*? Because it is written, 'So the priests shall put My name upon the children of Israel, and then I shall bless them' [Num. 6.27]. And the truest blessing of the Holy One is peace'" (Meg. 18a). The rabbis also made the prayer for peace the climax of our daily services, as a request for peace concludes the threefold priestly benediction: "May *Adonai* lift up His countenance to you and give *shalom*" (Num. 6:26). Today many worship services end with a petition from Psalms, affirming this paramount virtue in our tradition: "The Lord will give strength unto His people; the Lord will bless His people with peace" (Ps. 29:11).

"To Make Peace, It's Even Permitted to Tell a Lie . . ." (Yiddish Proverb)

We gain a good sense of just how dear peace was to the rabbis when we read some of their exaggerated statements they made to "prove" *shalom*'s importance. For example, they had *Adonai* compromise plans for our planet's basic structure in order to keep peace among God's creations. "When God created people, God said, 'If I create them as part of the heavenly world, there will be one more creation in heaven than on earth and there will be no peace in the universe. But if I create them as part of the earthly world, there will also be imbalance and controversy. So if I am to have peace in the universe, I will have to create humanity as partaking of both the heavenly and the earthly worlds.' And so God did" (Gen. R. 12.8).

A second instance of rabbinic hyperbole: "R. Ishmael taught: Great is peace, for we are commanded to treat God's name with the greatest sanctity. Look what God did for the sake of peace. If a husband suspects his wife of adultery, the Torah says that he should bring her to the Temple. There, the sacred letters of the Torah, with God's name among them, are written on paper and 'washed' into a cup. The accused adulteress must then drink this potion and is proven guilty if her body becomes swollen. God allows the blasphemy of having God's Name blotted out in water so that all the innocent women may be restored to their households in peace" (Num. 5:16–29, P. Hashalom 9, The Chapter about Peace, attached to the talmudic tractate Derekh Eretz Zuta, the "smaller" version of The Way of the World).

God, say some of the braver rabbis, even fudged the truth so that people might live in peace. "R. Ishmael said: Great is peace. When Sarah is told she will bear a son, she laughs, saying, 'Shall I, being so withered, have the joy of a child, my husband being so old?' But when the Torah relates that God asks Abraham why Sarah laughed, God diplomatically, though untruthfully, omits Sarah's reference to Abraham's age, all for the sake of peace [Gen. 18:12–13]" (B.M. 87a). "R. Simeon b. Gamaliel said: Great is peace, since an untrue statement is made in the Torah to maintain peace between Joseph and his brothers after Jacob had died, as it is written: 'And they sent a message to Joseph saying: Before he died, your father commanded that you forgive your brothers for the sin they committed against you' [Gen. 50:16–17]. But nowhere in the Torah do we find that Jacob had so charged him" (Lev. R. 9.9). Bar Kapara reports a similar subtlety after an angel visits Samson's mother-to-be: "He said to her, 'Behold, now you are barren . . . but you shall conceive and bear a son' [Judg. 13:3]. When she repeats this to her husband, she only says, 'Behold you shall conceive and bear a son' [13:7], and there is no mention of her infertility" (P. Hashalom 7). Such statements caused R. Simeon b. Gamaliel to observe: "See how much ink was spilled, how many pens broken, how many hides cured, how many children spanked—to learn in the Torah something that had never been said. Great indeed, then, is the power of peace!" (Tan. B., Tzav 10).

Traditional Jewish teaching cites four major areas meriting peace that touch us all: family, neighbors, community, and the hereafter. We moderns have extended *shalom* to two additional themes: the world of politics and our personal, inward search for meaning.

"Peace Be within Your Walls" (Ps. 122:7)

When the Torah records a false statement without comment, it does so in order to keep peace in the family, *shalom bayit*. About two millennia ago, R. Simeon b. Gamaliel taught that if our homes are filled with rancor and quarreling, dissension ripples out into the world, eroding the very foundations of human harmony: "Scripture esteems the person who makes peace in his house as if he made peace for every individual in Israel. But Scripture also demeans one who brings jealously and strife into his house as if he had infected the whole House of Israel with them" (A.R.N. 28.3). In our day, when we need healing time at home to remedy the grating realities of life in the "real" world, *shalom bayit* is particularly precious. Yet in many ways these tensions are nothing new. The Ladino proverb cynically jokes, "With one's family and relatives it is good to eat at a distance," and the Yiddish maxim unhappily notes, "Some people may be happy in public yet sad at home." But the general truth is captured in this Yiddish adage: "If there is peace in the house, one can be satisfied with an olive's worth, [the minimum of food that requires a blessing]."

A lovely rabbinic midrash dramatically illustrates how far one should go to create *shalom bayit*. "A woman once stayed at the synagogue so late into a Shabbat evening to listen to R. Meir's discourse that when she came home, she found that her Sabbath light had gone out. Her husband asked her, 'Where have you been?' She replied, 'I have been listening to R. Meir's discourse.' The husband didn't believe his wife. He said to her, 'You may not enter my house again until you have gone and spat in the face of R. Meir.' She left her home and went to pray for guidance. The prophet Elijah told R. Meir what had happened, so R. Meir also went to the town's *beit midrash* [study-house/synagogue]. When he saw the woman enter, he pretended to blink and asked, "Who knows how to cure a sore eye by a charm?' The woman replied, 'I have come to do so,' and she spat into his face. R. Meir then said to her, 'Go and say to your husband—I have spat in R. Meir's face—and become reconciled with him. See how great is the power of peace'" (Deut. R. 5.15). In another version of this story, R. Meir's students say that they could have cured their master by merely whispering a charm. To this R. Meir responds, "Isn't it good enough for R. Meir to act like God? If *Adonai* can let The Ineffable Name be blotted out by water in order to bring peace between a husband and wife [Num. 5], then Meir can also show how great is peace" (Lev. R. 9.9).

How Pleasant It Is When Neighbors Live in Harmony

Peace in the world begins with a simple hello, particularly if you mean by it, *shalom.* "It is reported of R. Yoḥanan b. Zakkai that no one ever preceded him in saying '*Shalom,*' not even an idol-worshiper he met in the marketplace" (Ber. 17a). "R. Ḥelbo further said in the name of R. Huna: . . . If someone's friend says '*Shalom,*' and he doesn't return the greeting, he deserves to be called a robber" (Ber. 6b).

Alas, casual cordiality doesn't settle everything, as anyone knows who has sat through a meeting that dissolved into a shouting match. If only these good people and others less well intentioned would dwell on the rabbinic teaching: "Should people strive with you, whether in the House of Study or at a social gathering, make peace with them, so that when you leave them, they no longer speak angrily about you" (D.E.Z. 9.11).

Our sages consider Aaron the greatest peacemaker. "R. Meir said: When two men quarreled, Aaron would go and sit with one of them and say, 'Do you know what that person you argued with is doing? He berates himself for that spat and wonders how he'll ever face you, he's so ashamed that he behaved so badly.' Aaron would sit with him until he removed all the rancor from the first man's heart. Then he'd go and do the same thing with the other person. When the two men finally met, they would embrace each other" (A.R.N. 12). As an apt Yiddish adage has it: "When you are slugging it out with someone, do it in such a way that later you can make up." Other Jewish writers suggest additional peacemaking tactics. The eighth-century Babylonian Ḥai Gaon warns: "When people start to quarrel, leave them and don't get caught in their snares" (*Musar Haskel* [Intelligent instruction]). The eleventh-century Spanish philosopher Solomon ibn Gabirol suggests: "Never argue with a bad-tempered person, for you'll only provoke him. And never let two people who argue only to win come to your house at the same time" (*Mivhar Hapeninim,* 444). Much closer to our own time, Eliezer Steinman, a near-contemporary Hebrew writer, affirms: "When someone tells you the reason for the quarrel between him and someone else, don't believe it. The cause of all quarrels is the desire to quarrel" (*Midor Lador* [From generation to generation]).

The most common cause of strife among acquaintances is cruel gossip, the near-slander we spread about one another, what our tradition calls *leshon ha-ra* and we term "bad-mouthing." As a Ladino proverb says, "A busybody is like a brooch that always sticks its wearer." If we hear awful things said about us, we physically recoil, for the pain can be that sharp. R. Samuel b. Nahman admonishes: "Why is the evil tongue called the thrice-slaying tongue? Because it slays the person saying it, the hearer, and the person spoken about" (Ar. 15b). R. Hana b. R. Hanina asks: "How shall we interpret the verse, 'Life and death are in the hand of the tongue' [Prov. 18:21]? A tongue certainly doesn't have a hand! What it means is that a tongue can kill as surely as a hand. But while a hand can only kill what is nearby, a tongue can kill everywhere its message goes" (Ar. 15b). *Leshon ha-ra* is so effective because slanderers are not stupid. Like the ten negative-speaking spies who scouted out the Land of Israel, they begin by repeating the truth, but end up by relating falsehoods (Tan. B., Shelah 17). And R. Meir suggests that if we build a small measure of truth into a report, we can get people to accept the entire statement (Sot. 35a). No wonder Shakespeare advises: "In thy right hand carry gentle peace, to silence envious tongues" (*Henry VIII,* act 4, sc. 2).

"Quarreling Is Like Setting Seven Villages on Fire" (Ladino Proverb)

Why do we stop at a red light and proceed at a green one? Why do we drive on the right side of the road in the United States and most other countries, England and Japan excepted? There isn't a good reason for doing it just this way, and we don't hold elections to determine if people feel like changing these arrangements. We set them up, arbitrary though they may be, because without such rules our communities would be chaotic, without order, much less peace. The Mishnah recounts a number of specific statutes designed to keep peace in the Jewish communities of rabbinic times: "The following rules were laid down in the interests of peace, *mipne dharkeh shalom.* A priest is called up first to read the Torah, and after him a Levite and then a lay Israelite. . . . In the interests of peace, the water-pit that is nearest the stream is the first one filled from it. In the interests of peace, seizing something found by a deaf-mute, an idiot, or a minor is reckoned as a kind of robbery, even though they are not legally competent in Jewish law. In the interests of peace, poor idol-worshipers may not be prevented from joining the Jewish poor in gathering gleanings, forgotten sheaves, and grain left in the corner of the field" (Git. 5.8).

The larger the group we try to persuade to live together, the harder it is to make everyone happy. One is fortunate, then, if one lives in a community where the justice system is sound and the political life healthy. But even the best social systems require a moral citizenry. The founders of America warned coming generations against fractiousness and factionalism. The need for social unity is equally strong in the Jewish tradition: "Hezekiah said: Great is peace, for the Torah says about the wilderness journeys of the Israelites, 'And they journeyed . . . and they pitched' [Num. 33:5]. There was sufficient dissension that the people are described in the plural. When, however, they came to Mount Sinai, they all became one camp, as it is stated, 'And there Israel camped before the mount' [Exod. 19:2]. God noticed that Israel had come together and knew that this was the time to give the Torah to the people of Israel" (Lev. R. 9.9). Knowing the degree of contention existing between Jews in our time, we are inclined to imagine the notion of a unified Jewish community as another of the Bible's miracles!

More significant, though historically questionable, is this report: "Although the school of Shammai and the school of Hillel were in disagreement—what the one forbade, the other permitted—the school of Shammai did not refrain from marrying women of the families of the school of Hillel, nor did the school of Hillel refrain from marrying those of the school of Shammai. This should teach that they showed love and friendship toward another, practicing, 'Love truth, but also peace' [Zech. 8:19]" (Yev. 14b). Trying to extend these attitudes from family and neighborhood to our nation and the world is a critical moral challenge of our time.

May You, at Long Last, Rest in Peace

Since even good lives are filled with toil and turmoil, we remember our beloved dead by saying, after we mention their names, *alav/aleha ha-shalom,* peace be upon him/her. This is a hope that dates back to the Bible: "R. Levi b. Ḥita said: One who leaves a funeral should not say to the dead, 'Go unto peace' but, 'Go in peace' . . . because God said to Abraham, 'You shall go to your fathers in peace' [Gen. 15:15]" (M.K. 29a). Particularly when someone has suffered protracted emotional adversity or physical pain, the release promised by the peace of death can almost be welcomed. As R. Meir taught: "When a righteous man departs from the world, three groups of angels warmly receive him with the greeting of *shalom.* The first says, 'Let him enter in peace,' the second says, 'Let him rest on his couch,' and the third says, 'Each one that walked in righteousness' [Isa. 57:2]" (Num. R. 11.7). But even those whose lives have not been particularly troubled hope for an ultimate peace. So we read about Judah ha-Nasi: "As Rabbi was dying, he raised his fingers toward heaven and prayed, 'Sovereign of the Universe, it is revealed and known to you that I have labored in the study of Torah with all ten of my fingers and that I did not seek the benefits of this world with even the littlest of them. May it be Your will, therefore, that there be peace in my final resting place.' A Heavenly Voice then proclaimed, 'He shall enter into peace; they shall rest on their beds' [Isa. 57:2]" (Ket. 104a). To this day at funerals and memorial services we intone the *El malei raḥamim* prayer, "God, full of compassion . . ." which in resounding conclusion appeals: May *Adonai* be his/her possession and may his/her repose be *shalom.*"

"A Bad Peace Is Better Than a Good War" (Yiddish Proverb)

Only within the last two hundred years have Jews had much of a say regarding international war and peace. Before that, Jews were not considered worthy of citizenship, since they lived isolated from the community in mandatory ghettos. Of course, only in a democracy, a fairly recently developed form of government, are ordinary people allowed to make their voices heard. Hundreds of years ago a wise sage said, "When kings are engaged in controversy, it is of little concern to the common folk" (Gen. R. 93.2). Nevertheless, the Torah admonishes the people of Israel to first offer peace to their enemies, and attack only if these efforts are rebuffed (Deut. 20:10, Deut. R. 5.13).

Our devotion to peace has received new expression in contemporary paraphrases of *sim shalom,* the prayer for peace said during each morning worship. Here is an early-twentieth-century translation from the morning service of the *British Authorized Daily Prayer Book* compiled by Rabbi Joseph H. Hertz, the late chief rabbi of Great Britain: "Grant peace, welfare, blessing, grace, lovingkindness and mercy unto us and all Israel, Thy people . . . may it be good in Thy sight to bless Thy people Israel at all times and in every hour with Thy peace." Its scope is the praying community, and the people of Israel and their needs. The second paraphrase was composed for the Reform Jewish prayer book at the end of the nineteenth century by Rabbi David Philipson, one of the first graduates of Hebrew Union College, the Reform Jewish seminary: "Grant us peace, Thy most precious gift, O Thou eternal source of peace, and enable Israel to be a messenger of peace unto the peoples of the earth. Bless our country that it may ever be a stronghold of peace, and its advocate in the council of nations. . . ." While these nationalistic sentiments may be implicit in the traditional prayer, here they have become explicit, in keeping with the expanded political enfranchisement and social consciousness of modern Jews.

The Inner Peace We Crave

The turmoil of contemporary society seems to have magnified our search for personal quietude. While we still reel from fallout from the almost century-old Freudian revolution, and our turn to meditation and introspection may be more intense than before, we find similar expressions in medieval Jewish tradition. Thus, the eleventh-century Jewish philosopher Solomon ibn Gabirol could say in his anthology of moral sayings: "He is the greatest of men whose mind is most tranquil and whose association with others is most happy" (*Mivhar Hapeninim*, 400). The late-thirteenth-century ethicist Bahya b. Asher relates our search for overtly religious solutions to the problems of the spirit: "All of the precepts of the Torah bring peace to the body and soul . . . because, through the fulfillment of the commandments, the soul gains a perfection and purity that links it to its Source" *(Kad Hakemah)*. Rabbi Simha Bunim of Przysucha captures the inwardness of hasidic messianic thought in his teaching: "Our sages say, 'Seek peace in your own place.' You cannot find peace anywhere save in your own self. . . . Only when we have made peace within ourselves, will we be able to make peace in the whole world" (Buber, *Tales of the Hasidim*, bk. 2, *The Later Masters*). When we look to Jewish practice as a spiritual discipline for the individual, Jewish duty becomes an intensely personal path to *shalom*.

Shalom is a Process, a Work Always Under Way

Peace is not so much a state of being as a process of becoming that illumines our lives. Judah the Pious had this in mind when he wrote: "We should think how far we would travel in order to see our sons or daughters when we want to see them, or the lengths we would go in order to see our love. Then we may realize how much more we should pursue peace within our actual ability to do so" (Judah Hehasid, *Sefer Hasidim*, 954). We are allowed to sample this peace every week when we celebrate the Sabbath. But we will not own this *shalom* until the coming of the Messiah, in whatever guise we anticipate the advent of the End of Days. As R. Yose the Galilean said: "Great is peace, for even the name of the Messiah is *Shalom*, as it states, 'And His name is called . . . *Sar Shalom*, a peaceable ruler.' . . . Great is peace, for when the Messiah reveals himself to Israel his first message will be peace, as it is written, 'How beautiful upon the mountains are the feet of the messenger of good tiding announcing *shalom*' [Isa. 9:5 and 52:7]" (P. Hashalom 11, 13). But it is Micah's vision that has captured human hearts: "In the days to come, the Lord's house shall stand firm above the mountains . . . and nations shall go and say, 'Come, let us go up to the mount of the Lord.' . . . And they shall beat their swords into plowshares and their spears into pruning hooks. Nations shall never again know war. But all of us shall sit under our vine and fig tree, and none shall make us afraid" (Mic. 4:–4).

From Our Tradition

Bar Kapara said: Great is peace, for even the angels, among whom there is no enmity, jealously, hatred, strife, rivalry, or dissension, need *Adonai* to keep peace among them. How much more so, then, do people, among whom all these evil dispositions are rife, need God's help that peace exist among them?

—P. Hashalom 8

There was once a fierce rivalry between a king's two best fighting legions. When the time came for the king to wage war, what did he do? He made peace between them, and they both marched out and executed the king's orders together.

—Exod. R. 12.4

R. Yehuda b. R. Simon said: The poor man sits and complains, saying, "How am I different from So-and-so? Yet he sits in his own house, while I sit here in this hovel; he sleeps on his own bed, while I sleep on the bare ground." So you come forward and give him something to ease his poverty. "Then," God says, " I will deem it as though you had made peace between him and Me."

—Lev. R. 34.16

Seek peace with your friend and pursue it with your enemy. Seek it in your place and pursue it in other places. Seek it with your body and pursue it with your money. Seek it for yourself and pursue it for others. Seek it today and pursue it tomorrow. And do not despair, saying, "I will never achieve peace," but pursue it until you do.

—Yehiel b. Yekutiel, *Sefer Maalot Hamiddot*

Rabbi David of Lelov and his disciple Yitzhak were invited to a community to make peace between two men who had a long-standing quarrel. On the Sabbath he acted as the reader of the prayers. The two adversaries were present. After the Sabbath ended Rabbi David ordered the horses harnessed for the journey home. "But the rabbi has not carried out what he came for," said his disciple. "You are mistaken," said Rabbi David. "When in the course of my prayer I said: 'He who makes peace in the high places, may He make peace for us,' the peace was made." And it was really so.

—Buber, *Tales of the Hasidim*, bk. 2, *The Later Masters*

Elijah the prophet comes down to earth only to make peace.

—Judah Hehasid, *Sefer Hasidim*, 508

Staying Worthy

$\mathcal{N}$othing shapes our character more than what we regularly do. But that doesn't seem to make sense. Isn't our nature significantly shaped by the thoughts that mirror our ideas and the emotions that color them? Of course it is! Otherwise we would not write a book that tries to point you toward the self you know you ought to be. Yet however much our sages loved a sharp mind and sought to cultivate our sense of values, they cared more about how we actually acted than what we said or felt. The idealistic realism of our teachers required that we always give priority to how, in fact, we behave. Since these long-range visionaries thought in terms of lifetimes and historic destiny, they valued our continued stability more than sporadic spontaneity. Our tradition built the good Jewish life around those personal traits we have been describing, a solid foundation of sacred habits.

Our musarists identified three areas of action that particularly mold the Jewish soul. The chief of these, unsurprisingly, is a life of Torah, both its study and observance. But people's enormous talent for sinning links *teshuvah*, repentance, so closely to Torah that we may call it Torah's "shadow." For Torah demands we fulfill the duty of *teshuvah* whenever we do what we shouldn't, or overlook what merits our doing. And since Torah and *teshuvah* are grounded in our ongoing relationship with God, we need to stay in touch with the Divine regularly. The continuous empowerment of *tefillah*, prayer, actively steers our efforts to stay worthy. Thus we say with our sages that Torah, *teshuvah*, and *tefillah* serve as the three pillars that support Jewish character. Let us now examine them.

CHAPTER 20

· · · · · · · · · · · · · · ·

Torah and Observing the Commandments—
Torah Vekiyum Mitzvot

$\mathcal{T}$orah is more than a scroll we keep, more than a book, a collection, or even all the books written in its name. Torah is the ideal that guides Jewish thought, words, and action. Torah is that primal wisdom that Jewish legend credits with assisting God in fashioning the universe: "*Adonai* created me at the beginning of His work, the first act of His acts of old. . . . I was there when God set the heavens into place, when God fixed the horizon upon the deep" (Prov. 8:22, 27). The rabbis imagined Torah as a kind of divinely authored blueprint: "Just as an architect does not build something out of his head but employs plans and diagrams . . . so God consulted the Torah and created the world" (Gen. R. 1.1). No wonder the Psalmist cannot contain his praise for all that Torah is and does:

> "Adonai's *Torah is perfect, restoring the soul;*
> Adonai's *testimony is trustworthy, making the simple wise;*
> Adonai's *precepts are just, rejoicing the heart;*
> Adonai's *commandment is pristine, brightening the eyes;*
> *the awe of* Adonai *is pure, lasting forever;*
> Adonai's *statutes are true, altogether righteous. . . ."*
> —Ps. 19:8–10

Like wisdom, *ḥokhmah,* the Torah has a feminine persona; indeed, to our mind's eye she is a most adored queen. We "dress"

251

her regally, wrapping her elegantly in a gold-embroidered mantle; she is bedecked with jewels and silver finery and dwells in royal splendor in a beautifully appointed home. When she comes into public view, we rise in her honor, singing her praises. Her officials lead her in procession, encouraging the people to press forward and eagerly touch or kiss her robe. The congregation sits only when she is brought to her proper place of authority, the Torah lectern, where she remains modestly covered until just before the Torah reading begins. Afterward, the community again stands as she is lifted for our adulation and then regarbed in her regalia. The community stands yet a third time as she returns to her dwelling place, the holy ark. Truly, she is "more desirable than gold, even than much fine gold; sweeter than honey, than drippings of the honeycomb" (Ps. 19:11).

The Literal Torah: Our Most Sacred Text

The Torah ideal is made concrete in the Torah scroll, our handwritten, one-sided, most holy book. Much of it describes what transpired between God and the Hebrews, brokered by the man who led these slaves to freedom. We honor the leader of the Hebrews when we refer to Torah as "the five books of Moses." Our tradition states that Moses reveals the Torah's religious significance as he briefs the people, now a religious group covenanted to God, as they are about to enter the Holy Land: "Gather the people—men, women, children, and the strangers in your communities—that they may hear this Torah and thus learn to revere *Adonai,* your God, and to observe faithfully every word of it" (Deut. 31:12).

Some scholars trace the origin of our regular communal Torah reading to a great moment late in the fifth century B.C.E., after the Jewish leaders Ezra and Nehemiah led a band of Babylonian exiles back to the land of Israel: "When the Israelites were settled in their towns, the entire people assembled as one in the square before the Water Gate, and they asked Ezra the scribe to bring the scroll of the Torah of Moses, *Sefer Torat Moshe.* . . . They read from the scroll, translating it and giving it sense, so that the people understood the reading" (Neh. 8:1, 8). This public study of Scripture inaugurates universal education as a means of teaching religious piety, leading the way to the ensuing rabbinic period in Judaism.

In its broad usage, Torah includes both the historical and prophetic books, and the miscellany called the "Writings." This gives us the Bible as Jews know it today, any part of which we refer to as Torah without lessening the special authority of the five books contained in the sacred scroll. In addition, the dynamism of Torah encompasses what the rabbis call "Oral Law," which, tradition tells us, was also revealed by God to Moses on Mount Sinai. We still call such works "Oral Torah," though they were soon written in book form. They are the primary arsenal of the dreams, ideas, and practices that enabled Jews to face all that history dealt them: "R. Samuel b. Naḥman used to say: the words of Torah are weapons. Just as arms stand up in battle for their owners, so too, words of Torah stand up for those who labor to understand these texts" (P.R.K. 12).

To this day, Judaism is the religion and the practice of the Torah books. Thus our *rite de passage* for adolescents, becoming a bar or bat mitzvah, involves publicly demonstrating competence in that most sacred of instruction manuals, the Torah. Extend this to the constant torrent of words heard in most Jewish households and the heated dinner table discussions, and we have discovered the cultural origins for our congenital need to debate and analyze that so many of us seem blessed (or cursed) with!

Torah: A Process That Never Ceases

Despite its bookish content, Torah is more a dynamic than a literature. It is the understanding that the Jewish people has chosen to carry forward in its ongoing covenant relationship with God. Nearly two thousand years ago Ben Azzai so described Torah's continued vibrancy: "Torah is not even as old as a decree issued two or three days ago, but is as a decree issued this very day . . ." (P.R.K. 12). New challenges make new Torah. For example, early in the twentieth century anesthesia became generally available to lessen women's pain during childbirth. Pious women wondered whether they could conscientiously use it, for did not God say to Eve, and thus to every female thereafter: "I will intensify your pangs in childbearing; in pain shall you bear children" (Gen. 3:16)? It did not take long for rabbinic authorities to permit its use, since they knew that the severe pain that women experience at this time could endanger their lives.

Today a host of such bioethical issues has introduced a vast literature on Jewish medical ethics. And this is only one field in which contemporary grappling with various interpretations of Torah continues. Major differences between Orthodox and various non-Orthodox groups center around just how this Torah process should most authentically proceed. Yet for all that diversity divides us, it validates Torah, agreeing with the ancient words: "The words of Torah are life to the one who finds them" (Prov. 4:22).

The First Path of Torah: Study as a Lifetime Ideal

In the middle of the second century C.E., when the Roman authorities wanted to punish the Jews of Palestine for rebelling against them, they sought to rob the people of their future: they forbade Torah study on pain of death. But rabbinic literature glories in the risks that our sages took to defy their enemies. Here is a tale of R. Akiba and his colleague R. Tarfon, one of the foremost (and wealthiest) rabbis of the period, hiding with their cronies in a farmer's loft, carrying out their "criminal" activity: "R. Tarfon and some elders were reclining in an upper chamber in the house of Aris in Lydda, when this question was raised: Which is greater—study or practice? . . . R. Akiba said, 'Study is greater'" (Sifre Deut. 41). [We shall return to this text to hear opposing opinions.] Hillel agreed, for he said with unaccustomed rigor: "The empty headed can't be sin-fearing, the ignorant can't be pious" (Avot 2.6). Maimonides neatly summarizes the unequivocal requirements of the law: "Every man, without exception, is obligated to study Torah. It makes no difference whether he is rich or poor, healthy or ill, young or old. . . . Every Jew must set aside definite times to study by day and by night. . . . One must continue to study until the day of his death" (M.T., Hil. Tal. Torah, 1.8–10). More pithily, a Yiddish maxim prescribes: "As long as you live, you study." A not-so-subtle tinkering produces a directive that echoes in most Jewish hearts: "As long as you study, you live." And the practical reason for this is given by still another Yiddish proverb: "You don't acquire Torah by inheritance." Something similar must have led the medieval Spanish scholar Solomon b. Isaac to write: "Each child should have in his house a chair on which a talmudic work rests, so he can always open the book as soon as he comes home" *(Hebrew Ethical Wills)*.

To our sages, the best of all possible worlds would be one in which we did not have to support ourselves and our loved ones, but could devote our lives to the study of Torah. Jewish folklore similarly fantasizes about studying with Moshe Rabbenu, Moses, our Teacher, in the world to come. Yet in this world, where we must produce our bread "with the sweat of our brows" (Gen. 3:19), most of us are able to devote only a few precious moments in our hectic schedules to a little Torah. Apparently that is not a new problem. A custom arose among eleventh-century French Jews of Rashi's time to include a "bare-bones" minimum of study texts that each Jew would recite at the start of the daily morning service. One's obligation to fulfill the commandment of Torah study is thus satisfied with three verses from the Torah and two rabbinic passages (T. Ber. 11b). Let us see how even this pittance of education helps to shape our lives.

Our French sages picked the three biblical verses that make up the Temple priestly benediction: "May *Adonai* bless and guard you; may *Adonai* glow with concern for you and be gracious to you; may *Adonai* pay special attention to you and grant you peace" (Num. 6:24–26). So we begin not with laws directing what we should do for God, or for others in God's name, but with a sense of what God may do for us! Yes, we all can use as much divine help as we can get! Though we are right to expect much of ourselves, our efforts alone cannot provide for everything. A quiet sense of our partnership with God empowers even as it humbles.

Our abbreviated daily study continues with two rabbinic passages we also have seen before: "These are the things about which the Law prescribes no acceptable amount—how large a corner you must leave in your farm field for the gleaners to reap, how many first fruits you need to bring to the Temple, how great an offering you need to bring when you come to the Temple on the three pilgrimage festivals, acts of *gemilut ḥasadim,* and how long you need to study Torah each day" (Pe'ah 1.1). *Gemilut ḥasadim,* we already know, involves us in a variety of duties toward others. In its own way, how we handle the harvest of our field makes a similar point. Content with our own well-being, we remember the poor by not completely harvesting our field; so we round the corner, *pe'ah,* and leave what remains for the needy. And whatever involves us, we should let our hearts, rather than our wallets, decide just how much is enough.

A talmudic passage from another tractate is appended to the Mishnah Pe'ah text as our second rabbinic study passage: "These are the things, whose 'dividends' we enjoy in this world, while the 'capital' remains for us in the world to come: honoring our parents, *gemilut ḥasadim,* early attendance at the house of study in the morning and evening, hospitality to travelers, visiting the sick, providing for a bride, escorting the dead to the grave, absorption in prayer, and making peace between people—but the study of the Torah is equal to them all" (Shab. 127a).

Now the full impact of study upon character becomes clear. This pedagogy involves us completely in routine, real-life situations, rather than encouraging an ivory tower retreat. The ideal life of Torah is one of total immersion, not contemplative theorizing. And the text speaks commandingly to both "them, then" and to "us, now." Thus through study we are reminded to reach out to others, breathing renewed life, warmth, and hope into our covenant community.

Torah Lishmah: **Study for Its Own Sake**

Talk of rewards we are to receive both in this world and the next does not seem high-minded enough for some of our teachers. If Torah is so wondrous a gift, then we should pursue it simply to fill our lives with its words and sacred meaning: "Do not say, 'I will read the Bible that I may be called a sage; I will investigate the traditions that I may be called a rabbi; I will study that I may be called an elder and sit in the assembly of elders'; but study out of love and let what honors come as may. . . . R. Eliezer b. R. Zadok said: Do good deeds because of your regard for their Commander and study the words of Torah for their own sake. Do not use them as a crown to magnify yourself with, or as a spade to hoe with" (Ned. 62a).

Though this idea is a noble one, it clashes with the dominant motifs of western civilization. Too often we are taught to become paragons of pragmatism or even opportunism, calculating our profit before investing much effort. Even if the understanding of "what's in it for me" is subtle and refined, like elevating our humanity or making us better people, we too often live with our eyes on the prize instead of the task before us. Of course, all of our sages believed there are great rewards in studying and living by the Torah. But those who preached the vision of *Torah lishmah* did so from their passionate conviction of the intrinsic worth of studying God's word. They want us not only to love God but to love God's Torah. And from this devotion grew a religious tradition that gives at least as much adulation to the learned as to those rare unabashedly good, saintly souls of our faith.

Torah Is Doing: Performing Mitzvot

Where the scholar par excellence R. Akiba championed the pre-eminence of Torah as study, R. Tarfon proclaimed in that same gathering in the attic of Aris in Lydda: "Practice is more important than study" (Sifre Deut. 41). R. Tarfon may well have had this verse from the Book of Proverbs in mind: "The keeper of a mitzvah keeps his soul" (Prov. 19:16). The Mishnah reiterates this teaching: "Whoever performs even a single commandment, it shall go well with him, and his days shall be prolonged, and he shall inherit the Land" (Kid. 1.10). Elisha b. Abuyah, a contemporary of R. Akiba and R. Tarfon, is chiefly remembered as the scholar who eventually became an apostate. Nonetheless, his accepted teachings are duly recorded in the Talmud: "A man who has good deeds to his credit and has also studied much Torah, is like one who builds a structure and lays stones below it as its foundation, and clay bricks above it for the structure. Then even should much water collect, the building will not wash away. But a man who has no good deeds to his credit, though he has studied Torah, is like one who builds a structure and lays down a foundation of clay bricks and puts the stones above that.

Then even a little water will undermine the building" (A.R.N. 24). Using language that belies the timidity we often associate with mystics, the thirteenth-century Franco-German adept, Judah the Pious, boldly states: "Better is a little done out of awe for God than a pack of rascals who sits all day studying but does not do much else" (Judah Heḥasid, *Sefer Ḥasidim,* 17).

For "doing Torah" forms the basis of Jewish character, shaping our lives by guiding our actions: "My rules alone shall you observe and faithfully follow my laws. . . . You shall keep My laws and my rules, by the pursuit of which a man shall live: I am *Adonai* your God" (Lev. 18:4–5). The next chapter of Leviticus deals with stealing and defrauding, with respecting laborers, not taking advantage of the deaf or blind, showing no partiality in a court of law, and calling for love, not grudges, between neighbors. These injunctions are not solely for analysis or intellectual musing. They demand doing. "Wherever you go, mitzvot accompany you. 'When you build a new house, make a railing for your roof' [Deut. 22:8]. When you make a door for it, a mitzvah accompanies you. 'And you shall write them on the doorposts of your house' [Deut. 6:9]. When you go to cut your hair, a mitzvah accompanies you. 'Do not round off the corners of your head' [Lev. 19:27]. And so with plowing, sowing, and harvesting, and so with everything!" [Deut. R. 6.3]. Naḥmanides, the great medieval Spanish commentator, directs us to learn so as to observe mitzvot: "Take care to study Torah always so that you will be able to fulfill its commands. When you rise from study, ponder carefully what you have learned; see what there is in it which you can put into practice" (Letter of Naḥmanides in Feuer, *A letter for the ages*).

R. Tarfon's formula "It is not your duty to finish the task, but neither are you free to desist from it" (Avot 2.16) has been cited so often in recent years that it has become something of a cliché. It was a soothing balm for the chronic Jewish overachievers who could not complete all that they had overextended themselves into attempting—and if that remains your complaint, we commend Tarfon to you. But familiarity and a change of social ethos have turned a sensible limitation into an excuse for being almost as satisfied with starting something as with carrying it through to its conclusion.

Perhaps for the foremost tasks of humanity, contentment with making a beginning contains sparks of moral grandeur. But for the myriad of small duties that make up responsible living, we prefer what we learn from the scoring rules of America's favorite spectator sport, major-league baseball. The pitcher who successfully concludes the game receives credit for the win, not the one who goes to the showers after a few innings. The Bible describes a similar situation. Moses, knowing Joseph's wishes to be buried in Canaan, exhumes the patriarch's bones in Egypt and schleps them through the desert for 40 years (Exod. 13:19). But since Moses doesn't enter the land, it is Joshua, Moses's successor, who buries Joseph's remains, which is why this is mentioned in the book that bears Joshua's name (Josh. 24:32). This observation leads the rabbis to comment: "Not the one who begins the task, but the one who completes it receives credit for it" (Gen. R. 85.4).

An Iraqi proverb reminds us of the special power of mitzvot: "Good deeds are like a menorah; out of its fire, others have light." Doesn't knowing or hearing of someone who quietly cares for others momentarily make us wish we were doing more of the same? Francie knows a woman who helps care for both her invalid mother and mother-in-law; in her spare time, she drives cancer patients to their doctor appointments. For years Gene's neighbor, among other good deeds, regularly has read for a blind person he did not previously know. We confess: we did not write this book merely to add to America's Everest of reading matter. We hope it will bring you to more Jewish doing. This is our tradition's hope as well: "A man has three loves in his life: his family, his wealth, and his good deeds. Before departing this world, he gathers his family around him and says, 'I pray you, free me of this stern judgment of death.' They reply, 'Have you not heard that there is no redemption from death?' [Ps. 49:8]. He then gathers his wealth and says, 'Free me of this stern judgment of death.' Wealth says, 'Have you not heard, wealth will not avail on the day of wrath?' [Prov. 11:4]. He then gathers his mitzvot and says, 'Rescue me . . .' They reply, 'Before you go, we shall precede you, "and your righteousness shall go before you"' [Isa. 58:8]" (P.R.E. 34).

When it comes to performing the commandments, regularity is the hallmark of piety. Sacred habit is the evidence of genuine Jewish devotion: "Ben Azzai says: Run to an easy mitzvah as to a difficult one, and flee from transgression, for one mitzvah leads to another mitzvah, and one transgression leads to another transgression" (Avot 4.2). And a later commentator affirms: "When a mitzvah presents itself, rejoice not in that one, but in the one that follows" (A.R.N. 33). As there is an ideal of *Torah lishmah,* there is also an ideal of *mitzvah lishmah.* The thirteenth-century Roman sage Yeḥiel b. Yekutiel explains: "If God had explicitly stated the reward for doing each of the mitzvot, they would not be performed for the sake of Heaven . . . people would do only those offering great benefits and neglect others, leaving some of them undone" *(Sefer Maalot Hamiddot).*

So Is Torah Mostly for Study or for Doing?
The Rabbinic Ruling

The rabbis often live by either/or—if the Pesaḥ wine cup won't hold a bird's egg in it, you can't drink four cupfuls and fulfill your Pesaḥ obligation; when you are making *kiddush,* the blessing for the wine precedes the blessing for the special occasion, Shabbat or *yom tov.* But as we have seen, often the rabbis are loath to abstain from any good idea, and they live by both/and. So let us return to our Akiba/Tarfon controversy over Torah: "R. Tarfon and some elders were reclining in an upper chamber in the house of Aris in Lydda when this question was raised: Which is greater—study or practice? R. Tarfon said, 'Practice is more important than study.' R. Akiba said, 'Study is greater.' At that all the rabbis present spoke up and said, 'Study is greater for it leads to practice'" (Sifre Deut. 41). To put this in more contemporary terms: "A man came to the Kotzker Rebbe and asked how he could make his children devote themselves to Torah. The rabbi answered: 'If you really want them to do this, then you yourself must spend time over Torah, and they will do as you do. Otherwise, they will not devote themselves to Torah, but, when they have a family, they will tell their children to do it, and so it will go on'" (Buber, *Tales of the Hasidim,* bk. 2, *The Later Masters).*

From Our Tradition

[We devote this entire section to a surprising but delightful story from the Talmud. We love its unique mix of what doesn't change in human nature and what can change. But do remember, please— this is only a story.]

R. Nathan said: There is not a single precept in the Torah whose reward is not enjoyed in this world. You may learn this from the mitzvah of *tzitzit,* which requires us to put tassels on the corners of any poncho-like garment.

Once a disciple of the sages heard of a harlot who was so desirable that her charge was 400 dinars, an extraordinary amount. He gathered and sent her the 400 dinars and set up an appointment with her. For this assignation she prepared a ladder-like arrangement of seven beds, six of silver leading to one of gold. She went up to the top bed and lay down upon it naked. He too went up after her and undressed, hot with his passion to lie with her.

But in the course of that his *tzitzit,* the four fringes of his garment, struck him across the face and awakened him to what he was doing. He slipped down the beds and sat on the ground. She also slipped down the beds and sat upon the ground beside him and said, "I will not leave you alone until you tell me what blemish you saw in me." He replied, "Never have I seen a woman as beautiful as you are, but there is a precept that God has commanded us called *tzitzit.* With regard to it, the expression 'I am *Adonai* your God' is written twice [in the verse, Num. 15:41]. It means, I am He who will exact punishment in the future, and I am He who will give reward in the future. The *tzitzit* appeared to me as four witnesses testifying against me. She said, "I will not leave you until you tell me your name, the name of your town, the name of your teacher, and the name of your school in which you study Torah." He wrote this down and handed it to her.

She went with her bedclothes to the *beit midrash* of R. Ḥiyya, and said to him, "Master, give me instruction that will make me a proselyte." He replied, "My daughter, perhaps you have met one of my disciples?" She took out the scrap of paper and handed it to him.

He said, "Go and enjoy your acquisition." Those very bedclothes that she had spread for the disciple for an illicit purpose she now spread for him lawfully.

—Men. 44a

CHAPTER 21

. . . .

Repentance—*Teshuvah*

Adonai *said to Moses . . . "take the rod and assemble the
community and before their very eyes, order the rock to yield
its water."* . . . *And Moses said to them, "Listen, you rebels,
shall we get water for you out of this rock?" Moses raised his
hand and struck the rock twice with his rod.*

—Num. 20:8, 10–11

*David flew into a rage when he heard the prophet Nathan's
story. It seems that a rich man had taken a poor man's
small ewe, rather than one from his own extensive flocks.
David said, "As* Adonai *lives, the one who did this deserves
to die!" Nathan then said to David: "That rich man is you!*
. . . *Why have you flouted* Adonai's *command?* . . . *You
took Bathsheba, the wife of Uriah the Hittite and made her
your wife, and then had Uriah killed by the sword of the
Ammonites."* . . . *David said to Nathan, "I stand guilty before
Adonai." Nathan said, "Adonai has remitted your sin."*

—2 Sam. 12:5–7, 9, 13

s if we didn't know already—nobody is perfect. And
no matter how hard we try, we will probably add to
our list of sins by the end of the week. True, we may
not directly disobey God's instructions like Moses or use our power
to commit murder and adultery like David. But as soon as we
assume that our next sin will be "only" as little as unintentionally
hurting someone's feelings, we have as good as issued an invitation
to the Evil Urge to work its wiles on us. And our next transgression
may be an act we didn't think ourselves capable of—big sins do
occasionally happen. Now add in all the things we should have been

263

doing but "forgot" to do—like calling our aged aunt, mailing the promised pledge check, or passing another Shabbat without a word of prayer, while stealing time for a work project—again. If our two most revered biblical role models, Moses and David, sinned grievously—and the authors of the Bible make sure to remind us that they did—we don't stand a chance in the halo department. The Bible's point is that you don't need to be perfect to win, playing the Jewish righteousness game. We all are human and must learn to live with those imperfections that so well define us. As the author of Ecclesiastes states: "For there is no one on earth who does what is best and does not sin." (7:20). Similarly, the Yiddish proverb reminds us: "Even the Temple High Priest had to repent for himself and his family before he sought atonement for others."

David is our model for the Jewish work of holy healing: "He who wishes to repent ought to look to King David as an exemplar. As the Psalm says: 'Many shall see and fear,' but seeing how his relationship with God was reestablished, they shall trust in *Adonai*" (Mid. Pss. 40.2).

The Way of the Penitent: The Great Rabbinic Creation

Our tradition calls this therapeutic enterprise *teshuvah*, literally, "turning around." In English we refer to it as "repentance." Though *sh-u-v*, the Hebrew root of this term, is often used in the Bible in reference to repentance—Ezekiel 18 is a well-organized sermon on *teshuvah*—the noun form only took on special connotations in later, rabbinic literature.

Our sages praise *teshuvah* highly. They saw what God had provided to help us make amends for our failings. So they teach: "God knew that humankind would sin. Therefore God created our means of healing, *teshuvah,* even before the heavens and earth, long before we were around to incur wounds because we had transgressed" (Pes. 54a). The rabbis are filled with admiration for someone who repents: "How can it be shown that if a man turns from his evil ways and does *teshuvah* for his misdeeds, his many iniquities are now regarded as merits? Consider the words of the prophet Ezekiel: 'If the wicked turn from wickedness and do what is just and right, by virtue of these things, they shall live' [Ezek. 33:19]" (Exod. R. 31.1).

A later midrash gives us a practical explanation for why our sages so adored the act of *teshuvah:* "Repentance is greater than charity. To give charity you must expend money, but *teshuvah* entails no expenses. The Holy One seeks from Israel no more than repentance by means of words, as the prophet teaches: 'Take with you words and return unto *Adonai*' [Hos. 14:3]" (Eliezer Zuta 22). And R. Yose b. Tzartzos hyperbolically equates doing *teshuvah* with doing everything admirable: "One who repents is esteemed as if he had gone up to Jerusalem, built the Temple and the altar, and offered upon it all the sacrifices mentioned in the Law" (Lev. R. 7.2). As R. Abbahu states somewhat more soberly: "Even the wholly righteous do not stand at the height the repentant sinner attains" (San. 99a).

The Torah prescribes Yom Kippur, with its elaborate Temple rituals, as an annual rite for the community to seek atonement for its sins. It remained for the rabbis to create practices by which individuals (and, after the Temple was destroyed, the community) might reconcile themselves with God. Well versed in human frailty, they want *teshuvah* to be as much a part of our daily lives as mitzvot, for each depends on the other. "R. Eliezer said to his students, 'Repent one day before you die.' His disciples said, 'Who knows when we will die?' 'All the more reason to do so,' he replied. 'Let us repent today, for, heaven forbid, we might die tomorrow; and also on the morrow lest we die the day thereafter. The result will be that all our lives will be spent in repentance'" (A.R.N. 15).

The rabbinic pattern for doing *teshuvah* has four overlapping aspects. We want to comment on each, from both a rabbinic and a contemporary understanding.

Self-Consciousness: Recognizing We Did Wrong and Becoming Remorseful about It

As we have seen, King David was a blissful sinner until the prophet Nathan's words punctured his fantasy of propriety. He then made no protestations of innocence and no effort to deny reality, a brutally honest self-awareness that took character and deserves emulation, as much as his immoral deeds deserve condemnation. For who of us has not resisted "facing the facts"? But denial is the enemy of healing; until we are truly remorseful, we will not be motivated to turn our lives around.

One of our chief aids to studying this topic is the late medieval *musar* book *Orḥot Tzaddikim* (The ways of the righteous). We don't know who wrote this substantial work more than 450 years ago, but its section on *teshuvah* is a fine digest of what previous sages had taught. Of all that *Orḥot Tzaddikim* says are necessary for repentance: "The first is that one must know his deeds. . . . If one does not know wherein he has transgressed, how can he regret what he has done? . . . As it is written, 'For I know my iniquities, and my sin is always before me' [Ps. 51:5]."

In this case, "knowing" immediately implies self-judgment, recognizing where we have come up short. As *Orḥot Tzaddikim* indicates: "If one thinks: 'What of it, if I've benefited from things in this world and never said a blessing over them, or if I've neglected Torah study? That's not so terrible.' One who thinks like this will never be filled with remorse and therefore will not repent with a full heart. For remorse is that quality wherein a person does something, and in retrospect regrets the deed." It is the emotional spur that moves us to repent, so we "must seize upon the trait of remorse and impress it upon our heart."

There is something logical about this first step. A basic tenet of Judaism teaches that God gave each of us free will, endowing us with the great dignity of being responsible for our deeds. If we do not continually evaluate what we do and change it when necessary, we are doomed to lives of ignorance and error. We can only hope to become mature people by learning to be self-correcting, often with the help of others. Our freedom is a freedom to do better, so *teshuvah* is a critical means to fulfill the promise of our humanity.

We may better understand this if we reflect how much we are the product of our relationships. Our words or deeds have hurt those who had every reason to expect better from us. A phrase thoughtlessly spoken or a confidence betrayed may destroy a friendship that once sustained us. When we involuntarily think of the wrong we did, something gnaws at our insides, testifying to our diminished selfhood. Now worry and anxiety find their proper roles as motives for repentance. The author of *Orḥot Tzaddikim* equates genuine sorrow with remorse, differentiating them as "sorrow is for what has already taken place, while worry concerns the future." Yiddish proverbs convey a similar realism: "Only fools and horses have no reason to be remorseful," and "Who has no reason to worry? Only the kings in a pack of cards."

Confession: Acknowledging to Others What We Have Done

When we first consider it, confessing our sins may seem more a Roman Catholic than a Jewish rite. Yet, while there is considerable difference between such practices in the two faiths, Judaism has long called for *viddui,* the verbal admission that we have sinned. Once again, King David is our model. After Nathan denounces him, he responds without hesitation: "I stand guilty before *Adonai.*" As we shall see shortly, we know by David's acts of genuine remorse that this is not a glib play for favor, but is a simple admission of a painful truth (2 Sam. 12:13). Each year our High Holy Day services unite the congregation in statements of our sinfulness before God and, incidentally, each other. Poignantly we pray: *Avinu Malkenu,* "Our Father, Our King"; *Al ḥet,* "For the sin" (which we have committed by . . .). We also pray the Hebrew alphabetic acrostic *Ashamnu, bagadnu,* "We have incurred guilt, we have been treacherous . . . ," a prayer that describes our talent for sinning as limited only by the number of letters in the alphabet.

The sages do not minimize the difficulty of facing those we have wronged and confessing our deeds to them; they know how hard this is for any of us. So they give us an extreme example of what we ought to do: "Let no one say, 'If I confess, I shall lose my office,' but let one hate office, and humble ourselves, and return in repentance. Let no one say after we have sinned, 'There is no restoration for us,' but let us trust in the Lord and repent, and God will receive us" (Mid. Pss. 40.4, in Montefiore and Loewe, *A Rabbinic Anthology*). A verse from Proverbs promises even more: "He who covers up his faults will not succeed; he who confesses and gives them up will find mercy" (28:13). And another rabbinic text even holds out God's absolution, if a person will only confess the evils done: ". . . when a man confesses, God remits the charge against him" (Mid. Pss. 100.2). Today most twelve-step support groups expect members to identify themselves and their problems when they introduce themselves at meetings: "My name is . . . and I am an alcoholic." They know the old truth that verbally acknowledging what we are and are likely always to be, empowers us to gain control over our problem.

Parson Weems may have been indulging in creative midrash when he praised George Washington for confessing his cherry tree escapade to his father, but most of us seem to prefer the ideal of the story to the realities of verifiable history. For confession erases the lie of our guilty silence. By this moral, though ego-bruising act, we return to the path of personal responsibility. If we don't approach the person we have offended to acknowledge our misdeed, we debase our claims of being ethical that are so central to our self-respect.

The hurt that lingers after our deed only intensifies if the one we have offended is our friend or our love and we fail to admit what we have done. Now we have not only injured them, but created an unapproachable void between us. Worse, should our friend/love know what we did, our sin of omission adds a special bitterness to all the other hurt we have inflicted. As humbling and humiliating as facing them may feel to us, nothing else will restore what we once meant to one another. When we can admit our wrong, we demonstrate how truly we care and how genuinely we have determined to act on our remorse. As the Ladino proverb counsels: "Admitting your guilt brings you half the necessary forgiveness." We would add, admitting your guilt is surely the harder half.

Resolution: Make Up for the Wrong and Determine to Live Differently

David could not bring Uriah the Hittite back to life, or restore his wife, Bathsheba, to him. But when he heard that his child by Bathsheba had become ill, David lay on the ground, fasted, and refused to bathe or change his clothes. He did what any of us would do if, God forbid, we found ourselves in a similar situation: he implored God to save the child. Only after the child died did he desist from his fast. David's acts testify to his remorse, and to his need to make up for his past sins by clearly turning his life around through *teshuvah*.

Usually our sins, and thus our efforts to compensate for them, are less demonstrative. Sometimes, as Jonah Gerondi, the thirteenth-century Spanish ethicist, instructs us: "We can be reconciled to God by means of the very thing in which we have sinned" (*Shaarei Teshuvah* [Gates of repentance]). So New York City graffiti "artists" who are found guilty of defacing public property must give art lessons to inner-city kids through community service, as well as clean the walls that they defiled, to successfully complete their sentence and do true *teshuvah*. More commonly: "If you have heaped up bundles of transgressions, heap up against them bundles of commandments" (Lev. R. 21.4). Referring to the biggest reprobates it knew, a midrash says: "It is difficult for repentant tax and custom collectors to make restitution. So they should directly compensate those whom they know they have defrauded, and the balance due to those whom they cannot identify or reach should be devoted to public needs" (T.B.M. 8.26). Moving from secular to more particularist peccadilloes, the author of *Orhot Tzaddikim* states: "If one has gotten into the habit of talking in the synagogue and engaging in jocularity and frivolity there, from the time one becomes penitent one should take care not to speak in the synagogue about any secular thing. . . . If one has stolen or taken usury, one must ask forgiveness from the man one has injured and fast for forty days."

While the angst of remorse is usually a private, interior emotion, restitution is more visible and routine. For ethics cannot be satisfied with mood and feeling alone; the deed we do to rectify the situation remains decisive. Fortunately we have the ability to change; our subsequent deeds will demonstrate that we have overcome our previously errant behavior. Medieval *musar* has a similar understanding: "When one exerts himself to uphold truth, and strengthens men of truth and elevates them, and lowers men of falsehood unto the very dust, he engages in the sanctification of the Name" (*Orhot Tzaddikim*).

Even a symbolic act can heal a fractured relationship. Is our friend/love's world falling apart? Then a sympathetic smile or word indicates that you are aware and you care. Or drag those recycling cans to the curb, even before you are reminded to do it. Whatever you do now should testify wordlessly that you are not now the person who did "that" hateful thing. As R. Ḥana b. R. Ḥanina remarks: "Great is penitence, for it brings healing to the world, as it is said: 'I will heal their affliction, generously will I take them back in love' [Hos. 14:5]" (Yoma 86a). And men, please note—sometimes honest tears can certify the depth of our *teshuvah*. As a Ladino proverb states: "When all the gates of repentance are closed, the gates of tears still remain open." But not if they are "crocodile" tears, as the Yiddish maxim reminds us: "Tears caused by onions don't break your heart."

"'Rabbi Simḥa Bunim of Przysucha once asked his disciples: 'In this day and age, when there are no prophets, how can we tell when a sin we have committed has been pardoned?' They gave him various answers, none of which he found acceptable. 'We can only tell,' he said, 'by the fact that we no longer commit that sin'" (Buber, *Tales of the Hasidim,* bk. 2, *The Later Masters*). "R. Eliezer b. R. Yose says: If one sins and repents and then continues uprightly, he is forgiven before he stirs from the spot." (A.R.N. 40). R. Judah was more direct: "How is one proved a repentant sinner? If that which caused his original transgression comes before him on two occasions and he keeps away from . . . the same woman, at the same time, in the same place" (Yoma 86b).

Having thus qualified ourselves, we can finally ask the one we have hurt to pardon us for what we did. This is the Jewish law: "For sins against a man's neighbor, the Day of Atonement brings no forgiveness until a man has become reconciled with his neighbor" (Yer. Yoma 8.9). "Samuel said: One who has sinned against his fellow must say to him, 'I acted wrongly against you.' If he accepts this apology, then the matter is settled. If not, the penitent brings other people and attempts to mollify the person wronged in their presence. . . . It is necessary to appease the one you have injured, even if you must go to his grave and there say, 'I acted wrongly towards you'" (Yer. Yoma 8.4).

When this is done, the offended person has a duty to accept the apology. Maimonides indicates how far this must go: "If the offended party is unwilling to forgive, the wrongdoer should bring three of his friends to the wronged person, whom they entreat to pardon the sinner. If they fail, the repentant one takes a second and then a third group to solicit a pardon. If the injured party still refuses to forgive, the repentant one leaves. The one that refused now becomes the sinner" (M.T., Hil. Tesh., 2.9).

In recent, post-apartheid years, South Africa has given us an extraordinary example of this effort to bring understanding between those who have been grievously wronged and their malefactors. After hearing the confessions of those who committed bestial crimes against them, its Truth and Reconciliation Commission has granted legal amnesty to the former persecutors, an uncommon but very substantial gift of forgiveness. While it may be too soon to expect a true understanding between Germans and Jews, Jewish hopefulness makes us pray that a reconciliation between us may yet be possible.

Atonement: In Humble Confidence, Asking God for Forgiveness

The final step remains. Our most primal relationship is the one we share with God. The more we become capable of loving God with all our heart, the more we shall care about being reconciled with our Creator. If the gut-wrenching candor of Psalms reflects David's true intentions to return to a good relationship with God, we shall have no problem knowing what ideally is required of us. Psalm 51 reads:

"For the leader. A psalm of David when Nathan the prophet came to him after he had intercourse with Bathsheba. . . .

Have mercy upon me, O God,
as befits Your faithfulness;
in keeping with Your abundant compassion,
blot out my transgressions.
Wash me thoroughly of my iniquity,
and purify me of my sin;
for I recognize my transgressions,
and am ever conscious of my sin.

> *Against You alone have I sinned,*
> *and done what is evil in Your sight;*
> *so You are just in Your sentence,*
> *and right in Your judgment. . . .*
> *The true sacrifice to God is a contrite spirit;*
> *God, You will not despise*
> *a contrite and broken heart"*
>
> —Ps. 51:1–6, 19

This cry of David is the last stage in seeking *teshuvah*. It is not a matter to be put off until next Yom Kippur, but grounds the foundation of our everyday spiritual well-being. The rabbis ritualized our efforts to restore our intimacy with God, despite our misdeeds, in our three daily services. We ask God in the second intermediary prayer of the *Shemoneh Esreh,* the Eighteen Benedictions: "Turn us toward You in perfect repentance. You are blessed, *Adonai,* who desires our repentance." And then, assuming that prayer has been granted, we continue: "Forgive us, our Father, for we have sinned; pardon us, our King, for we have done iniquity. You are blessed, *Adonai,* gracious one who abundantly pardons."

Alone and in private we continue our supplications. The eighteenth-century sage Alexander Suesskind writes: "If I perceive that I committed an unintentional offense against the Creator, whether in conduct, speech, or thought, I make a broken-hearted confession without delay before God, and resolve to watch against similar offenses" *(Jewish Ethical Wills).* Samson Raphael Hirsch, the nineteenth-century founder of Modern Orthodoxy, counsels: "If you recognize that you have sinned, then step into the presence of God and say, 'O God, I have erred and sinned. I have been disobedient before you, for this, specifically, is what I have done.' . . . Lay the future of your inner and outer life in the just and forgiving hand of God . . . and make this a permanent mood and frame of mind which can bear fruit in your practical conduct" *(Horeb,* 514).

Abashed as we are, humble before God as we must be, we approach God with some confidence, not because of anything we can now claim in God's presence, but because we know the depths of God's capacity to forgive: "A king had a son who was estranged from his father. . . . His friends said, 'Return to your father.' He said, 'I cannot.' Then his father sent him a message, 'Return as far as you can, and I will come to you the rest of the way.' So God says to Israel, 'Return to me, and I will return to you'" (Pes. R. 184b–185a, in Montefiore and Loewe, *A Rabbinic Anthology*). R. Samuel b. Naḥman said: "When we wish to bathe in the sea, we can bathe in it at any hour. So with repentance. Whenever we wish to repent, God will receive us" (Lam. R. 3.60). As the prophet Hosea writes and we read each year on Shabbat Shuva, the Sabbath between Rosh Hashanah and Yom Kippur: "Return, O Israel, to *Adonai*, your God, / For you have fallen because of your sin. / Take words with you / And turn to *Adonai* . . . / 'I will heal their affliction, / In generous love will I take them back; / For my anger has turned away from them'" (Hos. 14:2–3, 5).

The Distinctive Jewish Approach to Atonement

The Jewish way to expiation for sin is remarkably universal and democratic. God is available to everyone. As the Book of Jonah reminds us, you don't have to be Jewish to do *teshuvah*. Even the Ninevites, citizens of the capital of the hated Assyrian empire, gave up their evil ways when Jonah called them to account. Then, to Jonah's intense annoyance, God promptly forgave them. Jews still read this story every Yom Kippur afternoon to remind us that God listens to the sincere supplications of gentiles as well as Jews. And this narrative also makes plain the Jewish belief that every human being, without needing a "professional" clergy or special rite, can do *teshuvah* by directly asking for God's forgiveness. Our tradition teaches that people are capable and God is caring. As the rabbis said: "The only intercessors with God a person needs are repentance and good deeds" (Shab. 32a). "Even if your sins are as high as heaven, even unto the seventh heaven, and even to the throne of glory, and you repent, I will receive you" (Pes. R. 185a, in Montefiore and Loewe, *A Rabbinic Anthology*, cf. 44.7).

Scholars debate the reason that this belief achieved its prominence in rabbinic teaching. Did we ask for forgiveness in the wake of the Temple's destruction, blaming this massive catastrophe on our grievous sins? Or was it developed as a conscious tenet to counter beliefs in an emerging Christian church? An early midrash states the rabbinic view succinctly: "'And Cain went out' [Gen. 4:16]. On his way Cain met his father Adam [neither of them, of course, were Jews]. The latter, surprised to see his son, asked, 'What has happened to the judgment of death that God passed upon you for killing Abel?' Cain replied, 'I repented, and I am pardoned.' When Adam heard that, he smote his face and said, 'Is the power of repentance as great as that? I did not know it was so'" (Lev. R. 10.5).

In contrast to Jewish teaching as it emerged at this time, classic Christian doctrine teaches that people are born as sinners, an inheritance from what Adam and Eve did in the Garden of Eden. That being the inevitable human condition, people cannot reconcile themselves to God on their own. But out of God's abundant love for humanity, God sends the Christ into history. His self-sacrifice thus saves people from their sinful state.

Judaism teaches that God's love for people is so great, they only need to show God a genuine desire to turn away from their sin, and God will accept them. Indeed, the rabbis do not hesitate to suggest that God, so to speak, also participates in our repentance: "A king's son was sick, and the doctor said that if he would eat a certain thing, he would be healed. But the son was too frightened to eat it. His father said to him, 'So that you may know that it will not harm you, I will eat of it.' God said to Israel, 'You are ashamed to repent; behold, I will be the first to repent,' as it is written: Thus says *Adonai*, Behold I will turn' [Jer. 30:18]" (Pes. R. 44.7).

Are we exaggerating the rabbinic love of *teshuvah?* If so, we stand in good company: "R. Levi said: If the Israelites would but repent for one day, they would be redeemed, and the Messiah, the son of David, would come straight away, as it says, 'Today, if you would but hear His voice' [Ps. 95:7]" (S. of S. R. 5.2).

From Our Tradition

R. Elazar b. Durdaya was addicted to harlots. A famous, very expensive courtesan became upset with him and called out that he would never receive repentance from God. On his journey home, he sat between two hills and said, "Ye hills and mountains, pray for compassion upon me." But they said, "Before we seek compassion for you, we must seek compassion for ourselves." This continued as he vainly asked for exoneration from earth and heaven, sun and moon, and the stars and planets. Finally he said, "The matter depends wholly on me." And he cried until his soul departed from his body. A heavenly voice was then heard, saying, "R. Elazar b. Durdaya is appointed for life in the world to come." When Rabbi Judah ha-Nasi heard about this, he wept and said, "There are those who hope to attain the world to come in many years, and there are those who attain it in an hour! It is not enough that the repentant are received into the life to come, but they are even called rabbis."

—A.Z. 17a

Our Rabbis have taught: If a man is guilty of a sin and confesses it, but does not change his way, what is he like? He is like a man who holds a defiling reptile in his hand. Though he should immerse himself in all the waters of the world, it will avail nothing. But as soon as he throws away the defiling reptile, an immersion in a small measure of water will be accounted to him as a cleansing bath, as it is said, "But one who confesses and forsakes his sins shall obtain mercy" [Prov. 28:13].

—Taan. 16a

Rabbi Levi Yitzhak of Berditchev said: Some people, may God preserve us, sin from passion, and others do so simply to be perverse and without any desire for what they're doing. Of the latter we read that the rebellious sinners are without hope. But the lustful sinners can have hope, for they can always turn and do *teshuvah*.

—Levi Yitzhak, *Kedushat Levi*

The "turning" is the navel of the Jewish conception of the way of man. Our tradition teaches that the turning has the power to renew someone from within and to change his status in God's world. That is why the rabbis praised it so . . .

—Martin Buber, *The Way of Man*

. . . .

CHAPTER 22

Prayer—*Tefillah*

> *Reb Naftali, the Rebbe of Ropshitz, was taking an unaccus-*
> *tomed way home when he came across a magnificent estate.*
> *He approached the man he saw patrolling the grounds, and*
> *asked him for whom he worked. The guard mentioned the*
> *name of one of the great men of the city and said he was*
> *employed to protect the estate. He then asked Reb Naftali,*
> *"And for whom do you work?" That question hit the*
> *Ropshitzer so hard that he said to the man, "Will you come*
> *work for me?" The man replied, "What would be my*
> *duties?" Answered Reb Naftali, "To remind me."*
> —Martin Buber, *Tales of the Hasidim,*
> bk. 2, *The Later Masters*

Prayer is the guard religion employs to counter our forgetfulness of God. We are not the people Judaism calls us to be if we neglect the Source and the Standard of the virtues we esteem. For the world has a thousand ways of convincing us that it deserves all our attention. Even a brief prayer snatches us from the seductive embrace of the profane, reminding us Who granted us our lives and what we ought to do with this precious gift.

The prayer book *Shaarei Tefillah* (Gates of prayer) has paraphrased an homage to prayer by Abraham Joshua Heschel that beautifully captures the power of *tefillah:* "Prayer invites the Eternal Presence to suffuse our spirits and let God's will prevail in our lives. Prayer cannot bring water to parched fields, nor mend a broken bridge, nor rebuild a ruined city. But prayer can water an arid soul, mend a broken heart, and rebuild a weakened will." Perhaps this supportive aspect of prayer has influenced its tremendous resurgence; a recent poll reports that more than half of all Americans pray at least once each day. In recent years prayers for the sick have gone far beyond a brief *mi shebeirakh,* the traditional healing prayer that begins, "May the One who blessed . . . ," to become an important part of synagogue liturgy. In the early years of the twentieth century, it was taken as commonplace that science could explain everything, making prayer seem almost superfluous. More realistically, we now accept that doctors cannot know it all. So God and human expertise combine in that mystery we call healing. Prayer summons the help that God alone can give and prods us to work in concert with the Eternal.

Prayer once seemed so simple—we just talked to God. But today, growing up often means learning how to replace wonder with skepticism. Study may appeal to our minds, ritual to our hearts, and good deeds to our conscience. Yet talking to God seems to embarrass us, reducing us to an uncomfortable teen-age self-consciousness. Even in these days of increasing Jewish spirituality, many do not consider prayerfulness a high Jewish virtue. However, our biblical and rabbinic traditions did, and later ethicists strongly seconded them.

So let us explore the three types of prayer our tradition has commended: the spontaneous, the occasional, and the regular. The first two are said by individuals, praying by themselves; the last calls for a community of praying persons. Each has its special effect in shaping our Jewish character. Even if you are not yet ready for the full prayer regimen, see where you can comfortably begin, or look for your best path to intensify this aspect of your Judaism.

Spontaneous Prayer: "You Don't Get Punished, Just for Asking" (Yiddish Proverb)

No biblical figure exemplifies the power of Jewish prayer more nobly than Hannah, the barren wife of Elkanah. Her husband takes her, his other wife, and their children on their annual visit to the shrine at Shiloh. While they are all celebrating, Hannah "in her wretchedness, goes into the shrine and prays to *Adonai,* weeping all the while. . . . Now Hannah was praying in her heart; only her lips moved, but her voice could not be heard. The priest Eli, thinking she is drunk, upbraids her: 'How long will you make a spectacle of yourself? Sober up!' Hannah replies, 'Oh, sir, I am a desperately unhappy woman. I have drunk no wine or strong drink, but I am here pouring out my heart to *Adonai*. Don't think me a worthless woman. I have only been speaking all this time out of my great anguish and distress.' 'Then,' said Eli, 'go in peace, and may the God of Israel grant you what you have requested'" (1 Sam. 1:10, 12–17). God gives Hannah the child she longs for, and she calls him Samuel, meaning in Hebrew, "God heard." Samuel becomes the great seer-prophet who establishes the first Jewish monarchy. The sixteenth-century mystic Moses Cordovero explains Hannah's great devotion: "Prayer does not ascend according to one's spiritual expertise, but according to the measure of one's soul and its power" (*Pardes Rimonim* [Garden of pomegranates]).

"The Torah says: 'Love *Adonai* your God and serve God with all your heart' [Deut. 11:13]. How does one serve God with one's heart? You must say, by prayer" (Taan. 2a). To thus serve God, you don't always need to be in a special place: "When you pray, pray in the synagogue in your city; if you cannot pray in the synagogue in your city, pray in an open field; if you cannot pray in an open field, pray in your house; if you cannot pray in your house, pray in your bed; if you cannot pray aloud in your bed, commune with your heart" (Mid. Pss. 4.9). The outdoors often inspires us. Francie recalls focusing on a redwood tree in the Santa Cruz mountains while praying the daily morning service, and feeling an almost palpable sense of God's presence. We have even heard about worship—a *Minḥah*, afternoon service—that takes place when the Baltimore Orioles play day games in their home stadium!

It is easy to achieve this important ideal: wherever, whenever an urge to pray occurs, act on it. "The congregation of Israel says, 'We are poor; we have no sacrifices to bring as a sin offering.' God replies, 'I need only words,' as Scripture says, 'Take with you words' [Hos. 14:3]. But 'words' can mean words of Torah, so the congregation says, 'We aren't learned enough to do that.' God replies, 'Just weep a bit and say what you want, and I will receive you!'" (Exod. R. 38.4). "Even if all you can say to God is 'Help!' it is still very good.

Repeat this over and over again, until God opens your lips and the words begin to flow from your heart" (Naḥman of Bratzlav, in Mykoff, *The Empty Chair*).

For as the rabbis teach, God is always available: "R. Joshua b. Levi said: Even an iron partition cannot separate the people Israel from their Father in heaven" (Pes. 85b). "See how high the Holy One, blessed be He, is above His world. Yet a person can enter a synagogue, stand behind a pillar and pray in a whisper and the Holy One, blessed be He, hears his prayer" (Yer. Ber. 9.1). Though contemporary standards may find the next message offensive, the rabbis testify to their inclusiveness by the sexism they proudly overcome: "Before God, all are equal—women, slaves, poor and rich" (Exod. R. 21.5).

The Genre of Women's Spontaneous Prayers

Beginning in the seventeenth century, eastern European women developed a new genre of impromptu devotions, written in Yiddish, the *mamaloshen*. These *tkhines,* literally "supplications," came from the hearts of housewives who had not been given a formal Jewish education. But that did not stop them from praying and wanting to know what prayers were being said by other women. Collected in small books and pamphlets, the *tkhines* were widely distributed for several centuries, until their mass readership perished in the Holocaust. What follows are a few examples of this rich literature, which recent scholarship has begun bringing to our attention.

This apparently quite popular prayer was said by the many women left to care for children and their households for lengthy periods, while their husbands were peddling or otherwise seeking a livelihood far from home. Note what concerns them other than the physical dangers their husbands might encounter. "By Your faithful and gentle hand, give us a decent and honorable living so that we will not require any human *tsedokeh* [charity]. . . . Protect my husband from all the evil in the world and most of all, from the enemies who speak and think evil about him. Confound their thoughts, make their lips mute, send a fright and a trembling to their bones" *(The Merit of Our Mothers)*.

Another prayer from the same collection thanks God for helping women survive the dangers of giving birth: "Master of the entire universe! When the *beys hamikdesh* [the Temple] stood in *Yerusholayim* [Jerusalem], it was the custom that a woman who had just arisen from childbirth would bring a sacrifice to the Temple [Lev. 12:6–8]. Now that, because of our many sins, the *beys hamikdesh* is no more, we fulfill our obligation through prayer in a *mikdesh me'at* [the Talmud's term for the synagogue, literally, 'a small sanctuary'] [Ezek. 11:16]. So I go to the shul to thank You and to praise You, dear God, for all the lovingkindness which You have bestowed upon me to this very day . . ."

And finally, here is a general petition that is included in whatever else one wants to ask for: "Accept my request. Have mercy upon me and upon my entire family. Do not treat me, *kholileh* [God forbid] with Your attribute of justice, but instead with Your attribute of mercy . . ." *(New Yerusholayim Tikhine, in The Merit of Our Mothers)*.

Occasional Prayer: "Even a Rooster, after Drinking Water, Lifts His Eyes to Heaven" (Iraqi Proverb)

Spontaneous prayer is a tribute to the power of the self and its many impulses—but no one ever became admirable living merely by the mood of the moment. And no one ever solidifies a relationship by leaving it to emotional happenstance. For instance, of course we mean to stay in touch with those we care about. But let's be honest—how often do we remember to call or even e-mail them, outside of birthdays or other greeting card–driven occasions? Those we love deserve better than sporadic attention; surely God is no exception. For a Jew, prayer is a duty. Abraham Joshua Heschel puts it this way: "I am not always in a mood to pray. I do not always have the vision and the strength to say a word in the presence of God. But when I am weak, it is the law that gives me strength; when my vision is dim, it is duty that gives me insight" ("The Spirit of Jewish Prayer," in *Moral Grandeur and Spiritual Audacity*).

The rabbis specify certain occasions when this duty to speak to God occurs. They gave us a relatively simple prayer formula we use in almost all *berakhot*, blessings: *Barukh atah Adonai, Elohenu melekh ha-olam,* "You are the Blessed One, *Adonai* our God, Ruler of the universe . . ." Then we attach the phrase appropriate to the occasion, for example, "who creates the fruit of trees." Since talmudic times Jews have recited some of these blessings several times a day; others we say less frequently. The second-century sage R. Meir assigned us an extremely high goal. He declared it the duty of each Jew to say 100 blessings every day (Men. 43a). While no sage suggested that we go around with a daily tally sheet, they hoped our lives would receive their proper orientation if our days were filled with thankful contacts with God.

Let us look at the most obvious of these prayers, the *motzi* blessing, "who brings forth bread from the earth," which we say before eating anything larger than an "olive-sized" piece of bread. This usually comes into play three times a day—for many of us, several additional times! How does it affect us? Gene relates a story that shows the way saying a *motzi* often works in his life. Dashing over to a close-by McDonald's between teaching classes at the HUC-JIR, he reviews his afternoon's activities while awaiting his fish sandwich and diet drink. He must eat fast to get back to his office early to see a student before the next class. After that class, for which he's not sure he's adequately prepared, he will chair a meeting involving some dicey issues he really cares about. Finally finding a not too greasy table amid the hubbub, he unwraps his sandwich and remembers he should say the blessing before he eats, even if he does so silently. But before that, he must take a moment to recenter himself. In these few seconds, carried through to reciting the blessing, he is aware that something has changed. It's not a monumental defrazzling, for the craziness will quickly close in again. But for a moment, sanity and ultimacy reassert themselves. If Gene can let his *berakhah* experience impose itself on what he has to do, he will be able to approach them quite differently, and probably much better. For this is what *berakhot* are for, to express and restore our covenanted existence.

We'd like to share some of our favorite occasional blessings with you. Those in the first group are said more frequently; those in the second, rather rarely.

Occasional Prayers We Say Regularly

There are two wake-up blessings connected with getting dressed every morning. The one, *malbish arumim*, "who clothes the naked," hearkens back to those garments God made for Adam and Eve and thanks God for the clothes we wear. The other, *ozer Yisrael bigevurah*, "who girds Israel with might," has overtones of putting on armor, and so our ethicists connected it to fastening a belt or girdle. In his ethical will, Rabbi Eliezer Hagadol advises: "My child, never attire yourself without a blessing. Even as we should offer thanks for food, so must we do the same for the gift of clothing" *(Hebrew Ethical Wills)*.

Everyone knows the blessing over wine, but few people realize that there is another blessing over liquor or, for that matter, over iced tea, cola, or any drink other than water. We thank God *shehakol nihyeh bidevaro*, "by whose word everything came to be." Remembering this prayer when next negotiating another too-crowded cocktail party can be a momentary antidote to the dissoluteness we often sense about ourselves.

But there is no reason we should limit prayers for specific occasions to traditional *berakhot*. Thus we read in the Mishnah that R. Neḥunya b. Hakanah would regularly say a prayer when he entered and left the Study House: "When I enter, I pray that no offense should occur through me. When I leave, I express thanks for my lot at being a disciple of the wise" (Ber. 4.2).

The practice of saying prayers on certain repeated occasions has not died out, as the following two recently composed prayers indicate. The first is written by a forensic pathologist, Gregory J. Davis, M.D., to be said before rendering a legal opinion: "*Adonai*, let me be an instrument of your will in utilizing all the resources I am able to call forth in fulfilling your command to pursue justice. Grant that I may use the strength of my learning, scholarship, and experience to formulate and articulate opinions for no special interests, only for the truth" (*Sh'ma* 28/542). Here are excerpts from the second, written by Elisheva S. Urbas: "To Be Recited before Nursing: God of our mothers, Sarah, Rivkah, Rachel and Leah, You remembered me when I longed for this child. . . . Now I turn to You again, hoping to feed this child as You feed all living creatures, out of Your boundless lovingkindness. . . . May Your goodness teach me to help my child grow both now in my arms and in all the years You grant us together . . ." (*Sh'ma* 28/545).

The "Thank You, God" Prayers Said at Special Times

Francie lives for the wide-open spaces out west. Whenever she's fortunate enough to hike in the desert, she says the classic *berakhah* for the grandeur of nature: "Blessed are You, *Adonai* our God, Ruler of the universe, who makes the creation." Gene's floriferous suburb practically demands the classic blessing for the first time each spring that we see trees in bloom: "Blessed are You, *Adonai* our God, who left nothing lacking in Your world, but who created for it beautiful creatures, and these beautiful trees for people to see and enjoy" (Ber. 43b). There is also a blessing for seeing an ocean: "Blessed are You, *Adonai* our God, Ruler of the universe, who made the great sea." And if you see a friend for the first time in a year, R. Joshua b. Levi prescribes this blessing: "Blessed is God, who revives the dead" (Ber. 58b).

The blessing for seeing an unusually beautiful person or landscape occasioned this charming anecdote: "Once it happened that R. Gamaliel saw a beautiful gentile woman, so he uttered a blessing at the sight of her. . . . When this surprised some of the rabbis, others responded that all he had said was: 'Blessed are You, *Adonai* our God, who has created such beautiful creatures in Your world.' For even if he had seen a beautiful camel, a beautiful horse, or a beautiful donkey he would have recited the same blessing. Was it then R. Gamaliel's habit to gaze at women? No, but the road must have been narrow and winding so that he could not help looking at her" (Yer. Ber. 9.1).

Regular, Communal Prayer: "God Does Not Reject the Prayer of the Multitude" (Sifre Num., Pinḥas 135)

Even the minimally observant Jew understands our last type of worship. Communal prayer, if only by way of a Pesaḥ seder and High Holy Day services, still serves as a critical means of joining Jews to

God. By worshipping through these prayers, we reconstruct our-selves as the people who once stood at Sinai and continue the social religiosity we call Torah.

The minyan, the ten Jews who constitute the quorum needed for a full service, was probably fixed before rabbinic times. But there is no question about its importance for the rabbis. "When the Holy One, blessed be He, enters a synagogue and does not find ten wor-shipers, God immediately becomes angry, as the prophet said: 'Why was no one there when I came? Why did no one answer when I called?' [Isa. 50:2]" (Ber. 6b). R. Joshua b. Levi ruled: "A man should always get up early so that he can have the merit of being counted among the first ten for that day's service. Even if a hundred people then follow him . . . he is given a reward equal to all of theirs" (Ber. 47b). This love of the minyan is reflected in the proper eti-quette for going to and from a synagogue. "R. Helbo taught in the name of R. Huna: When we leave the synagogue, we should not take big steps. Abaye added: We may walk slowly only when coming from the synagogue. But when we go to it, it is a duty to rush, as is said, 'Let us hurry to know *Adonai*' [Hos. 6:3]" (Ber. 6a).

Later teachers have focused on the human value of communal prayer. Rabbi Naḥman of Bratzlav puts it simply: "The presence of many worshipers heightens devotion" (Newman, *The Hasidic Anthology*). The great-grandfather of the Bratzlaver and the founder of Hasidism, the Baal Shem Tov, pragmatically comments: "A wet log placed in a stove will not burn, but if placed between ten dry logs with proper kindling, it will indeed burn. So too, the worship of pious men whose ardor cannot kindle a similar fervor among the doubters who have joined them is not genuine worship" (*Keter Shem Tov* [Crown of a good name], 30a). Rabbi Israel I. Mattuck, then of London's Liberal Jewish Synagogue, echoes this view: "Some will pray together who cannot pray alone, as many will sing in chorus who would not sing solos" (*Shaarei Tefillah*).

There is a widespread custom to inscribe a phrase over the syna-gogue ark derived from the last words of R. Eliezer: "Know before Whom you stand" (Ber. 28b). To that we would add, we must be especially conscious of those *with whom* we stand, those included in the ubiquitous "we" and "our" of the Jewish service. For then we better understand our sacred relationship with God, extending it to all those created in God's image. Moses Hasid, a seventeenth-century Prague kabbalist, is not too mystical to note: "It is the merging of one's personality in the congregation that makes prayer unselfish. It shows that the worshiper is not speaking or begging for things solely for his own advantage . . ." (*Hebrew Ethical Wills*). We hear that echoed in Aaron Berechiah b. Moses of Modena's warning not to shirk our primary responsibility to another, even to fulfill our duty to pray: "If one is with a critically ill person and the time for communal prayer comes, do not leave him unless there is someone else there to care for him" (*Maavar Yabbok* [The ford of the Jabbok]). The contemporary rabbi Chaim Stern sums up this wisdom: "Why fixed prayers? To learn what we should value, what we should pray for. To be at one with our people, the household of Israel. To ensure that the ideals painfully learned and purified, and for which many have lived and died, shall not perish from the community, and shall have a saving influence upon the individual" *(Shaarei Tefillah).*

"Lengthy Prayers Are an Ugly Custom" (Yiddish Proverb)

Though regularity and community are critical to Jewish prayerfulness, we have been given well-defined limits to the praying we should do. "How many services should one recite each day? Our masters taught: One is to utter no more than the three services that the Great Assembly ordained. David came and specified the times: 'Evening, morning, and noon' [Ps. 55:18]" (Ber. 31a). Furthermore, our individual prayers are supposed to be brief and to the point: Rav said in the name of R. Meir: "When addressing the Holy One, Blessed be He, a person's words should be few, for Scriptures says, 'Be not rash with your mouth to proclaim a word before God' [Eccles. 5:1]" (Ber. 61a). That sage wisdom has had to contend with the continual love that certain rabbis or communities had with a particular prayer or poem, often causing the traditional morning service to be quite lengthy. Nonetheless, Jewish practice has never suggested that praying, whether spontaneously, occasionally, or regularly in a minyan, should exert a monopoly on our time. Some

Jews have tried to make study the constant of their lives. But no movement among us has sought for the life of continual prayer that animates some Catholic orders or Tibetan Buddhists.

However, our teachers did not minimize the importance of having fixed prayers for the community (and individuals, wherever they were) to say three times a day—morning, noon, and night—plus upon awakening and going to bed. Nonetheless, they knew that what makes prayer so precious is intention, *kavannah*. Abaye, in a notable outburst of rabbinic hyperbole, rejects R. Papa's efforts to defend rote recitation of prayers: "Dare anyone behave presumptuously with God? If someone does not pray with *kavannah* from the very beginning of his prayers, we hit him with a smith's hammer until he does" (Ber. 33b–34a). The hasidic master Menaḥem Mendel of Kotzk agrees: "The person who prays today merely because he prayed yesterday is worse than a sinner" (Elkins, *Melodies from My Father's House*). On another occasion he called to some of his Hasidim and asked: "What is all this talk of praying earnestly? Is there anything at all that one ought not to do earnestly?" (Buber, *Tales of the Hasidim*, bk. 2, *The Later Masters*).

Yes, *tefillah* is a high ideal our sages set before us. The twentieth-century German philosopher Franz Rosenzweig identifies their basic concern: "The sum and substance of the whole of historical Judaism will ever be the Prayer Book. The one to whom these volumes are not a sealed book has more than grasped the 'essence of Judaism.' He is informed with it as with life itself; he has within him a 'Jewish World'" ("Zeit ists [It is time]" in *On Jewish Learning*). So it continues to be our fondest joy to show our devotion to the One who gave us everything, every time we chant these words from our prayer book: "Eternal God, open my lips, that my mouth may declare Your glory" (Ps. 51:17).

From Our Tradition

R. Eliezer said: God said to Moses, "My children are in trouble; the sea shuts them off on one side, the enemy pursues them on the other, and you stand and make long prayers. There is a time to lengthen prayer, and a time to shorten it."

—Mekh. Beshallaḥ 3

*W*ith my voice I cry unto *Adonai;* with my voice I make supplication unto *Adonai.* I pour out my complaint before You. I declare before You my trouble.

—Ps. 142:2–3

*R*abbi Naḥman said, Make every effort to pray from the heart. Even if you do not succeed, in the eyes of the Lord the effort is precious.

—Newman, *The Hasidic Anthology*

*T*he Roman emperor Antoninus asked R. Judah ha-Nasi: " Is one allowed to pray every hour?" Rabbi said, "It is forbidden, so that one should not become irreverent toward the Almighty." Antoninus refused to accept this explanation. What did Rabbi do? Early in the morning, he went to the palace and called out, "Hail O Lord." An hour later he came again, "Hail, Emperor." After another hour, "Peace upon you, O king." At this Antoninus asked, "Why do you treat royalty with such contempt?" Rabbi replied, "Let your ears hear what your mouth utters. If you, who are no more than flesh and blood, think that he who salutes you every hour holds you in contempt, surely one should not bother the King who is the King of kings every hour [with his prayers]."

—Tan. B. Miketz 10.11

R. Isaac asked R. Naḥman: Why does the master not come to the synagogue to pray? R. Naḥman: I have not the strength. R. Isaac: Then let ten men gather at the master's house and pray with him. R. Naḥman: There is too much trouble for me in such an arrangement. R. Isaac: Then let the master ask the reader to come and tell the master that the congregation is about to pray so he can pray at the same time. R. Naḥman: Why go to such trouble? R. Isaac: Because of what R. Yoḥanan said in the name of R. Simeon b. Yoḥai:

"With regard to the verse 'But as for me, my prayer is unto You, O Lord, in an acceptable time' [Ps. 69:14]. When is the time acceptable? The time when the whole congregation is praying.'"

—Ber. 7b–8a

Rabbi Uri of Strelisk said: Whoever said that one must pray with a whole heart? Perhaps it is preferable to pray with a broken heart?

—Elkins, *Melodies from My Father's House*

PART VIII

Our Guide, Our Ground, Our Goal

$\mathscr{M}$any people become uncomfortable when talk turns to God. They believe that such discussions unnecessarily involve people in primitive or infantile ideas. Sometimes their unease comes from concerns that others might try to force their ideas on them. Or, more pointedly, they simply refuse to discuss what they do or don't believe. Still others view intelligent people as having better things to think about. This judgment often comes from becoming learned in other areas, while letting their knowledge of Judaism remain at a Hebrew school level. If any of these reactions occasionally arise in you, we ask only that you try to keep them from prejudicing your reactions to our final three chapters. For they are all about God, or, more precisely, about three ways Jews understand their relationship to God.

The musarists affirm that Jewish character and observance grow from our sense of what is most real in the universe, and therefore ought to be most important in people's lives. Our teachers urge us to live in the ways we have been describing here because of who our God is, a God so complex as to not be beyond either good and evil, yet not mean or indifferent or inaccessible. For our God is *Adonai*, the mysterious, yet talkative Holy One of the Bible, the Ultimate that draws endless speculation from rabbis, mystics, and philosophers alike. Our God is the *Atah*, the You, served over the centuries by all those ordinary and extraordinary people, our biological and spiritual predecessors, who shaped the details of sacred Jewish living.

So it is to "the foundation of all foundations," as Maimonides termed *Adonai*, that we now turn our attention. We once again follow the guidance of the musarists, who bid us build our lives on three themes: knowing God, "fearing" God, and loving God.

Knowing God—
Yediat ha-El

> *Rabbi Schneur Zalman of Lyady said: Sovereign of the*
> *Universe! I don't fear Your Hell, I don't long for Your*
> *Heaven, and I will gladly pass up Your celestial angels.*
> *Do you know all I truly desire? You, only You!*
> — Elkins, *Melodies from My Father's House*

Everyone knows that the Bible often speaks of both loving and fearing God. There is also a third approach that biblical authors consider critical: knowing God. The prophet Ezekiel is so taken with this theme that he mentions it over sixty times. For the rabbis, the Torah itself commands this: "Know then this day, and take it to heart, that *Adonai* is God in the heaven above and the earth below and there is no other" (Deut. 4:39). If that sentiment sounds familiar, it is because the Hebrew is used in the summary prayer of our traditional Jewish service: *Alenu leshabe'ah la-adon ha-kol.* It is incumbent upon us to praise the Master of all things.

The command "to know" immediately arouses our contemporary craving for precise definition, one that concisely explains what our spiritual geniuses mean by "knowing God." Unfortunately, such knowledge is not to be. When it comes to matters of belief, our teachers have discovered that religious reality is inevitably greater than any of their attempts to express them in a few pithy remarks. Thus they shift into highly symbolic rhetoric and continue to multiply these symbols in the hope that their number and variety eventually reveal what they have in mind. So it is with "knowing God."

Some Biblical Meanings of *Yediat ha-El*

As we begin our own not-so-symbolic journey, let us quickly track seven layers of meaning for the word "know" found in the Bible. Seeking to comfort Job, his friend Zophar reminds him of the fate of the wicked: "He shall not know quietness in his innards or escape this in one of his diversions" (Job 20:20), indicating that knowing can mean being aware of one's inner state. More commonly, knowing can be as simple as recognition. Late one night, Saul, Israel's first king, hears someone taunting his bodyguard for not sufficiently protecting him. Saul knows that voice to be that of his nemesis and calls out to him: "Is that your voice, my son, David?" (1 Sam. 26:17). But it also can happen, as we are told it did in the Garden of Eden, that we gain insight and see the familiar in a new, sometimes startling, way: "And the eyes of both of them were opened and they knew that they were naked" (Gen. 3:7). Such an abstract perception can expand into the complex emotions that describe human relationships. Moses describes the tribe of Levi as having such loyalty to God that "they did not know their own children" and ignored familial affection in order to remain true to their covenant with God (Deut. 33:9). And we all know "know" as a term for sexual intimacy, from that often-quoted biblical verse: "And Adam knew his wife Eve, and she conceived and bore Cain" (Gen. 4:1).

Yet knowing is usually associated with having precise understanding. King Ahashuerus consulted his astrologers, "the wise men who knew about times," to determine the most propitious moment to punish Queen Vashti, Esther's predecessor (Est. 1:13). This connection between the self within and the world without reaches its full potential when we become certain that we possess the truth, however unpleasant it may be: "When Mordecai knew that Haman had persuaded Ahashuerus to sanction the death of the Jews and the plundering of their possessions . . ." (Est. 4:1).

All these shades of meaning pointed the biblical authors in one direction, to the One who is as near as the air we breathe and as far as the most distant galaxy. Today, the many-leveled desire for connection with the Ultimate Unity resonates throughout our society. For we, too, seek to know God. Just think of all of the popular music whose lyrics speak of this yearning: from former Beatle George Harrison's "My Sweet Lord" ("I really want to know You") to Joan Osborne's matter-of-fact message ("What if God were one of us, just a slob like one of us, just a stranger on the bus, trying to make His way home? If God had a name, what would it be? Would you say it to His Face?. . .").

The Easier Part of Knowing: What God Is Not

Jews disdain what doesn't make sense. Still, there are folks in almost every generation who make hash of Judaism's basic beliefs about God. From biblical times on, our prophets and sages have done their best to explain certain ideas that Jews *should not* believe; these "negations" have proven their worth over the centuries. Yet human nature being what it is, today some otherwise intelligent people will cite one of these long-discarded notions to justify their views. Here are the four beliefs our thinkers have deemed incompatible with mature Jewish faith.

First, God is not an idol. Our God cannot even remotely be so symbolized. This notion already seemed so unbelievable to the prophet Isaiah, who lived about 2500 years ago, that he satirized it: "The idol? A woodworker shaped it, and a smith overlaid it with gold, forging links of silver . . . he chooses mulberry, a wood that will not rot, and then seeks out a skillful woodworker to make a firm idol, one that will not topple" (Isa. 40:19–20). God cannot be a "thing" like all other created things, for God is the Source and Sustainer of all the things that ever were, are, or might yet be. And it makes no difference if the things we worship aren't statues, but ideals like power, youth, or wealth or, more devastatingly, "isms" like fascism, socialism, or capitalism. Just because they're abstractions doesn't make them any less idolatrous, or any less dangerous.

Second, don't take the Bible or the prayer book's anthropomorphisms literally. For the authors of the Bible didn't; they never hesitated changing descriptions of God when a different aspect of the Divine more deeply moved them. In the Moses/Miriam song of the sea, God is "a man of war" (Exod. 15:3), but in Daniel's vision the Eternal is an "Ancient of Days" with white hair (Dan. 7:9). The rabbis were not fazed by this multiplicity of images. They merely reminded their listeners that these various portrayals all referred to the same God, the One behind all the metaphors (Mekh. Shirata 4). The medieval commentator Baḥya ibn Pakuda explains this philosophy: "The aspect of God made manifest in various places in the Bible is revealed to us only as a matter of human necessity, since we have a limited ability to comprehend God. These descriptions are not in proportion to God's true ability, which is limitless. . . . The clever and intelligent man will try to peel the anthropomorphic husk from the term and abstract its meaning. . . . Only the ignorant, simple man . . . would believe in the Creator according to the Bible's literal sense" (Hovot Halevavot).

Thirdly, no comparison of God to any "thing" can be anything more than a metaphor. That's what the Torah indicates in a verse of such significance that the rabbis made it a prominent part of the daily service, placing it in the prayers concluding the Shema: "Who is like You among those that people call gods? Who is like You, majestic in holiness, awesome in our praise, working wonders?" (Exod. 15:11). The obvious answer is "No one." So we have metaphors, images taken from daily life, that both do and don't properly speak of God. We like the positive side of such usage so much—for God does, in a sense talk to us, hear us, love us—that we try to tolerate the people who assume this is what God is truly like. Of course we could put quotation marks around the metaphors— "talk," "hear," "love," as we sometimes do in this book—but that quickly becomes tedious.

The medieval mystics solve this problem by boldly stating that we have two ways of understanding God. One, by way of the sefirot, the ten interactive nodes of God's action, has room for not only all the metaphors the Bible uses but any that an imaginative soul will later think up. But the other is radically different. A participant in the sixteenth-century kabbalistic community in Safed, Eleazar Azikri gives a précis of this other Zoharic doctrine of God: "With regard to the Ein Sof, the Limitless One, we are not permitted to make any comparison whatsoever. We may not make an imaginative construction out of the letters of the alphabet, or any other conceivable product of the imagination. (Azikri and de Vidas, *Sefer Haredim* [The book of the rigorous], 5). As to how it is possible for the one God to be utterly describable yet utterly indescribable at the same time, that is perhaps the greatest mystical secret of them all.

And fourth, we cannot know God as God really is, for the simple reason that we would have to be as great as God, in order to do so. Job's friend Zophar poetically describes our problem: "Would you discover the mystery of God? Would you discover the limit of the Almighty? Higher than heaven—what can you do? Deeper than Sheol—what can you know?" (Job 11:7–8). The fourteenth-century Spanish talmudist, Nissim b. Reuben Gerondi, agrees: "A certain sage was asked, 'What is God?' and he answered, 'If I knew God I would be God'" (Sermon "A," *Sermons of Rabbenu Nissim*). And the later mystics concur: "Know that the truth of God's existence cannot be known except to *Adonai* alone, for such knowledge has no end and God has no end" (Azikri and de Vidas, *Sefer Haredim*). As the twelfth-century ethicist Berachyah warns: "If we tax our minds to investigate the subject of God's glorious Essence as it really is . . . then the result will be that we shall lose the very limited knowledge we have of God" *(The Ethical Treatises of Berachyah).*

What God Is

Perhaps the most rationalistic of our medieval sages, the physician-philosopher Maimonides resolved the logical problem of not being able to say exactly what God is in his famous work, *Guide of the Perplexed.* He reminded us that this higher ignorance does not prevent us from saying what is far more important: we can see and say what God *does* and therefore what we must do. Even our logic can grasp that if God is one, then "God's essence is . . . wholly unitary and simple, having no aspect that is added or is a distinct part of it" (*Guide,* 1.53). However, there is no reason why we can't go on to say: "The various actions of God the Bible describes, proceed from one simple essence in which there is no shred of multiplicity. . . . All attributes of God that are found in God's books . . . are therefore attributes of God's actions, and not at all descriptions of God's essence" (*Guide,* 1.53).

Most ethical writers who followed took Maimonides's guidance with at least one grain of salt. They did not hesitate to draw inferences about God from their religious appreciation of creation. So the later sage Simḥah Zisel Ziv of Kelm wrote: "When people see a table or a chair made by a distinguished craftsman, they immediately inquire about the extraordinary artisan who fashioned it. But when they see the orderliness of this great universe, whose smallest part all the wise men of the universe are not able to duplicate . . . they do not ask who made this great and expansive world, and why, and for whom, and for what purpose was it set up" (*Hokhmah Umusar* [Wisdom and instruction], 1.26). "What is the implication of the text: 'The earth is *Adonai*'s as is all that fills it' [Ps. 24:1]? Even in this world there is no place devoid of *Adonai*. Therefore one need not ascend a mountain to seek God, for the whole earth is full of God's glory" (*Hokhmah Umusar,* 2.76).

Our folk wisdom assimilates this lesson. As the Ladino proverb says: "We may not be able to see God, but we can get a sense of God by our thinking." And the Yiddish maxim only makes this more specific: "Even the worms under the stones are fed by God." The arguments having been noted and their elaboration of the Torah having been celebrated, we settle this ancient controversy with the judicious comment of the contemporary Jewish philosopher Kenneth Seeskin: "The difference between Maimonides and his opponents is that they think God stands at the top of the scale, while he thinks God is entirely off the scale" (*Maimonides: A Guide For Today's Perplexed*). But whether one is a Maimonidean in this matter or not, it is clear that our tradition says that a good Jew is commanded to know God.

Thus we can say at least three positive things about God.

God Is Eḥad: *One, Unique, Alone*

We know this simply from the way our minds function, continuously trying to make order out of our usual jumble of thoughts. And we know this from the way the world works—not capriciously, but predictably, in ways we can know or hope to decipher. Doesn't the central assumption of cosmology, the scientific study of the universe, state that there is only *one* set of laws describing everything happening in every part of nature, no matter how intergalactic or subatomic? To the Judaically learned, this is reminiscent of the classic Jewish affirmation of God's singleness. For example, Schneur Zalman, the founder of Lubavitch Hasidism, wrote: "God is an absolutely simple unity, without any mixture of multiplicity at all. God is one and utterly integrated. God and God's knowledge are all really one. Yet by God's self-knowledge, God knows all creatures of the upper and lower domains to the smallest minnow in the sea . . ." (*Tanya*, "Shaar Hayihud Vehaemunah" [The gate of unity and truth], 8 and 9).

God Is Real, Not an Illusion Or Wish

The medieval sage Berachyah borrows an image from his slightly earlier contemporary Solomon ibn Gabirol, who compares trying to know God to a search that leads to an understanding of the sun. As long as we examine the sun's effects—its rays—and its characteristics—it is bright, not dark—we can know the sun is real. So too, when we appreciate the effects of God's power and wisdom, acknowledging God's defining characteristics of unity and benevolence, we gain the knowledge of God the Bible talks about (*The Ethical Treatises of Berachyah*, 204). The fifteenth-century Sephardic philosopher Isaac b. Moses Arama adds: "How shall the creature comprehend its Creator? The Torah directs us to the truth of God's being and God's renewal of creation, as well as God's knowledge and providence over the rules that order nature. We have no reason to raise questions about them" (*Akedat Yitzhak* [The binding of Isaac], to Gen. 22:1). And the sixteenth-century Safed mystic Moses Cordovero affirms: "Just as a person does not perceive the soul inside him, but nonetheless the soul has its influence on him and he knows the soul by its effects, so one comes to know God" (*Elimah Rabbati*).

We Know God by What God Has Done for Our People

There is a mythic story about an exchange between Napoleon and the astronomer Laplace. When Napoleon asked about God's role in the creation of the various heavenly bodies, the scientist responded, "I have no use for that hypothesis." The Emperor next inquired, "Is there then no proof that there is a God?" Laplace replied, "Yes, your majesty, the existence of the Jews." This certainly is how we Jews have interpreted what has happened to us, from biblical days to the present. Despite periods of utter darkness and incomprehension, our people has retained its sense of God's presence in our history.

This communal sensibility rests upon each Jew's individual religious experience. How astonishing it is that the inner, often troubled, lives of the Hebrew poets who composed the Psalms three thousand years ago echo our own intimate response to the Ultimate One. These poets might have been speaking about our epoch and our inquisitive searching for the Divine: "Where shall I go from Your spirit? Where can I flee from Your presence? If I ascend to heaven, You are there; if I descend to Sheol, You are there, too. If I ride on the wings of the morning to reach the end of the sea, even there Your hand will be guiding me; Your right hand will be holding me fast. If I say, 'Surely darkness will cover me, night will cover me up,' the darkness is not too dark for You; night is as light as day; darkness and daylight are all the same to You" (Ps. 139:7–11). It helps to know that, since the one who penned these marvelous images found God, there is hope for us as well.

What Have We Learned about God and Evil?

R. Yannai said: "We cannot explain why some evildoers live happily, while some good people must endure severe suffering" (Avot 4.15). So let us say at once: The Jewish tradition knows no way of satisfying our desire for a clear, logical answer to the problem of how the good God could create a world in which real evil exists. As the Yiddish proverb puts it: "If God lived on earth, people would break the windows in God's house." But even in our pain, what we know of God can soothe us.

There can't be a world unless there is matter. And, if you have matter, there is going to be decay—mostly slow, sometimes disastrously fast. Occasionally wind blows ferociously, ground heaves unpredictably, rivers flood towns, DNA degenerates. One way or another, people inevitably die. This is the price we pay for being part of God's world. As Maimonides says: "This type of evil must necessarily exist" (*Guide*, 3.12).

More disturbing is the evil that doesn't have to exist, but that we human beings choose to create. Ever since the Garden, our abuses of freedom have practically defined our humanity. Hear the words of one of our prophets as he describes his late seventh-century B.C.E. community: "*Adonai* looked for justice, but behold, injustice; for equity, but behold, iniquity. . . . Woe to those who chase liquor from early morning, and are inflamed by wine till late in the evening! To those whose banquets feature lyre and lute, timbrel, flute, and wine, but never reflect *Adonai*'s plan" (Isa. 5:7, 11–12). In a melancholy moment we are tempted to feel that the universe would be a better place if we were created without free will, acting like the animals, who cannot choose evil over the good. But then, we could never be good in that special human way we call righteousness.

There is one clear, logical answer to the problem of evil. Following various twentieth-century theologians, we can resolutely insist that God's power is finite. Evil exists because, despite doing incomparably more good than anyone or anything else can, God can't do everything that needs doing; God simply isn't omnipotent. And that is why God needs humanity: to complete the work of creation. Mordecai Kaplan is the outstanding Jewish advocate of this position. His notion of a finite God, the only intellectually coherent response to the problem of evil, has appealed to a significant number in the Jewish community.

But many others think that making God conform to our logic, cutting God down to our size, so to speak, says far too much about us and has far too little an appreciation of God. This new humility is the corollary of our declining confidence in what science can do, as it attempts to solve our old problems without creating new ones. So, too, we now find it difficult to have faith in the basic goodness of people. The truth is that, for all the good people can do, most of us behave so badly much of the time, that it is difficult to see us as the yardstick by which God should be measured.

Over the millennia our tradition has admitted that we can't fully understand God. But all the same, we are able to trust God, regardless. The chastened Job speaks for generations of later Jews when he concludes: "Indeed, I spoke without understanding things far beyond me, matters about which I did not know" (42:3). And this is what some Jewish teachers call for today. Martin Buber believes that knowing God means having a personal relationship with the Eternal, not merely a mental construct of God. But anyone who has loved knows that there are times when our beloved hurts us for reasons that cannot ever be made clear. We don't understand, but often, we love them anyway—and love, not philosophy, is what the Torah prescribes for Jews. Buber's great contemporary, Abraham Joshua Heschel, opposes putting ourselves first and God second. When we get the order right, we realize: "God pursues man. . . . Religion consists of God's question and man's answer. It is beyond all reason, beneath the ground, where a seed starts to become a tree, that the act of faith takes place" *(God in Search of Man)*.

Knowing God, a Messianic Goal

While it is a worthy task to seek to know God, it is a task whose ultimate success is forever denied us. For the more we know, the more we know we don't know. But that only makes each bit of wisdom particularly precious to us, increasing our yearning to know as much as we can. We pray for the day "when all who dwell on earth will recognize and know that it is to You every knee should bend in fealty, and by Your name every tongue should swear truthfully" (the *Alenu* prayer). For surely we long for the consequences of this knowledge: "Then I will make the peoples pure of speech, so that they all invoke *Adonai* by name and serve God with one accord" (Zeph. 3:9). Then "*Adonai* will finally rule over all the earth; on that day, what people call God and what God truly is will be One" (Zech. 14:9). "They shall nor hurt or destroy in all My holy mountain, for the earth shall be filled with knowledge of the Lord as the water covers the sea" (Isa. 11:9).

Knowing God, then, means acting as God does. The medieval sage David Kimḥi taught: "Knowing God is following God's ways, doing righteous acts, justice and charity. . . . The one who follows in God's ways knows Him" (Commentary to Jer. 9:23, in *Mikraot*

Gedolot). Indeed, long ago the prophet told us what kind of knowing God asks of us: "Let not the wise glory in wisdom; let not the strong glory in strength; let not the rich glory in riches. But only in this should people glory: That they understand and know Me. For *Adonai* acts with kindness, justice, and equity in the world; for in these I delight, declares *Adonai*" (Jer. 9:22–23).

From Our Tradition

What is that small verse on which hang all the critical principles of the Torah? "In all your ways, know God" [Prov. 3.6].

—Ber. 63a

When Rabbi Yitzḥak Meir of Ger was a little boy, his mother once took him to see the Maggid of Koznitz. There someone said to him: "Yitzḥak Meir, I'll give you a gulden if you tell me where God lives!" He replied, "And I will give you two gulden if you tell me where God doesn't!"

—Buber, *Tales of the Hasidim*, bk. 2, *The Later Masters*

"But you, Israel, My servant, Jacob, whom I have chosen, [are] seed of Abraham My Friend" [Isa. 41:8]. Abraham discovered God for himself; he recognized that above the celestial sphere there is a Unique Being. He knew that from actual demonstration, for it was not a tradition from his father, nor did he acquire it from his contemporaries. He originated the idea. . . .

—Joseph ibn Kaspi, in *Hebrew Ethical Wills*

Yes, if you cry out for insight and raise your voice for understanding, if you seek it like silver and search for it as for hidden treasures, then you will understand the fear of *Adonai* and find the knowledge of God.

—Prov. 2:3–5

*S*aid the rabbi: There is a great difference between a believing Jew and a philosopher. The Jew seeks to know God for worthy consequences, as well as for the intrinsic value of knowing God. The only reason that the philosopher seeks to know God is to have an accurate description of Him. . . . It makes no difference to him otherwise whether he is a righteous person or a complete scoffer.

—Judah Halevi, *Kuzari,* 4.13

*G*od is unique, for what God does, no one sees.

*W*e may not be able to see God, but we can get a sense of Him by our thinking.

—Yiddish proverb

*G*od may delay, but God doesn't forget.

—Ladino proverb

*E*ven if one doesn't see God, one serves Him from what one recognizes of Him.

—Iraqi proverb

"Fearing" God— *Yirat ha-El*

*Y*our old friend who drives himself crazy with work asks you to help straighten him out. You tell him that he needs to take a little time to smell the roses. The next thing you know, he has torn up his already lovely garden and planted every variety of odoriferous rose carried by the most extravagant local nursery.

Oy—the pains of taking things too literally! No other Jewish idea has suffered more misplaced precision than this notion of "fearing" God—note our quotation marks around the term. Some people insist that, since Judaism makes "fearing" God, *yirat ha-El*, so central a concept, Jews are expected to perpetually cower before Adonai. It is true that our prophets and sages have discouraged treating God as a chum and have stressed the inexplicable difference between us and God. But if ever a religious motif required nuancing, it is this one, for it goes to the heart of who God is, who we are, and the ever-deepening relationship between created and Creator.

Gene remembers his HUC-JIR philosophy professor Samuel Atlas, drawing himself up to his full five-foot-five height, as he responded to a challenge, "I can either be clear or correct!" While he might be saddened by our fawning dedication to clarity, we suggest thinking about *yirat ha-El* along a spectrum that ranges from the plainly literal to the murky figurative. We shall attempt to "fear" God all along our journey, as we cover both extremes of our spectrum to reach its balanced midpoint.

God's Awesome Power

No terms have been used more frequently to express the roots of Jewish piety than *yirat ha-El;* its biblical synonym, *yirat Adonai;* and its rabbinic parallel, *yirat Shamayim,* fear of Heaven. Classically, this awareness contrasts a puny and ephemeral humanity with the inconceivable might of the One Who Spoke and the World Was. The thirteenth-century mystic, Judah the Pious, describes this mood: "When one thinks about the greatness of the Creator, one recoils on one's heels and becomes fearful, anxious about being so tiny and lowly a creature, one who stands before the Creator with so weak and small an understanding" (Judah Heḥasid, *Sefer Ḥasidim,* 14). One psalmist has experienced the same sensation while gazing at the nighttime sky: "When I look at Your heavens, the work of Your fingers, / The moon and stars that you set in place, / Who are we that you pay attention to us, / Human beings that you take note of us?" (Ps. 8:4–5). Another psalmist reacts similarly after being caught in a thunderstorm: "*Adonai*'s voice—that is power, / *Adonai*'s voice—that is majesty. / *Adonai*'s voice smashes the cedars, / It shatters the cedars of Lebanon. /. . . *Adonai*'s voice kindles flames of fire, / *Adonai*'s voice convulses the wilderness; / *Adonai* convulses the wilderness of Kadesh. / *Adonai*'s voice causes the hinds to give birth / And brings ewes to early birth. / While in God's temple all say, 'Glory'" (Ps. 29:4–5, 7–9).

When Francie was ten years old, she almost drowned in a treacherous undertow that caused the normally placid Lake Michigan waters to churn and heave. On that day, her concept of God changed forever. Now, God was no longer our typically kind old Grandfather, but had become the One who, though doing mostly good for us, also ruled the universe in inscrutable ways. She learned quite traumatically that God could be much more threatening than she had previously imagined.

Be it undertow or earthquake, mighty mountain or grand vista, we occasionally find ourselves gasping for air, almost afraid to breathe. We know of nature's power, of course, but this is awesome—literally, awesome. And so are the two ultimate humblers, birth and death. The former overwhelms us with its creative goodness, the latter with its mysterious finality, yet we know the same inscrutable Power lies behind both of them. Thus we render *yirat ha-El* without hesitation, "awe of God."

Life Demands Bravery—and Humility

From the time we were small, we were taught to admire and aspire to bravery. The characters in the stories our parents told us created both positive and negative role models. We laughed at the Cowardly Lion, who searched for a wizard to supply him with the courage he thought he lacked; when we were frightened, Jiminy Cricket told us to whistle away our fears. Reaching adulthood, newly liberated young women became empowered by their sisterly strength of millions. So they believed: "If we had to, we could do anything." And many "can-do" guys breathlessly pant to each other after an overly long run or weight-lifting session: "No pain, no gain."

Yet in recent years a new humility has overtaken us. Now the word "vulnerable" creeps into our more honest self-assessments. Men begin to abandon the image of omni-competence, finding pleasure in their gentler selves; women allow themselves to admit that they can't nearly do it all, and have good reason to feel overwhelmed. To resurrect an old phrase, the world isn't "our oyster." We attribute much of this newly found realism to our understanding that the One who shapes reality is very much greater than we might ever aspire to be.

Our *yirat ha-El* constantly moves us. For no matter how great our theoretical knowledge and technical competence, we know that humankind is not now and never will be ultimately in charge. God is the fearsome power behind nature's might; as our understanding of nature's incredible energies expands, *Adonai*'s power stuns us into silence. The folk wisdom of our Yiddish-speaking ancestors plainly speaks this truth: "If God starts toying with you, you can go to pieces even as you dance"; "Without God's will, no fly moves on a wall"; "Don't play around with God. You are not only forbidden to do so, but truthfully, God won't let you!" (Yiddish proverbs).

"If You Do This, or Don't Do That, God Will Punish You"

Much of what once made the religious notion of the "fear" of God so harmful was the harsh way others used it to control behav-

ior. A major strand of biblical thinking, closely associated with the
Book of Deuteronomy, states that God rewards those who obey the
commandments and punishes those who do not. The second of the
three paragraphs following the *Shema* typifies this: "If you obey the
commandments I am giving you today . . . I will send the rain for
your land in due season, both early and late. You shall have a fine
harvest of grain and wine and oil. I will also provide grass in your
fields for your cattle, to give you plenty to eat. Don't get involved
with other gods, and don't serve them. If you do, *Adonai*'s anger will
flare up against you, shutting the skies so that no rain falls and your
fields cannot yield their produce. And then you will soon perish
from the good land that *Adonai* has allotted to you" (Deut.
11:13–17). Sometimes the threat of God's punishment reaches horrific proportions. In one case, the warning to the people about to
enter the land of Israel (Deut. 28:16–68) is so fearsome that when
this passage is read from the Torah, it is done as quickly and as quietly as possible.

Many of these texts dealing with divine retribution are directed
to the people of Israel. To modern eyes, they seem to say more
about a prior generation's need for social controls than about what
God wants or what God will do. Still, this fear was so basic to premodern Jewish thinking, and, in one form or another, to most other
world religions, that it was also a way of understanding God's relation to individual behavior. It was irresistible to people in power,
certainly to parents, to say that not just they, but God demanded
that their underlings/children do just this, and not do that, or suffer divine punishment. These "guilt trips" had such a harmful effect
that much of Freud's early work dealt with "damage control,"
administering psychological antidotes to relieve people of the tox-
ins that poisoned their psyche.

Of course, it was already plain to some of the Bible's authors, and
to the rabbis who followed, that this tit-for-tat version of how God
responds to us often doesn't pan out. So somewhere between the
last biblical and the first rabbinic texts, during the final two or three
centuries before the Common Era, Jews began to believe that God's
judgment extends beyond this world to the *olam ha-ba*, the world to
come. In this scenario, each person must appear before God. Any

lapses in executing God's justice in this world will surely be paid for in the next one. No wonder Yehiel b. Yekutiel could write: "The fear of God is a great thing. When you have it and live by it, it stands up for you in this world and in the judgment you will face in the world to come, as is written, 'The fear of *Adonai* is pure, it stands forever' [Ps. 19:10]" *(Sefer Maalot Hamiddot).*

For nearly two millennia then, Gehenna, hell, was a very real and terrifying place. Avoiding the terrible torments that awaited sinners was a powerful deterrent to wrongdoing: "God will reward those that fear Him by saving them from the judgment of Gehenna" (Yev. 102b). Conversely, traditional Judaism taught that, though this world may bring us nothing but problems, our reward for continuing to "fear" God will be a marvelous afterlife. We will be welcomed into Paradise, the Garden of Eden, while evildoers suffer eternal tortures. Now biblical verses that even hinted at the concepts of "forever" or "eternally" were interpreted as referring to the *olam ha-ba.* A text that once was associated with God's justice in *this* world, has become a testimony to the *next.* Even today, we often read it at funerals: "How abundant is the good that You have in store for those who fear You . . ." (Ps. 31:20).

About two hundred years ago, as the Jewish community entered the modern age, many Jews abandoned this belief, at least in their more mature moments. They came to believe that not God, but relatively impersonal natural processes ruled the world. Thus no modern Jewish thinker has defended the narrow understanding of divine retribution that Deuteronomy teaches. When the 1903 and 1905 Kishinev pogroms captured international attention, no one suggested that this was God's punishment on a sinful generation. Instead, the Jewish community responded by forming Jewish self-defense groups and international agencies dedicated to political action.

Yet the doctrine refuses to die, despite its loss of intellectual legitimacy. Often we return to it when we are traumatized, asking: "How could God do this to me?" This is more a cry of pain than a serious theological inquiry. Nonetheless, though our minds tell us otherwise, most of us seem to retain some intuitive sense that God rewards and punishes us, though exactly how that works, either in this world or in the next one, few can fathom.

For proper divine respect demands that we do not turn God into an overprotecting nanny. But neither do we want to abandon our loving relationship with our Creator, substituting one marked by distant detachment. "Fear" of God as described in our tradition occupies a similarly ill-defined place, somewhere between God the utterly transcendent and God the intimately available. This ambivalence characterizes R. Yehuda b. R. Simon's tale about a group of men who had supported a king but now rebelled against him. The king offered a handsome reward to the one who apprehended the renegade group's leader. A man succeeded in catching the rebel chief, only to find himself placed under guard with the very man he had captured. Both men were filled with fear: the one for the punishment that awaited him, the other because he would have to appear before the king to claim his prize (Gen. R. 48.6). They both "feared," but they did not have the same experience.

"Fearing" God, Honoring Our Parents

We learn a good deal about this intermediate kind of *yirah* by looking at its human consequence: "I might not know what the implications of 'fear' are, but when the Torah tells us that we shall rise when the elderly enter and thus fear God, it indicates that we are also required to have deep respect for our teachers as well as our parents and God" (Tan. Beha'alotekha 11). More specifically, the Torah directs us to link *yirah* with *kavod*, honor. Leviticus thus commands: "You shall 'fear' your mother and father" (19:3). Yehiel b. Yekutiel learns from this: "Just as we must fear and honor the Holy One, Blessed be He, so must we fear and honor our father and mother, as the Decalogue says: 'Honor your father and your mother' [Exod. 20:12]. God connects anyone who honors and fears his father and mother with fear and honor of the Holy One, Blessed be He. . . . Both men and women are obligated to carry out this mitzvah" *(Sefer Maalot Hamiddot)*. This discussion is based on talmudic analysis: "Which aspect of one's service is termed 'fear,' and which 'honor'? Fear: One must not stand or sit in his father's place, or contradict his words, or uphold another in an argument against him. Honor: One must feed his father, give him drink, bathe him, anoint him, clothe him, shod him, and bring him in and take him out" (Kid. 31a). Our parents did all this and more for us; shouldn't we at least do the same for them, should they require it?

Yet there is more to this duty than simple repayment, for our parents evoke a certain awe in us, a reflection of our respect for them. "Issi b. Judah taught: If your father asks you for some water and you have other mitzvot to do, if they can be done by someone else, let them be done by others so you may occupy yourself with the mitzvah of honoring your parents" (Kid. 32a). When Rabbi Eliezer Hagadol was asked by his students how far they must extend themselves in honoring their parents, he replied: "You can learn a good lesson about this from the conduct of Dama b. Nethina. When his senile mother would strike him in the presence of his friends, he would only say, 'Enough, my mother'" (Deut. R. 1.14). Our special sensibility to parents often increases after they die. The Talmud records a practice that continues to this day. When mentioning a deceased parent, people quickly add: "of blessed memory for life in the world to come" (Kid. 31b).

"Fearing" God Means Fearing Sin

Some Jewish thinkers emphasize the general sense of *yirat ha-El* as sufficient reason for avoiding sin. "Antigonus of Sokho used to say: Be like servants who serve the master without the expectation of receiving a reward, and let the fear of God simply bring you to it" (Avot 1.3). R. Joshua b. Levi interprets the verse from Psalms: "Happy is one who fears God" (112:1) to mean: "Happy is the one who can master the evil inclination, as God meant for human beings to do" (A.Z. 19a). As the fourteenth-century rabbi of Toledo, Judah Asheri said: "Keep your mind open to whatever may remind you of the fear of Heaven; be not diverted by the jibes of others, nor by your own lusts" (*Hebrew Ethical Wills*). The fifteenth-century philosopher Joseph Albo tells us: "The fear of God is not like the fear of a human being. If one is in fear of an [earthly] ruler, one is in constant terror and dread, which shortens one's life, whereas fearing God prolongs it. . . . He who is happy is he who fears God, for this fear does not lead to timidity but to might, so that his seed shall be mighty on earth" (*Sefer Haikkarim* [The book of principles]). And the sixteenth-century Italian sage Ovadiah Sforno teaches: "Anyone who knows how greatly God ought to be praised will fear God because of this, rather than because of any punishment God may visit on us" (commentary on Exod. 15:11, in *Mikraot Gedolot*).

But most premodern Jewish thinkers followed the old punitive pedagogy. Jonah Gerondi gives his warning in the form of a blanket condemnation: "One who does not keep busy with good deeds . . . violates the command to fear God, and deserves to be called 'rasha,' a wicked person" (*Shaarei Teshuvah* [Gates of repentance], 3.12). Typically, medieval thinkers considered human guilt our major religious concern. "What do we mean by the fear of Heaven? That we humble ourselves before God and evidence all the attitudes of submission and obeisance common to servants before their master, fearing lest we err in our service or otherwise arouse God's displeasure" (Yehiel b. Yekutiel, *Sefer Maalot Hamiddot*). Of course, we exert every effort not to succumb to the sins that patiently wait for us at every turn: "The best means of guarding oneself from sin is the fear of God's punishment. . . . When temptation comes upon us, it will arouse our spirit and remind us that God oversees all of our acts" (*Sefer Hahinukh* [The book of instruction], Ekev, 432).

But despite its troublesome associations, the "fear" of God still has special power for Jews today. Drawing on our common experience, our near contemporary, the Hebraist editor and author, Meir Meiseles, makes this plain: "Religious fear is neither sorrow nor pain. . . . It may be compared to the protective thrill of concern felt by a father lest his little son fall when he mounts him on his shoulder so as to dance and play with him. He is full of joy, yet the fear this maneuver involves is equally pleasurable. It does not interfere with the carefree attitude with which he throws himself into the enjoyment of the game. To the contrary, it fortifies it and adds charm" (*Judaism: Thought and Legend*). Likewise, Abraham Joshua Heschel insists: "Awe precedes faith; it is at the root of faith. We must grow in awe in order to reach faith. . . . In Judaism, *yirat hashem*, the awe of God, is almost equivalent to the word 'religion.' In biblical language, the religious one is not called 'believer' . . . but, '*yare hashem*' [one who holds God in awe] (*God in Search of Man*).

Heschel here echoes the sentiment of Judah the Pious, who shrewdly observed: "Humility without a measure of fearfulness is like food without any spicing" (Judah Heḥasid, *Sefer Ḥasidim,* 15).

The Torah and all its wisdom and commandments rest on our *yirat ha-El.* Without it, we lose Judaism's critical anchor. With it, we embrace this vision of Ecclesiastes: "The end of the matter, all having been heard: Fear God and keep God's mitzvot, for that is why you were created a human being" (12:13).

From Our Tradition

The king of Egypt spoke to the two Hebrew midwives, the one named Shifrah and the other Puah. He said to them: "When you deliver the children of the Hebrew women, be alert. If the child is a boy, kill him; if it is a girl, let her live." But the midwives feared God and did not do as the king of Egypt said. They let the boys live.

—Exod. 1:16–17

R. Samuel went to Rome shortly after the queen lost her bracelet. He found it. A crier went through the kingdom and said: "Whoever returns the bracelet within 30 days shall receive a reward, but if it is found upon him after 30 days, his head shall be cut off." R. Samuel did not return it within 30 days, but did return the bracelet the next day. The queen said to the rabbi, "Haven't you been in the kingdom?" He said, "Yes I have." She said, "Haven't you heard the proclamation?" He said, "Yes I have." She said, "What did the crier say?" R. Samuel told the queen. She said, "So why didn't you return the bracelet within 30 days?" He said, "So that you should not say, I feared you, but I returned it because I feared God." The queen said, "Blessed be the God of the Jews."

—Yer. B.M. 11.5

Rabbi Levi Yitzḥak of Berditchev saw a man in the marketplace, so intent on his business that he never looked up. The rabbi stopped him and asked: "What are you doing?" The man answered hurriedly, "I have no time to talk to you now." He repeated his question, "What are you doing?" Impatiently the man cried, "Don't delay me. I have to attend to my business." The rabbi insisted, "All right," he said. "But you yourself—what are you doing? Everything you are so worried about is in the hands of God, and all that is in your hands is to fear God." The man looked up—and for the first time he knew what the fear of God was.

—Buber, *Tales of the Hasidim,* bk. 1, *The Early Masters*

If reverence of the Lord is someone's stored-up treasure, all is well; if not, nothing else matters. This can be compared to a man who said to his messenger, "Bring me a *kur* of wheat to the upper floor." The messenger brought it. The man asked him, "Did you mix in a measure of the preservative?" He answered, "No." The master then said, "It would have been better if you had not carried it up here."

—Shab. 31a

Rabbah recounted what certain sailors once told him: "Once we were on a voyage, and a wave lifted us up until we saw where the smallest of the stars rests. Then there was a flash as if someone had shot forty arrows of iron. Had the wave lifted us up any higher, we would have burned from the heat. Then one wave called to his friend: Did you leave behind anything in the world that you did not wash away? I will go and destroy it. The other wave replied: Go and you will see the power of the Master by whose edict I must not go beyond the sand by even as little as a thread's width, as it is said: 'Will you indeed not fear Me?' says the Lord. 'Will you not tremble before Me who placed the sand as a boundary of the sea, who made an eternal law that it can go no further?' [Jer. 5:22]."

—B.B. 73a

The people of Israel were united in the fear of Heaven when they stood at Mount Sinai, teaching us that without faith there is no fear, and vice versa.

—Isaac Arama, *Akedat Yitzhak*

.   .   .   .

Loving God—
Ahavat ha-El

Set me as a seal upon your heart,
As a seal upon your arm
For love is as fierce as death,
Jealousy as mighty as Sheol;
Its darts are darts of fire,
A blazing flame of God.
Vast floods cannot quench love,
Nor rivers inundate it.
If one offered all one's wealth for love,
People would sneer and laugh.

—S. of S. 8:6–7

*T*he onset is evident. We can't eat; we don't sleep; we're miserable; we're ecstatic; we can't concentrate, yet feel we could move mountains. We walk but do not seem to touch the floor; we collide with desks and chairs and start apologizing to them. In the mirror, we see a familiar face with a sappy look on it; in conversation we find ourselves giggling. People look at us knowingly; they recognize this variety of temporary insanity. It's just that we've lost our mind, and know exactly where to find it.

The later symptoms are more subtle: a new level of personal aspiration and a quiet power to work at it; a joy that multiplies in the other's smile and the solace their touch brings when things go wrong; a sense of worth greater than any compliment could create; a reason for living as fully and decently as one can; a sustaining togetherness that lets us go our own ways, yet always reunites us; an

315

awe at the incomparable you who, knowing me as you do, still embraces and upholds me. It is the most precious thing in the world. We speak as experts, for we have been married to our same spouse for a total of more than eighty years. Thus we know love when we see it, and choose it as the final, climactic theme of our *musar.*

What Has This "Divine Madness" To Do with Religion?

Judaism has often been described as a religion of law; yet few of its commandments are as central to Judaism as is *ahavat ha-El,* the love of God. On this score the Torah is uncommonly emphatic, putting a threefold stress upon our duty, an excess typical of true love: "You"—singular—"shall love the Lord your God with all your heart, with all your soul, and with all your might" (Deut. 6:5). By what spiritual genius did this sentence follow immediately upon: "Hear, O Israel, *Adonai* is our God, *Adonai* is One" (Deut. 6:4)? (Of course, this was not yet "The *Shema,*" as it came to be in postbiblical days.) But to say that *Adonai* is the Only One, the Unique, the Whole, the Primary, is to indulge in a passion of admiration and exclusivity that parallels what can happen between two people.

By the rabbinic era, the *Shema* was a critical component of the prayers we say twice each day. Each time we recite these prayers, we engage in a dialogue of love. For not only do we follow the *Shema* by recounting the command to love God, but we always introduce the *Shema* with prayers reminding us of God's love for us. Thus in the evening we say: *Barukh atah Adonai, ohev amo Yisrael,* Blessed are You, *Adonai,* who loves Your people Israel; and in the morning service we say: *Barukh atah Adonai, ha-boḥer be-amo Yisrael be-ahavah,* Blessed are You, *Adonai,* who in love chooses Your people Israel. The heart of Jewish prayer is this affirmation of our mutual love.

The Reality of the Love We Are Commanded to Feel

Our tradition gives us no reason to turn the love we are ordered to have for God into some bloodless spiritual abstraction. When the Bible talks of love, it is describing the same extraordinary emotion that we thrill at today. Thus we read in Genesis: Though Jacob served seven years for Rachel, they seemed to him but a few days because he loved her (29:20). Biblical love takes the many forms that fill fortunate lives: Jacob's love for Joseph, Ruth's devotion to her mother-in-law Naomi, and the classic story of David and Jonathan, a love threatened by King Saul's enmity for David. But Jonathan's "soul became bound to the soul of David; Jonathan loved David as himself" (1 Sam. 18:1).

And then there is that whole book devoted to love, the rapturously named Song of Songs. On the surface, it seems like a passionate series of exchanges between two lovers. But then, how did it become part of Sacred Scripture? Something about human love must have indicated a similar relationship between God and people. Still in rabbinic times, when the final canonization of Scriptures was taking place, there were those who thought Song of Songs too earthly to have been God-inspired. Yet not only did the rabbis insist that Song of Songs be included, but they began reading it as the love-talk between God and the people of Israel. They would not deprive love of its full libidinous nature, even as they understood it as modeling the most sublime Divine-human intimacy.

In medieval mysticism, these erotic connotations came into full play. The Zohar, the most important kabbalistic text, relates in one of its less overtly sexual metaphors: "The angels in the hall of love introduce love between Israel below and the Holy One above. And they all arouse love and remain in a state of love. And when love is aroused from the lower to the upper realms, and from the upper to the lower realms, this hall becomes filled with many good things . . . and the love of the lower world penetrates the love of the upper world and they are united together" (Zohar II, 253b).

Love Affects Us as Religion Should

Why would R. Simeon b. Eleazar say: "Greater is he who acts from love than he who acts from fear" (Sot. 31a)? We can turn to the eleventh-century Spanish philosopher Baḥya ibn Pakuda for an extended response. Baḥya, in awe of his love's very being, describes his tremendous joy as he looks forward to the favor of his loved one and his happiness in knowing that others also admire his beloved (*Ḥovot Halevavot*). Needless to say, he is not rhapsodizing over an earthly love, but about one that millions share without the usual pangs of jealousy—*ahavat ha-El*—the love of God.

What makes love so attractive in religion is that "Love upsets the natural order" (Gen. R. 55.8). Its very extremism helps us break through the fascination of everyday profaneness. Consider the rabbis' interpretations of the tripartite behest to love God. "Simeon b. Azzai said: 'with all thy soul', love God until your soul departs from you" (Ber. 61b). "R. Eliezer said: Since 'with all thy soul' is stated, why is 'with all thy might' stated? Or if 'with all thy might' is desired, why also write 'with all thy soul'? For the one to whom life is more precious than wealth, 'with all thy soul' is written, while he to whom wealth is more precious than life must accept, 'with all thy might'" (San. 74a). Loving God must be paramount. Any lesser love needs to be our instrument in serving God.

And this is exactly our Jewish religious ideal—to learn to love God with an all-powerful, all-consuming passion. The thirteenth-century Franco-German sage Judah the Pious says: "You need to love the Creator with a great and mighty love that makes you lovesick as over a woman, thinking about her constantly—sitting or rising, going or coming. Even when he eats or drinks, his love never ceases. More than that should be our love of God, so that we continually think of *Adonai*" (Judah Hehasid, *Sefer Hasidim*, 14). Bahya b. Asher, a Spanish commentator who lived half a century or so after Judah, wants even more: "Although the quality of loving God is indeed great, that of desiring God is even greater. In the case of love, one can occasionally forget the object of his love when he is preoccupied with other matters, but this is not so in the case of desire, which is all-consuming. Even when one is asleep, he sees the object of his desire in a dream. The Psalmist compared his longing for God to a person who extends himself so that he is in danger of dying: 'My soul thirsts for You, my body yearns for You, as a parched and thirsty land that has no water' [Ps. 63:2]" *(Kad Hakemah).*

Consider How Love Motivates and Empowers Us

If we truly love someone, we will do anything to get and, more important, keep this love. The late-sixteenth-century Italian sage Isaac Aboab remarks: "A man who is in love with a woman will endanger his body, his soul and his possessions in order to acquire the one his soul desires" (*Menorat Hamaor* [The illuminating lampstand]). Continuing to follow the lead of the rabbis, Aboab's younger compatriot Ovadiah b. Jacob Sforno comments: "The Deuteronomic command 'You shall love' means you should rejoice to do anything that God indicates is good, since you understand that there could be no goal more worthy than this" (Commentary to Deut. 6:5, in *Mikraot Gedolot*). In contemporary jargon, may we suggest behavior like sending your significant other to bed while you stay up late, cleaning up after guests leave, or getting up before dawn to make your spouse a nutritious breakfast, when you have an equally hectic day ahead. Jacob Zvi Hirsch of Mecklenburg, a mid-nineteenth-century commentator, explains the invigorating effect of religious love with an important nuance: "Some love is limited and some unbounded. When one has a limited kind of love, one is enthusiastic about God's commandments . . . but within the limits which the Torah sets for it. To be sure, one cannot attain this level of attachment except after very great effort and exertion. Yet there is a love which is very much greater and more important . . . this is the love which is unbounded. . . . Then one expands the doing of the commandments in every way and measure" (*Haketav Vehakabbalah* [Scripture and tradition], to Exod. 20:6).

Love also means defending your beloved from attacks by others. For medieval Jews, this often meant responding to Christian polemics. Baḥya ibn Pakuda was uncompromising: "Never associate the love of anyone else with the love of God" (*Ḥovot Halevavot*). His later colleague, Naḥmanides, was the most significant defender of Judaism during the increasingly troubled times of thirteenth-century Spain. "Who are those whom God calls 'those that love Me'? They are the people who acknowledge God's exclusive divinity and deny that there is any other God, refusing to serve false gods, even if this puts their lives in danger. . . . For they dedicate their souls to loving God and refuse to link themselves with a strange deity" (*Commentary on the Torah*, to Exod. 20:6).

"A Love without Deeds Is No Love" (Ladino Proverb)

As we would for a human lover, we care passionately about what God wants of us and eagerly seek to do it. In the words of Yeḥiel b. Yekutiel: "When one is firmly bound in love to one's Creator, God's mitzvot are etched upon his heart forever" *(Sefer Maalot Hamiddot)*. Joseph Albo, the last of the great medieval Jewish philosophers, agrees: "The love of God must consist of serving God and observing God's commandments as far as possible and at all times" *(Sefer Haikkarim)*. And this, as Jacob Zvi Hirsch of Mecklenburg observes, has a limiting effect as well: "When one truly loves God, one is constantly concerned lest, heaven forbid, one causes a blemish to God's proper respect" (*Haketav Vehakabbalah,* to Gen. 22:12). In this sentiment, he echoes that of the Psalmist: "O you who love the Lord, hate evil!" (97:10).

Love also means bringing our whole self to our efforts on behalf of our beloved. Thus we are cautioned against doing the commandments only by rote. Once again, Joseph Albo is our guide: "Even bringing an offering to the Temple in Jerusalem, which is surely a good act, if a person brings it without distinguishing between good and evil but merely as a result of habit and custom, that act is worth nothing" (*Sefer Haikkarim*).

"Another characteristic in the lover of God," Baḥya ibn Pakuda teaches, "is that he leads and instructs others in the service of God, gently or severely, in accordance with time and place . . . from kings to ordinary folk" *(Ḥovot Halevavot)*. That is to say: "The commandment 'You shall love' may be read 'You shall cause to be loved.' So you are to cause the name of Heaven to be loved by mankind. Hence you are to be loving in the give-and-take of everyday life—in your going about in the marketplace and in your dealing with people" (T.B.E. [28] 26).

Our nomination for someone who well exemplified this aspect of *ahavat ha-El* is the pathfinding pediatrician and social activist Benjamin Spock. Baby doctors before him had cautioned parents not to stray from following rigid schedules and certainly not to spoil their babies by picking them up and cuddling them. Spock changed all that, encouraging bewildered adults to trust their instincts, to hold and soothe crying babies, loving them even if they did not behave "by the book." When the first generation raised by Spock's recommendation of love and affection reached maturity, the now young adults demanded that we "make love, not war." Spock continued to join them on the picket line in the ensuing decades of ethical activism until shortly before his death.

True Love Fills Us with Joy and Does Not Fade

Loving God, like loving a mortal, may make heavy demands on us. But as long as love is real, it is grounded in the happiness that our love uniquely engenders. More than seven hundred years ago, Judah the Pious wrote: "The source of our love of God is that the love in our soul is bound up with God's soul in joy, in love and good will" (Judah Hehasid, *Sefer Hasidim*, 14).

But how shall we know when love is true, when what we feel is what we had hoped to attain? R. Eleazar offers us the following test: "A man may love God because he is wealthy, has lived long, is surrounded by children, has triumphed over his enemies, and is prosperous in all his ways. Because of all this, he loves God. But if his situation were to be transformed, and the Holy One were to turn the wheel of strict judgment in his direction, taking away some or all of his many blessings, he would then hate God. This is love without roots. Perfect love is love in both conditions: when one is in favor, or in disfavor" (Ber. 61b).

Later, medieval Jewish philosophers were more analytic. Thus Joseph Albo distinguishes among three varieties of love, but comes to the same conclusion: "The love of the good, the love of the useful and the love of the agreeable. . . . The love of the good for the sake of the good itself cannot change or be destroyed, for the lover does not love the loved one merely because he is good to him . . . but because he has found that the loved one is good in himself. . . . A love which is solely for the sake of the beloved and for no other cause, will last as long as the beloved endures. Now, since God endures forever, love for God never ceases" *(Sefer Haikkarim)*.

Yet as in life, the ultimate test of whether our love is real rests on whether it can survive those trials that love inscrutably but inevitably brings upon us. "R. Jacob taught: By the similarity of the sounds of *me'od* ('might') and *midduh* ('measure'), we may learn that loving God 'with all your might' means with whatever measure God metes out to you. Whether it be the measure of good or of chastisement, love God. Love God with all your heart" (Sifre Deut. 32). This is very much like R. Akiba's dictum: "'Love God . . . with all thy soul' means that you are to love God, even if God takes away your soul" (Ber. 61b).

Love of God is a lofty ideal indeed. Yet through the ages there have been Jews who achieved a good measure of it. Alexander Suesskind, writing his ethical will two hundred years ago, says he lived by this philosophy: "It was ever my wont to thank God for whatever happened to me. If some misfortune befell, I would acclaim with joy the justice of the decree. On any good occasion, I would offer thanks for the Lord's bountiful kindness. I have rendered this service of praise to God out of the great love which is fixed in my heart, which has made it thankful for evil as for good, seeing both as God's handiwork" (*Hebrew Ethical Wills*). In this, Suesskind was observing what had already been determined by the Mishnah as the standard to which Jews should aspire. So too, "We are required to bless God over the evil that befalls us, just as we bless God for the good that comes our way. As it says: 'You shall love *Adonai* with all your heart'" (Ber. 9.5). The blessing over personal good is the familiar *she-heḥeyanu:* "who has kept us alive, and sustained us, and brought us to this day." The blessing over evil, which most people only encounter when there is a funeral in their immediate family, is *Barukh dayyan ha-emet,* "Blessed be the judge of truth," a reference that likely refers to God's judgment on Adam and Eve, when God banished them from the Garden and its tree of life.

"God Does Not Punish with Both Hands" (Ladino Proverb)

But now we must face up to the truly black moments of existence, those times when it seems as if all the love and intimacy that had sustained us for so long has disappeared. Such days are doubly bitter, because we cannot help but contrast them to the times when we were able to emerge from this engulfing sadness. Let us say straight out: love is not all sweet sentimentality and joyful victory over difficulties. Love, too, has its limits. It cannot always overcome everything that life may throw at it and us. Evil is real. The desperate darkness of real evil should never be minimized. Often, what pains us most deeply is that the one that we love has betrayed us so badly. Love itself, then, is a cause of our pain.

Franz Rosenzweig, the early-twentieth-century Jewish philosopher, explores the gap between what we can do and what we'd like to do. He explains why the love of God is necessarily blemished. "But love is difficult. Even love for God. That is the most difficult love. Unhappy love, which is in all love, even the happiest, through the tension between the infinitude of the desire for loving, the having to love, and the finitude of the capacity for loving, here ascends by degrees to the infinite. The love of God is always at once happy and unhappy, the happiest and the unhappiest love" (Galli, "Note to 'The Lovers,'" in *Franz Rosenzweig and Jehuda Halevi*).

That leaves us with mere rationalizations concerning our very human constraints to ease our despair, small comforts indeed. Yet two things further must be said about love and evil. The first: Love helps us understand how to live with a God that we may have concluded is necessarily limited. Such an intellectual resolution of the problem of evil may seem difficult for the pious to live with, until we consider the totality of our experience with those we love. In the first flush of romance, we are overwhelmed by the almost limitless ways that our love fulfills our long search for companionship. They are our saviors, who redeem us from the unsatisfying lives we lived before them. But with time we learn that they have faults, as do we. And now a fantasy-less love becomes possible for us, a relationship in which we discover that we love despite the real imperfections of the other—sometimes, it seems, we love them for just these imperfections. And so it should be with God, who perhaps is not yet powerful enough to overcome all evil.

The second: We want a personal relationship with God rather than merely a logical, analytic connection. Again, the experience of great intimacy gives us a model for what it is to love, even though we often do not understand the one we so adore. For often, those we care about most deeply wound us for reasons—if there are any—that they cannot provide and we cannot imagine. Strangely enough, such traumas do not automatically end our relationship, even if we have sworn that another such occurrence will be the last straw. Love often manifests a mysterious power to surmount the unthinkable and the inexplicable. But it is also true that some trivial thing, a matter that never occasioned discussion, can arise and suddenly snap the tie that once seemed so permanent. The mysterious power of love is real, but it operates with a double edge.

Giving Our *Ahavat ha-El* Staying Power

When love is strong, it seems invincible; when it is threatened, it seems as weak as wet paper. Paradoxically, we need to work at love, even though we cannot force it into being or keep it solid. Yet we must do what we can, reaching out, being there for and with them. Much of Jewish religious life seeks to facilitate this powerful/feeble bond by the deeds it commends. But that must be accompanied by a genuine focusing of our soul. Our frequent guide in this matter, Baḥya ibn Pakuda, who wrote of the "duties of the heart," does not fail us here. He reminds us of our direct as well as of our indirect paths to reach the open heart. As he says, sometimes we can easily point to what renews our love: "It is the soul's yearning for the Creator, turning to God of its own accord, cleaving to God's sacred light." At other times: "When we realize the Almighty's infinite power and essential sublimity, we will bow down and prostrate ourselves, until the Creator assures and quiets us. . . . Then our thirst will be assuaged by drinking deep out of the cup of love of God" (*Ḥovot Halevavot*).

Others point to the surges of gratitude that sweep over us when we realize what God does on our behalf: "Said the Alexanderer Rebbe: If a physician not only cured a poor patient, but also donated a sum of money to him, wouldn't the sick person feel everlasting love for the generous friend? The Lord gives us life and the means of maintaining it, so our love for God need not be dictated by the Torah alone" (Newman, *The Hasidic Anthology*). God's wonders surround us. The freshness of the early morning air reminds us we have been given another day; the shouts of children playing remind us of how much vitality and goodness God has implanted in us. Our minds work, our souls create, our hearts are touched and reach out to others. Even if it only lasts a moment, this simple thanksgiving transforms into our love for God.

We Jews have another reason for loving God—*Adonai* gave our people the Torah. It is not chauvinism, a violation of the Torah's own principles, to thrill in our delight, our treasure, unique in human history. And as long as humankind exists, the Torah's original text remains Hebrew, testifying to the culture of an otherwise small, obscure people. Why were we so blessed? Why are we so blessed, that this Torah tradition continues to sanctify us? Yes, as in any great love, we wonderingly inquire, why did You "choose us from among all peoples and give us Your Torah"? We dare not, as the Torah tells us, claim it because of our merit. It must be because You, God, love us. So we, small of faith and weak of soul, dare say, we love You, for giving us this goodly heritage.

But not being saints, we know we cannot live only in the steady consciousness of our love. We must live mainly out of *yirat ha-El,* our "fear" of You. Yet, as the sixteenth-century biblical commentator Moses b. Ḥayyim Alshekh tells us: "If we only served God out of fear, we would not be serving God with all our soul, or exerting ourselves with all of our power" (*Commentary to Deuteronomy, Torat Mosheh,* to Deut. 10:12). So "fear" needs the elevating partnership of love. And this mix of love and awe, we are convinced, is what sustained Jewish piety over the ages. "In truth, the fear and love of God are simply one thing. Love is the cause of fear, and this fear is the fulfillment of love . . ." (Hirsch, *Haketav Vehakabbalah,* to Gen. 22:12). Love knows and fears the threat of loss; "fear" transcends itself as awe becomes appreciation. And that is the climax of the three linked requests we make of God in the morning prayer that introduces the *Shema:* "Enlighten our eyes in Your Torah; make our hearts cling to Your commandments; integrate our hearts in the love and fear of Your name." Amen, Selah.

From Our Tradition

Rabbi Levi Yitzḥak of Berditchev used to sing this song:
Where I wander—You!
Where I ponder—You!
Only You, You again, always You!
You! You! You!
When I am gladdened—You!
When I am saddened—You!

Only You, You again, always You!
You! You! You!
Sky is You! Earth is You!
You above! You below!
In every trend, at every end,
You, You again, always You!
You! You! You!
—Buber, *Tales of the Hasidim*, bk. 1, *The Early Masters*

A certain famous rabbi once said to the Tzaddik, Abraham of Stretyn, "I have heard that you provide people with charms and amulets for all sorts of things. Perhaps you can let me have a charm for godfearingness." The Tzaddik replied, "There is no charm for godfearingness, but there is one for love of God." "Good," said the rabbi. "Give me one for that then." The Tzaddik replied, "The charm for love of God is love for our people Israel. The one who possesses love of Israel will easily achieve love of Heaven."

—Zeivin, *Sippurei Ḥasidim*

How strong and overpowering is the joy of the one who loves God? Compare it to a man who has not had intercourse with his wife for many days and has an intense desire for her. Finally, he consummates it. The joy he feels at that moment is nothing compared to the strength and power of our love of God and the joy we have in our Creator.

—Judah Heḥasid, *Sefer Ḥasidim*

When young Rabbi Eleazar of Koznitz was a guest in the house of Rabbi Naftali of Ropshitz, he once cast a surprised glance at the window, where the curtains had been drawn. When his host asked him the cause of his surprise, he said, "If you want people to look in, then why the curtains? And if you do not want them to, why the window?" "And what explanation have you found for this?" asked Rabbi Naftali. "When you want someone you love to look in," said the young rabbi, "you draw aside the curtain."

—Buber, *Tales of the Hasidim*, bk. 2, *The Later Masters*

CHAPTER 26

Epilogue— Post-Modern *Musar*

*O*ore than seven hundred years have passed since Yeḥiel b. Yekutiel made his pioneering selection of the Jewish moral virtues for his book, *Sefer Maalot Hamiddot*. His age did not know a printing press—he was, in fact, a scribe—or a steam engine, or a cell phone, much less interchangeable human body parts. Most of all, he did not know what it meant for a Jew to be a free and equal member of the state in which he lived. Indeed, thirteenth-century Italy was moving toward the creation of the first ghettos, a word that still betrays its Italian origins. Democracy would have to await the economic and technological advances of the Industrial Revolution. This began only two centuries ago; in many places, it still awaits meaningful fulfillment. Thus Yeḥiel's list of moral virtues are very much more personal than communal. While the social implications of the standards he commends are always evident, we cannot end our work without saying a few words pointedly directed at the civic virtues, which now so prominently inform our Jewish morality.

We would like to speak briefly about three contemporary values. As Ecclesiastes puts it: "A three-fold cord is not easily broken" (4:12). Surely the first of these must be a passion for social justice, for few themes are as central to the Jewish sense of God. Justice is a primary Divine concern, a notion reinforced by the modern regard for conscience. Our charge to pursue justice is not confined to face-to-face activities, but applies to the very structure and functioning of our society. It thus creates a vision of the social order in which justice expands to care for the powerless: the widow, the orphan, and the stranger within our gates. Not merely a holding action against individual human sinfulness, doing justly honors everyone, since we are all created in "the image." Bitter experience has taught us that only if there is justice for all members of society, most particularly for downtrodden minorities, will the freedom and security of Jews remain secure. Wherever Jews have become free members of their society, they have almost instinctively known these truths.

Democracy also demands and celebrates its own special virtue, tolerance. True, Yeḥiel may have been "tolerated," but only in a cursory, medieval way. His was not an environment that rejoiced in the benefits of pluralism and diversity, as does our own.

Here we find two beneficial forces in seeming competition. The first, centrifugal one, spins out of the restrictions of our neighborhood existence, involving us in a vast nation with its amazing array of problems. Ultimately we find ourselves part of a world teeming with people whose lives we frankly could not imagine just a few decades before. Some contend that we have brought down everyone else to our low level of American mass culture. Yet this alleged leveling itself reminds us that there is one humanity on earth, as there is only one God in heaven. And something about this surging homogenization has also generated a second force, this one centripetal. So we rejoice in regional and near-at-hand aspects of life. We celebrate our diversities, exulting in differences that add to everyone's horizon. Of course it is easy to get so caught up in our own small group that we forget about the rest of humanity. But only by starting where we are, can we then make meaningful contributions to the common welfare. Thus these two forces need to balance each other. Certainly we Jews, long treated as a pariah-people, find the ideal of tolerance to be particularly precious.

Unfortunately, our personal and social gains have come at a price. Flush with the rewards of modernity, we once thought that our genius would fashion an up-to-date contemporary equivalent of the biblical vine and fig tree, with none to make us afraid. Alas, we not only have suffered the shocking disappointment of failing to solve old problems, but have seen the creation of new ones. Amid the greatest and most widespread affluence the world has ever known, we are anxious, fearful, depressed. We tried to play God and discovered that we are still only too human, seriously limited in our ability to re-create the world as we would like it to be. In such an environment, we cannot overemphasize our second virtue, that of hope.

Yehiel would be appalled at our clutching at hope almost as an afterthought. He and the rest of our Jewish sages rarely discussed this virtue, because they knew that the future did not depend solely on their actions, but on God's. They knew that God's power would one day show itself unmistakably. We see proof of this when we read the *Alenu* prayer in our worship service. The first paragraph tells us: "Know this day, and keep in your heart the truth that *Adonai* is the only God in the heaven above and the earth beneath. There is no one else to serve" (Deut. 4:39). Then, the prayer's second paragraph gives us the key: "Therefore, we put our hope in You, *Adonai, our God,* soon to see the glory of Your power . . ." Jewish hope comes from being satisfied, indeed thrilled by knowing Who our Senior Partner is.

Our last word must return to the personal. For as much as we have held our various themes in high regard, we must not pursue them too one-sidedly, thereby missing another all-important ideal, our third contemporary virtue, balance. Thus we have commended zeal, *zerizut,* but not without a corresponding measure of contentedness, *histapkut,* to accompany it. And wealth, *osher,* without charity, *tzedakah,* becomes a caricature of Jewish character. We even suggest having a sense of balance about being balanced, for there are some virtues that should never be compromised. Justice for all, the pursuit of Torah, and devotion to God rightly demand such wholehearted commitment.

This is our *musar.* We hope it encourages you to think of your own life as one great work of *musar* teaching, one that you create by the acts that you do. So we take our leave, as the rabbis have advised, with words of Torah: "Three offerings that are to be made in the Temple—the whole-offering, the burnt-offering, and the meal-offering—are all described as having a 'sweet savor,' teaching that it makes no difference whether it is great or small, as long as our hearts are directed to Heaven" (Men. 13.11).

Glossary

All foreign words are in Hebrew unless otherwise noted.

(F)—French; (S)—Spanish; (Y)—Yiddish.

Adonai: "My Lord"; euphemism substituted for the ineffable name of God.

Adonai, Adonai, El raḥum ve-ḥanun: "*Adonai, Adonai* is a God of mercy and graciousness" (Exod. 34:6); the beginning of God's unique self-description to Moses.

aggadah: Narrative or homiletic writings of rabbinic literature, as opposed to *halakhah,* legal texts.

ahavat ha-El: Loving God.

Al ḥet: "For the sin"; opening of a confessional prayer said as part of High Holy Day liturgy.

Alenu leshabe'aḥ la-adon ha-kol: "It is incumbent upon us to praise the Master of all things"; the summary prayer of our traditional service.

Amidah: "[The] standing [prayer]"; one of several titles for the group of petition-blessings that is the center of each Jewish service.

anavah: Humility.

Ashamnu, bagadnu: "We have sinned, we have been treacherous . . ."; opening terms of an alphabetic acrostic confessional prayer in the High Holy Day liturgy.

Ashkenazi: Jew from non-Mediterranean European countries, or their culture.

Avinu Malkenu: "Our Father, our King"; first words of a confessional petition; most notably, a High Holy Day prayer.

Baal Shem Tov: "Master of the Good Name"; common late medieval mystic title, most notably used for the founder of Hasidism in the early eighteenth century.

Barekhu: "Blessed/praised are You"; first word of the formal opening of the morning and evening service.

barukh: "Blessed/praised," referring to God.

beit din: Rabbinic court of law.

beit midrash: "House of study"; where adults gather to study texts.

berakhah(ot): Blessing(s).

beys hamikdesh: (Y) The Jerusalem Temple.

bikkur holim: Mitzvah of "visiting the sick."

birkat hamazon: Blessings and prayers said after eating.

boshet: Shamefacedness.

Converso: (S) Jew forced by the Inquisition to publicly renounce his or her faith, yet practiced it secretly.

derekh eretz: Common decency.

Diaspora: Jewish communities outside the Land of Israel.

Ein Sof: In Kabbalah, God as the utterly Limitless One.

El Emunah: "The faithful God," a biblical phrase often used in later prayers.

El malei rahamim: "God, full of compassion"; prayer said at funeral or memorial service.

emet: Truth.

emunah: Trustworthiness.

etrog: Lemon-like fruit that is part of the Sukkot observance.

gabbaei tzedakah: Trustees of the community charity fund.

Gehenna: Hell.

gemilut hasadim: Lovingkindness.

genevat da'at: "Stealing someone's mind"; deceit.

golem: (Y) Legendary semi-human creature mystically fashioned to protect Jews from danger in late medieval Europe.

grager: (Y) Purim noisemaker; during the reading of the Book of Esther, sounded each time the villain Haman's name is mentioned.

haggadah: Book containing order of Pesaḥ ceremonial dinner, explanations, prayers, special songs, and readings.

ḥakham: "Wise person"; Sephardic term interchangeable with "rabbi," used particularly of distinguished leaders.

halakhah: Jewish law; the legal parts of rabbinic literature.

ḥanufah: Flattery.

ḥasid: "Pious one"; particularly applied to adherents of Hasidism.

Hasidism: Form of mystic Judaism started in the early eighteenth century by the Baal Shem Tov, emphasizing joy and community.

hatzne'a: Modestly, privately.

havdalah: "Difference, separation"; ceremony concluding Shabbat, during which prayers are said over wine, spices, and the distinctive braided candle.

ḥet: Sin.

ḥevrah kadishah: "Sacred fellowship"; Jewish burial society.

hiddur mitzvah: "Adorning a commandment"; to beautify one's ritual objects.

histapkut: Contentedness.

hokhmah: Wisdom.

ḥumrot: "Stringencies," as in especially rigorous observances.

ish tam: Pure-hearted soul.

Judah ha-Nasi: Judah the "Nasi"; Prince or Patriarch of the Palestinian Jewish community under Roman rule, compiler of the Mishnah about 200 C.E.

Kabbalah: Medieval and later Jewish mystical thought.

kal ve-ḥomer: Hermeneutic principle that proves that the greater must be true, since the lesser is true.

kavannah: "Intention," used frequently to describe directing the self to God in prayer.

kavod: Honor, respect.

kever avot: The custom of visiting parents' graves during the month of Elul, which precedes Rosh Hashanah.

kholileh: (Y) "God forbid."

kibud av va-em: Honoring one's father and mother.

kibud ha-met: Showing respect for a corpse.

kiddush: Blessing over wine on the Sabbath and festivals.

Kohen: Descendant of a Temple priest.

lashevet: "For habitation"; biblical term (Isa. 45:18) used by the rabbis for the duty to lead a socially constructive life.

leshon ha-ra: "Tongue of evil"; gossip.

levayyat ha-met: "Accompanying the dead"; a funeral.

Levite: Descendant of an assistant to the Temple priests; one of the biblical tribe of Levi.

lishmah: Task done "for its own sake."

maggid: Preacher; storyteller.

malbish arumim: "Who clothes the naked"; one of the Jewish blessings on awakening.

mamaloshen: (Y) "Mother tongue," i.e., Yiddish.

mamzer: Jew of illegitimate birth, as defined under Jewish law.

manna: Foodstuff sent by God to feed the people during their forty years of wandering in the wilderness.

mi shebeirakh: " May the One who blessed . . ."; opening words of prayers for individuals, most famously a prayer for healing.

midrash: Homiletic interpretation of biblical text.

mikdesh me'at: (Y) "Small sanctuary"; talmudic term for the synagogue, as opposed to the Jerusalem Temple.

Minḥah: Daily afternoon service.

minyan: Ten adult Jews, the quorum needed for full worship.

mipnei darkhei shalom: Rules "in the interest of peace."

mishkan: Portable sanctuary used during the Israelites' forty years of wandering in the wilderness.

Mishnah: Law code compiled in Palestine in 200 C.E.; basis of the Talmud.

mitzvah(ot): A commandment; figuratively, a good deed.

mitzvah lishmah: A commandment done for its own sake.

modeh ani: "I give thanks . . ." ; opening words of the traditional prayer said upon waking up.

Moshe Rabbenu: "Moses, our teacher"; respectful way of referring to the greatest prophet.

motzi: "Who brings forth [bread from the earth]"; blessing said before eating bread.

musar: Pietistic ethical teaching.

Musar movement: Nineteenth-century Jewish effort emphasizing a rigorous, ethical pietism in the traditional life of study and observance.

Nazirite: In biblical times, a Jew who voluntarily assumed the self-denial of hair-cutting, wine-drinking, or other practices for a given period, sometimes for life.

nedivut: Generosity.

nikayon peh: "Pure mouth"; the Jewish term prohibiting foul speech.

olam ha-ba: The world to come.

ona'at devarim: Fraudulent representation.

oneg: Joy.

Oral Law, or Oral Torah: Traditionally, that aspect of God's revelation at Sinai not revealed in written form, but formalized and gradually put into writing, beginning in the second century C.E.

osher: Wealth.

ozer Yisrael bigevurah: "Who girds Israel with strength"; opening words of a Jewish blessing, said on arising.

perutah: Smallest coin used in the rabbinic period.

Pesaḥ: "To pass over"; spring festival celebrating the Hebrew slaves' exodus from Egypt.

Rabbi: When standing alone, refers to Judah ha-Nasi, Patriarch of the Palestinian Jewish community, compiler of the Mishnah about 200 C.E.

raḥamim: Compassion.

Ramban: "Naḥmanides," Moses b. Naḥman, thirteenth-century Spanish thinker.

rasha: Wicked person.

ratzui: "Popular."

rebbe: (Y) Hasidic leader.

reḥem: Womb.

rite de passage: (F) Significant event in life, a transition from one stage to another.

Rosh Hashanah: "The head of the year," Jewish new year; period of self-examination.

Sar Shalom: "Peaceable ruler"; a messianic title.

seah: Small biblical unit measuring volume.

Sefer Torat Moshe: Scroll of the Torah of Moses.

sefirot: "Spheres"; in kabbalistic teaching, the ten emanations of the Godhead.

Sephardi: Jew coming from countries bordering the Mediterranean Sea, or their culture.

"Shabbat Shalom": "Sabbath peace"; words of greeting on Friday night and Saturday.

Shabbat Shuva: "Sabbath of Repentance"; Sabbath between Rosh Hashanah and Yom Kippur.

Shabbat Zakhor: "Sabbath of Remembrance"; the Sabbath before Purim.

shalom: "Peace," "hello," "good-bye."

shalom bayit: "Peace of home"; the peaceful home environment to be cultivated.

shehakol nihyeh bidevaro: "By whose word everything came to be"; closing words of the blessing said over anything eaten or drunk (except water) when no other blessing has been prescribed.

shehitah: Laws pertaining to ritual slaughtering of animals.

sheker: Lie, deceit.

Shekhinah: Rabbinic name for God's Indwelling Presence, personified in feminine, nurturing terms.

sheliah tzibbur: "Messenger of the community"; cantor or other prayer leader.

shem tov: Good name.

Shema: "Hear/listen!"; first word of the most important statement in Jewish liturgy.

Shemoneh Esreh: The "Eighteen Benedictions"; one of several names for the group of petition-blessings that is the center of each Jewish service.

She'ol: The Bible's term for the place of the afterlife; in rabbinic literature, a term for Hell.

shivah: "Seven"; the period of most intense mourning.

shohet: Ritual slaughterer.

shtetl: (Y) Jewish village in eastern Europe.

sim shalom: "Grant peace"; opening words of prayer for peace in morning worship service.

Sitra Aḥra: "The other side"; ten negative *sefirot* or spheres matching God's ten positive *sefirot.*

sukkah: Temporary hut erected during Sukkot, the festival of tabernacles.

Talmud Torah keneged kulam: "Torah study is equal to all other mitzvot" (Pe'ah 1.1).

Tefillah: "The Prayer"; one of several names for the group of petition-blessings that is the center of each Jewish service.

tefillin: "Phylacteries"; square leather boxes tied to the hand and head for the morning service, containing the following biblical passages: Exod. 13:1–10, 13:11–16; Deut. 6:4–9, 11:13–21.

temimut: Pure-heartedness.

teshuvah: "Repentance"; formal rabbinic legal response to a halakhic inquiry.

tkhines: (Y) Prayers of supplication written in Yiddish, often by women.

Torah vekiyum mitzvot: Torah and observing the commandments.

Tosefta: Teachings of the rabbinic period, not included in the Mishnah, but accepted as secondarily authoritative.

tov ayin: "Good eye"; generous person.

tsedokeh: (Y) Charity.

tsu feel iz umgezunt: (Y) "Too much isn't healthy."

tzaddik: "A righteous person"; used as a title of respect for a pious Jew; a hasidic leader; the ideal of ordinary Jews.

tzar ayin: "Narrow eye"; stingy person.

tzar ba'alei ḥayyim: "The pain of living things"; the rabbinic term for prohibiting cruelty to animals.

tzedakah: Charity.

tzseniyut: Modesty.

tzenu'im: Pious, virtuous persons.

tzitzit: "Fringes" on a four-cornered garment, from Num. 15:37–41.

viddui: "Confession"; most commonly communal confession said during Yom Kippur worship, but also the personal confession made on one's deathbed.

Yad Vashem: "A hand and a name" (Isa. 56:5); Israeli institution and memorial honoring those who died in the Holocaust.

yediat ha-El: Knowing God.

Yerusholayim: (Y) Jerusalem.

yetzer ha-ra: Inclination to do evil.

yetzer ha-tov: Inclination to do good.

Yiddishe kop: (Y) Alluding to allegedly typical Jewish intelligence and cleverness.

yiḥus: (Y) Family background.

yimakh shmo: "May his name be blotted out"; curse invoked on evildoers.

yirat ha-El: "Fearing" God.

Yom Kippur: Day of Atonement.

zekher tzaddik livrakhah: "May the memory of the righteous be a blessing"; invoked in appreciation of good people.

zeriz: Industrious person.

zerizim makdimim le-mitzvot: "The diligent rush to do a mitzvah"; a common maxim in rabbinic literature.

zerizut: Zeal.

Bibliography

One of our goals in writing this book is to acquaint you with some Jewish thinkers whose names may be unfamiliar to you. Two Hebrew anthologies have been particularly helpful to us in this regard. *Aspaklaria* is a work in progress by an indefatigable scholar named Shmuel Adler, who is working his way through the Hebrew alphabet, letter by letter, collecting a great array of Jewish writing on a vast number of themes. As we went to press, his work had reached the letter *Kuf,* in twenty-three volumes. The other, a three-volume work by Zevi Scharfstein, *Otzar Harayonot Vehapitgamim* (Treasury of concepts and proverbs), has been quite useful in directing us to more modern Hebrew writers as well as medieval sages. All the renderings from the Hebrew are ours. In this bibliography we have tried to list the most accessible English edition of the Hebrew work cited.

Aaron, b. Joseph Halevi, of Barcelona. *Sefer Haḥinukh* (The book of instructions). Jerusalem: Mossad Harav Kook, 1952.

Aboab, Isaac. *Menorat Hamaor* (The illuminating lampstand). Vilna: Romm, 1890.

Abrahams, Israel, ed. *Hebrew Ethical Wills.* Pts. 1 and 2. Philadelphia: Jewish Publication Society, 1926.

Adler, Shmuel Avraham. *Aspaklaria.* Jerusalem: Aspaklaria, 1975–.

Ahai Gaon. *Sheiltot.* Ed. S. K. Mirsky. 6 vols. Jerusalem: Mossad Harav Kook, 1964.

Albo, Joseph. *Sefer Haikkarim* (The book of principles). Trans. Isaac Husik. 6 vols. Philadelphia: Jewish Publication Society, 1946.

Alshekh, Moses b. Hayyim. *Commentary to Deuteronomy, Torat Mosheh.* Warsaw: N.p., 1874/5-79. Reprint, Brooklyn: N.p., 1959–60.

Altschuler, David. "Metzudat David" (David's Fortress). In *Nakh Malbim.* New York: E. Grossman, 1964.

Arama, Isaac ben Moses. *Akedat Yitzhak* (The binding of Isaac). Lemberg: A. J. Medfis, 1868.

Aristotle. *On Rhetoric: A Theory of Civic Discourse.* New York: Oxford University Press, 1991.

Avot de Rabbi Natan (The Fathers according to Rabbi Nathan). Trans. Judah Goldin. New Haven: Yale University Press, 1955.

Azikri, Eleazar, and Elijah de Vidas. *Sefer Haredim* (The book of the rigorous). Lublin: N.p., 1896–97.

Baal Shem Tov. *Keter Shem Tov* (Crown of a good name). Piotrkow: H. H. Folman, 1912.

Babylonian Talmud (The Talmud). Ed. Isidore Epstein. London: The Soncino Press, 1935–50.

Bacon, Francis. "Of Judicature." In *Essays and New Atlantis.* New York: Walter J. Black, Inc., 1942.

The Bahir. Trans. Aryeh Kaplan. Northvale, N.J.: Jason Aronson, 1995.

Bahya b. Asher. *Kad Hakemah* (Encyclopedia of Torah thoughts). Trans. Charles B. Chavel. New York: Shilo Publishing House, 1980.

Bahya b. Joseph ibn Pakuda. *Hovot Halevavot* (Duties of the heart). Trans. by Menachem Mansoor. London: Routledge & Kegan Paul, 1973.

Bargeloni, Judah b. Barzillai. *Perush Sefer Yetzirah* (A commentary to book of creation). Ed. Z. H. Halberstamm. Jerusalem: Makor, 1971.

Berachyah. *The Ethical Treatises of Berachyah.* Ed. and trans. Hermann Gollancz. London: David Nutt, 1902.

Berechiah, Aaron b. Moses, of Modena. *Maavar Yabbok* (The ford of the Jabbok). New York: Omanut, 1919.

Bialik, Hayyim, and Yehoshua Hana Ravnitzky. *Sefer Ha-aggadah* (The book of legends). Trans. William G. Braude. New York: Schocken Books, 1992.

Birnbaum, Philip. *Hasidur Hashalem* (Daily prayer book). New York: Hebrew Publishing Co., 1995.

———. *A Treasury of Judaism.* New York: Hebrew Publishing Co., 1962.

Bloch, Abraham P. *A Book of Jewish Concepts*. New York: KTAV Publishing House, 1984.

Blue, Lionel, and Jonathan Magonet. *The Jewish Guide to the Here and Hereafter*. New York: Crossroad Publishing Co., 1989.

Browne, Lewis. *The Wisdom of Israel*. New York: Random House, 1945.

Buber, Martin. *Images of Good and Evil*. London: Routledge and Kegan Paul, 1952.

———. "The Silent Question." In *At the Turning*. New York: Farrar, Straus and Young, 1952.

———. *Tales of the Hasidim*. Book 1, *The Early Masters*. Book 2, *The Later Masters*. Trans. Olga Marx. New York: Schocken Books, 1991.

———. *The Way of Man, According to the Teachings of Hasidism*. London: Collins Books, 1964.

Cohen, Hermann. *Religion of Reason: Out of the Sources of Judaism*. New York: Frederick Ungar Publishing Co., 1972.

Cohen, Seymour J., trans. *Orhot Tzaddikim* (The ways of the righteous). Jerusalem and New York: Feldheim Publishers, 1969.

Coles, Robert. *Simone Weil: A Modern Pilgrimage*. Reading, MA: Addison Wesley, 1987.

Cordovero, Moses. *Elimah Rabbati*. Lvov: N.p., 1881.

———. *Pardes Rimonim* (Garden of pomegranates). 2 vols. Jerusalem: N.p., 1962.

Dan, Joseph, ed. *The Teachings of Hasidism*. West Orange, N.J.: Behrman House, 1983.

De Vidas, Elijah. *Reshit Hokhmah* (Beginning of wisdom). 3 vols. Jerusalem: Vagshal Publishing, 1997.

Dessler, Eliyahu E. *Mikhtav MeEliyahu* (Strive for truth). Trans. Aryeh Carmell. 3 vols. Jerusalem and New York: Feldheim Publishers, 1978–1989.

Elkins, Dov Peretz, ed. *Melodies from My Father's House*. Princeton: Growth Associates, 1996.

Encyclopedia Judaica. Ed. Cecil Roth. Jerusalem: Keter, 1971.

Entzihlopediyah Talmudit. Jerusalem: Encyclopaedia Talmudica with assistance of Mossad Harav Kook, 1947–.

Etkes, Immanuel. *Rabbi Israel Salanter and the Mussar Movement*. Trans. Jonathan Chipman. Philadelphia: Jewish Publication Society, 1993.

Feyer, Avrohom Chaim. *A Letter for the Ages.* (Iggeres Haramban). Brooklyn: Mesorah Publications, 1989.

Fox, Everett, trans. *The Schocken Bible: Volume I, The Five Books of Moses.* New York: Schocken Books, 1995.

Frankl, Viktor E. *Man's Search for Meaning.* 3rd ed. New York: Simon & Schuster, 1984.

Galli, Barbara. *Franz Rosenzweig and Jehuda Halevi.* Montreal: McGill Queens University Press, 1995.

Gerondi, Jonah. *Shaarei Teshuvah* (Gates of repentance). Trans. and Ed. Shraga Silverstein. 2 vols. New York: Feldheim Publishers, 1971.

Gluckel. *The Memoirs of Gluckel of Hameln.* Trans. Marvin Lowenthal. New York: Schocken Books, 1977.

Ḥafetz Ḥayyim. *Ahavat Ḥesed* (The love of kindness). Trans. Leonard Oschry. New York and Jerusalem: Feldheim Publishers, 1976.

Ḥai Gaon. *Musar Haskel* (Intelligent instruction). Odessa: Beilinson, 1888.

Hertz, Joseph H. *The Authorized Daily Prayer Book, Revised Edition.* New York: Bloch Publishing Co., 1975.

————. *A Book of Jewish Thoughts.* London: Oxford University Press, 1920.

Heschel, Abraham Joshua. *God in Search of Man: A Philosophy of Judaism.* New York: Farrar, Straus & Giroux, 1955.

————. *The Insecurity of Freedom.* New York: Farrar, Straus & Giroux, 1966.

————. *(Man's) Quest for God: Studies in Prayer and Symbolism.* New York: Crossroad Publishing Co., 1954.

————. *Moral Grandeur and Spiritual Audacity.* Ed. Susannah Heschel. New York: Farrar, Straus & Giroux, 1996.

Hirsch, Jacob Zvi of Mecklenburg. *Haketav Vehakabbalah* (Scripture and tradition). Leipzig: N.p., 1836. Reprint, New York: N.p., 1946.

Hirsch, Samson Raphael. *Horeb.* Trans. I. Grunfeld. London: Soncino Press, 1962.

————. *The Pentateuch.* Trans. Isaac Levy. London: N.p., 1958.

Hoffman, Lawrence A., ed. *Shaarei Binah* (Gates of understanding). New York: Central Conference of American Rabbis and Union of American Hebrew Congregations, 1977.

Horowitz, Isaiah. *Shenei Luḥot Habrit* (Two tablets of the covenant). Ed. and trans. Eliyahu Monk. Jerusalem: E. Monk; Brooklyn: M. S. Spiegel [dist.], 1992.

Ibn Ezra, Abraham. *Perushe R. Avraham Ibn Ezra* (Commentary of Rabbi Abraham Ibn Ezra). Ed. Asher Weiser. Jerusalem: Mossad Harav Kook, 1976.

Ibn Ezra, Moses. *Selected Poems*. Tel Aviv: Dvir, 1935.

———. *Shirat Yisrael* (Song of Israel). Berlin and Jerusalem: Schocken Institute, 1935–41.

Isserles, Moses. *Mappah* (The tablecloth). In Joseph Karo, *Shulḥan Arukh*. Reprint, Vilna: Romm, 1911.

Jacob b. Asher. *Arbaah Turim* (Four pillars). 1550. Reprint, New York: Grossman, n.d.

Jacob b. Meir (Rabbenu Tam). *Sefer Hayashar* (The book of the righteous). Ed. and trans. Seymour J. Cohen. New York: KTAV Publishing House, 1973.

Jacob Joseph of Polnoye. *Toldot Yaakov Yosef* (The progeny of Jacob Joseph). Jerusalem: N.p., 1967.

Jerusalem Talmud (The Talmud of the Land of Israel). Ed. and trans. Jacob Neusner. Chicago: University of Chicago Press, 1983–94.

The Jewish Encyclopedia. New York: Funk & Wagnalls Co., 1901–07.

Judah Heḥasid. *Sefer Ḥasidim* (The book of the pious). Ed. Reuven Margaliot. Jerusalem: Mossad Harav Kook, 1960.

Judah Halevi, *Kuzari* (Book of Kuzari). Trans. Hartwig Hirshfield. New York: Schocken Books, 1964.

Judah Loew b. Bezalel. *Tiferet Yisrael* (The book of divine power, pt. 1). Trans. and ed. Shlomo Mallin. New York: S. Goldman–Ber Aryeh, 1979.

Kaidanover, Zevi Hirsch. *Kav Hayashar* (An honest measure). Vilna: Romm, 1888.

Kaplan, Mordecai M. *The Future of the American Jew*. New York: Macmillan, 1948.

Karo, Joseph. *Shulḥan Arukh* (The properly set table). Reprint, Vilna: Romm, 1911.

Kimḥi, David. "Commentary to Jeremiah." In *Mikraot Gedolot*. New York: Pardes, 1950.

Kimḥi, Joseph. *Shekel Hakodesh* (The holy shekel). Trans. Herman Gollancz. London: Oxford University Press, 1919.

Klagsbrun, Francine. *Voices of Wisdom*. Middle Village, N.Y.: Jonathan David Publishers, 1980.

Klirs, Tracy Guren, ed. and trans. *The Merit of Our Mothers.* Cincinnati: Hebrew Union College Press, 1992.

Kumove, Shirley. *Words Like Arrows: A Collection of Yiddish Sayings.* New York: Schocken Books, 1985.

Lamm, Norman. *Torah Lishmah: Torah for Torah's Sake in the Works of Rabbi Ḥayyim of Volozhin and His Contemporaries.* Hoboken: KTAV Publishing House, 1989.

Levi Yitzḥak. *Kedushat Levi.* Jerusalem: Mossad l'Hotzaat Sifrei Musar V'ḥasidut, 1958.

Luzzatto, Moses Ḥayyim. *Mesillat Yesharim* (The path of the upright). Trans. Mordecai M. Kaplan. Philadelphia: Jewish Publication Society, 1936.

Macquarrie, John, ed. *Dictionary of Christian Ethics.* Philadelphia: Westminister Press, 1967.

Maimon, Judah Leib. *Sarei Meah* (The century's princes). Jerusalem: Mossad Harav Kook, 1944–47.

Maimonides, Moses. *Shemoneh Perakim* (Eight chapters). Ed. and trans. Joseph I. Gorfinkle. New York: Columbia University Press, 1912.

———. *Mishneh Torah, Hilkhot Yesodei Hatorah* (The laws being the foundation of the Torah). Trans. Eliyahu Touger. New York and Jerusalem: Moznaim Publishing Corp., 1989.

———. *Mishneh Torah, Sefer Hamada* (The book of knowledge). Trans. Moses Hyamson. Jerusalem: Boys Town Jerusalem Publishers, 1965.

———. *Moreh Nevukhim* (The guide of the perplexed). Trans. Shlomo Pines. Chicago: University of Chicago Press, 1963.

———. *The Preservation of Youth.* Trans. Hirsch L. Gordon. New York: Philosophical Library, 1958.

———. *Sefer Hamitzvot* (The commandments). Trans. Charles B. Chavel. London and New York: Soncino Press, 1967.

Meiseles, Meir. *Judaism: Thought and Legend.* Trans. Rebecca Schonfeld-Brand and Aryeh Neuman. New York: N.p., n.d.

Mekhilta de Rabbi Ishmael. Trans. Jacob Z. Lauterbach. 3 vols. Philadelphia: Jewish Publication Society, 1933.

Midrash Rabbah. Vilna: Romm, 1921.

Midrash Rabbah (The Midrash). Eds. H. Freedman and M. Simon. 10 vols. London: Soncino Press, 1948.

Midrash Tanḥuma. Ed. Solomon Buber. Vilna: N.p., 1885.

Midrash Tanḥuma. Jerusalem: Levin-Epstein, 1964.

Midrash Tehillim (The Midrash on Psalms). Trans. William G. Braude. 2 vols. New Haven: Yale University Press, 1959.

Mishnah. Trans. Herbert Danby. Oxford: Clarendon Press, 1933.

Mishnat Rabbi Eliezer. Ed. Hyman G. Enelow. New York: Bloch Publishing Co., 1933.

Montefiore, C. G., and H. Loewe. *A Rabbinic Anthology.* Philadelphia: Jewish Publication Society, 1960.

Moskonah, Yitzḥak, and Moshe-Giyora Elimelech, eds. *Penine Sefarad: Alpayim Pitgamim Meotzar Hahokhmah Shel Yehudei Sefarad* (Sephardic pearls: two thousand proverbs from the treasury of Sephardic Jewry). Tel Aviv: Hotza'at Sifriat Ma'ariv, 1981.

Mykoff, Moshe, ed. *The Empty Chair.* Woodstock, Vt.: Jewish Lights Publishing, 1994.

Naḥman of Bratslav. *Sefer Hamiddot* (Book of virtues). New York: N.p., 1965.

Naḥmanides (Moses b. Naḥman). *Commentary on the Torah.* Trans. Charles B. Chavel. 5 vols. New York: Shilo Publishing House, 1971–1976.

———. *Iggeret Hakodesh* (The holy letter). Trans. Seymour J. Cohen. New York: KTAV Publishing House, 1976.

———. "Torat Haadam." In *Kitvay Ramban* (Writings of Naḥmanides). Jerusalem: Mossad Harav Kook, 1963.

Newman, Louis I., ed. and trans. *The Hasidic Anthology.* New York: Schocken Books, 1963.

Nissim, b. Reuben Gerondi: *Derashot ha-Rabbenu Nissim* (Sermons of Rabbi Nissim). Jerusalem: Makhon Shalem Yerushalayim, 1973.

Otiot R. Akiva. Warsaw: Traklin, 1927.

Paine, Thomas. *Common Sense.* Amherst, N.Y.: Prometheus Books, 1995.

Papo, Eliezer. *Pele Yoetz* (The essential Pele Yoetz). Trans. and ed. Marc D. Angel. New York: Sepher-Hermon Press, 1991.

Paxichas, George A., ed. *The Simone Weil Reader.* New York: David McKay Co., 1977.

Pechter, Mordecai ed. *Kitvey Rabbi Yisrael Salanter* (Writings of Rabbi Israel Salanter). Jerusalem: Mossad Bialik, 1972.

Peretz, I. L. "Bontshe the Silent." Trans. Angelo S. Rappoport. In Nathan Ausubel, ed. *A Treasury of Jewish Folklore.* New York: Crown Publishers, 1948.

Pesikta de Rav Kahana (Pesikta de-Rab Kahana). Trans. William G. Braude and Israel J. Kapstein. Philadelphia: Jewish Publication Society, 1975.

Pesikta Rabbati. Trans. William G. Braude. New Haven: Yale University Press, 1968.

Pirke de Rabbi Eliezer. Warsaw, 1852. Trans. Gerald Friedlander. London: N.p., 1916. Reprint, New York: Ohm, 1946.

Rosenbloom, Noah H. *Luzzatto's Ethico-Psychological Interpretation of Judaism, A Study in the Religious Philosophy of Samuel David Luzzatto.* Studies in Torah Judaism, Vol. 7. New York: Yeshiva University Press, 1965.

Rosenzweig, Franz. "Zeit ists (It is time)." In *On Jewish Learning.* New York: Schocken Books, 1955.

Saadiah Gaon. *The Book of Beliefs and Opinions.* Trans. Samuel Rosenblatt. New Haven: Yale University Press, 1948.

Salanter, Israel. "Iggeret Hamusar." In Menahem G. Glenn, *Israel Salanter: Religious-Ethical Thinker.* New York: Bloch Publishing, 1953.

Satanov, Isaac Halevi. *Mishle Asaf* (The proverbs of Asaf). Berlin: Juedische Freischule, 1792.

Scharfstein, Zevi. *Otzar Harayonot Vehapitgamim* (Treasury of concepts and proverbs). Tel Aviv: Yavneh, Shilo Publishers, 1966.

Schneur Zalman. *Tanya.* Perth, Australia: Otzar Hahasidim, 1981.

Seder Eliyahu Rabba Veseder Eliyahu Zuta (Tanna debe Eliyahu). Trans. William G. Braude and Israel J. Kapstein. Philadelphia: Jewish Publication Society, 1981.

Seeskin, Kenneth. *Maimonides: A Guide for Today's Perplexed.* West Orange, N.J.: Behrman House, 1991.

Sforno, Obadiah b. Jacob. "Commentary to Exodus" and "Commentary to Deuteronomy." In *Mikraot Gedolot.* New York: Pardes, 1950.

Shaarei Tefillah (Gates of prayer). New York: Central Conference of American Rabbis, and London: Union of Liberal and Progressive Synagogues, 1975.

Shakespeare, William. *The Complete Works of William Shakespeare.* Ed. William Aldis Wright. Garden City: Doubleday & Co., 1936.

Shaw, George Bernard. *Four plays: Candida, Caesar and Cleopatra, Pygmalion and Heartbreak House.* New York: Modern Library, 1953.

Sherwin, Byron L., and Seymour J. Cohen. *How to Be a Jew: Ethical Teachings of Judaism.* Northvale, N.J.: Jason Aronson, 1992.

Sholom Aleichem (Shalom Rabinovitz). "Tevye Wins a Fortune." In *The Old Country*. Trans. Julius and Frances Butwin. New York: Crown Publishers, 1946.

Sifra: An Analytical Translation. Trans. Jacob Neusner. 3 vols. Atlanta: Scholars Press, 1988.

Sifre on Deuteronomy. Trans. Reuven Hammer. New Haven: Yale University Press, 1986.

Sifre to Numbers. Trans. Jacob Neusner. 2 vols. Atlanta: Scholars Press, 1986.

Simon, Solomon. *The Wise Men of Helm*. New York: Behrman House, 1952.

Solomon ibn Gabirol. *Mivhar Hapeninim* (The choicest pearls). Trans. A. Cohen. New York: Bloch Publishing Co., 1925.

Solomon Luria. *Yam Shel Shelomo* (The sea of Solomon). Sidelkov, 1836.

Steinberg, Judah. *Mishle Yehoshua*. Vilna: Romm, 1871.

Steinman, Eliezer. *Midor Lador* (From generation to generation). Tel Aviv: M. Neuman, 1951.

Stuchkoff, Nahum. *Thesaurus of the Yiddish Language*. New York: Yiddish Scientific Institute [YIVO], 1950.

Tanakh: The Holy Scriptures (The New JPS Translation According to the Traditional Hebrew Text). Philadelphia and New York: Jewish Publication Society, 1985.

Thoreau, Henry David. *Walden*. Mount Vernon, N.Y.: Peter Pauper Press, 1966.

Tishby, Isaiah. *Mishnat Hazohar* (The wisdom of the Zohar). Trans. David Goldstein. Vols. 2 and 3. Oxford: Oxford University Press, 1989.

Tosefta. Ed. Moses Samuel Zuckermandel. 3rd ed. Jerusalem: Wahrmann, 1963.

Union Prayer Book II. New York: The Central Conference of American Rabbis, 1945.

Vilna Gaon (Elijah of Vilna). *Kol Eliyahu*. Photo offset of Vilna Edition. Jerusalem: 1961.

———. *Sefer Mishlei im Biur Hagra*. Petah Tikvah: N.p., 1985.

Wiesel, Elie. *The Night Trilogy*. New York: Noonday Press, 1985.

Yalkut Shimoni. 2 vols. New York: Pardes, 1944.

Yehiel b. Yekutiel b. Binyamin Harofe. *Sefer Maalot Hamiddot* (The book of virtues). Trans. Shraga Silverstein. New York and Jerusalem: Moznaim Publishing Corp., 1994.

Zborowsky, Mark, and Elizabeth Herzog. *Life Is with People*. New York: Schocken Books, 1962.

Zeivin, S. J. *Sippurei Ḥasidim* (Hasidic stories). Tel Aviv: Abraham Zioni, 1955.

Zelda. "Each Man Has a Name." In *The Penguin Book of Hebrew Verse*. Ed. and trans. T. Carmi. New York: Penguin Books, 1981.

Ziv, Simḥah Zisel. *Ḥokhmah Umusar* (Wisdom and instruction). New York: N.p., 1956–57.

Index